PRENTICE HALL
LITERATURE

PENGUIN EDITION

Skills Development
Workbook

The British Tradition

PEARSON

Prentice
Hall

Upper Saddle River, New Jersey
Boston, Massachusetts

Copyright © by Pearson Education, Inc., publishing as Pearson Prentice Hall, Boston, Massachusetts 02116. All rights reserved. Printed in the United States of America. This publication is protected by copyright, and permission should be obtained from the publisher prior to any prohibited reproduction, storage in a retrieval system, or transmission in any form or by any means, electronic, mechanical, photocopying, recording, or likewise. The publisher hereby grants permission to reproduce these pages, in part or in whole, for classroom use only, the number not to exceed the number of students in each class. Notice of copyright must appear on all copies. For information regarding permission(s), write to: Rights and Permissions Department, One Lake Street, Upper Saddle River, New Jersey 07458.

Pearson Prentice Hall™ is a trademark of Pearson Education, Inc.
Pearson® is a registered trademark of Pearson plc.
Prentice Hall® is a registered trademark of Pearson Education, Inc.

ISBN 0-13-165295-8

2 3 4 5 6 7 8 9 10   10 09 08 07 06

Contents

UNIT 1

"The Pardoner's Tale" from *The Canterbury Tales* by Geoffrey Chaucer

"The Wife of Bath's Tale" from *The Canterbury Tales* by Geoffrey Chaucer

from *Sir Gawain and the Green Knight* translated by Marie Borroff

from *Morte d'Arthur* by Sir Thomas Malory

Letters of Margaret Paston by Margaret Paston, "Twa Corbies" Anonymous

"Lord Randall" Anonymous, "Get Up and Bar the Door" Anonymous

"Barbara Allan" Anonymous

© Pearson Education, Inc., publishing as Pearson Prentice Hall. All rights reserved.

UNIT 2

© Pearson Education, Inc., publishing as Pearson Prentice Hall. All rights reserved.

UNIT 3

© Pearson Education, Inc., publishing as Pearson Prentice Hall. All rights reserved.

© Pearson Education, Inc., publishing as Pearson Prentice Hall. All rights reserved.

"On Spring" by Samuel Johnson

"The Aims of The Spectator" by Joseph Addison

From The Author's Desk: Richard Rodriguez

Listening and Viewing: Richard Rodriguez

"A Modest Proposal" by Jonathan Swift

© Pearson Education, Inc., publishing as Pearson Prentice Hall. All rights reserved.

UNIT 4

© Pearson Education, Inc., publishing as Pearson Prentice Hall. All rights reserved.

© Pearson Education, Inc., publishing as Pearson Prentice Hall. All rights reserved.

UNIT 5

© Pearson Education, Inc., publishing as Pearson Prentice Hall. All rights reserved.

© Pearson Education, Inc., publishing as Pearson Prentice Hall. All rights reserved.

UNIT 6

© Pearson Education, Inc., publishing as Pearson Prentice Hall. All rights reserved.

"The Soldier" by Rupert Brooke

"Wirers" by Siegfried Sassoon

"Anthem for Doomed Youth" by Wilfred Owen

"Birds on the Western Front" by Saki (H. H. Munro)

Literary Analysis: Tone 271

Reading Strategy: Make Inferences 272

Vocabulary Builder 273

Grammar and Style: Using *Who* and *Whom* in Adjective Clauses 274

Support for Writing 275

"Wartime Speech" by Winston Churchill

"Defending Nonviolent Resistance" by Mohandas K. Gandhi

Literary Analysis: Speech 276

Reading Strategy: Identify Main Points and Support 277

Vocabulary Builder 278

Grammar and Style: Parallel Structure 279

Support for Writing 280

"Follower" and **"Two Lorries"** by Seamus Heaney

"Outside History" by Eavan Boland

Literary Analysis: Diction and Style 281

Reading Strategy: Summarize 282

Vocabulary Builder 283

Grammar and Style: Concrete and Abstract Nouns 284

Support for Writing 285

"No Witchcraft for Sale" by Doris Lessing

Literary Analysis: Cultural Conflict 286

Reading Strategy: Analyze Cultural Differences 287

Vocabulary Builder 288

Grammar and Style: Correct Use of *Like* and *As* 289

Support for Writing 290

"The Lagoon" by Joseph Conrad

"Araby" by James Joyce

Literary Analysis: Plot Devices 291

Reading Strategy: Picture the Action and the Situation 292

Vocabulary Builder 293

Grammar and Style: Adverb Clauses 294

Support for Writing 295

© Pearson Education, Inc., publishing as Pearson Prentice Hall. All rights reserved.

"The Lady in the Looking Glass: A Reflection" by Virginia Woolf

"The First Year of My Life" by Muriel Spark

"The Rocking-Horse Winner" by D. H. Lawrence

"A Shocking Accident" by Graham Greene

"Do Not Go Gentle into That Good Night" and **"Fern Hill"** by Dylan Thomas

"The Horses" and **"The Rain Horse"** by Ted Hughes

"An Arundel Tomb" and **"The Explosion"** by Philip Larkin

"On the Patio" by Peter Redgrove

"Not Waving but Drowning" by Stevie Smith

"B. Wordsworth" by V. S. Naipaul

© Pearson Education, Inc., publishing as Pearson Prentice Hall. All rights reserved.

Name _____ Date _____

"The Seafarer," translated by Burton Raffel
"The Wanderer," translated by Charles Kennedy
"The Wife's Lament," translated by Ann Stanford

Literary Analysis: Anglo-Saxon Lyrics

Anglo-Saxon lyrics were recited or chanted aloud to an audience by wandering poets. In order to make the poems easier to listen to and to be memorized, they were developed with strong rhythms. Each line has a certain number of beats, or accented syllables—almost always four. Many lines have a **caesura,** or pause, in the middle, after the second beat. Anglo-Saxon poetry also contained **kennings,** two-word metaphorical names for familiar things. Note these examples of rhythm, caesura, and kennings in these lines:

Rhythm: No hárps ríng in his héart, nó rewárds

Caesura: No pássion for wómen, [pause] no wórldly pléasures

Kenning: Nóthing, only the oceán's heáve

1. Mark the syllables that have a strong accented beat (´) in these lines from "The Seafarer."

   But there isn't a man on earth so proud,

   So born to greatness, so bold with his youth,

   Grown so brave, or so graced by God

   That he feels no fear as the sails unfurl.

2. In the lines in passage 1, how many caesuras are there? Write the word that appears before each caesura.

   _____

3. Mark each syllable that has a strong accented beat (´) in these lines from "The Seafarer."

   Those powers have vanished, those pleasures are dead.

   The weakest survives and the world continues,

   Kept spinning by toil. All glory is tarnished.

4. Underline the kenning in these lines from "The Wife's Lament."

   First my lord went out away from his people

   over the wave-tumult. I grieved each dawn

   wondered where my lord my first on earth might be.

© Pearson Education, Inc., publishing as Pearson Prentice Hall. All rights reserved.

1

Name _____ Date _____

"The Seafarer," translated by Burton Raffel
"The Wanderer," translated by Charles Kennedy
"The Wife's Lament," translated by Ann Stanford
Reading Strategy: Connect to Historical Context

Recognizing the **historical context** and the characteristics of the period in which a work was written helps you notice relevant details and ideas. For example, if you know that Anglo-Saxon culture was male-dominated, you may be able to understand the poet's line: "My lord commanded me to move my dwelling here."

DIRECTIONS: *Use your understanding of Anglo-Saxon historical context to help you understand the following excerpts. In the right column, record how your comprehension is affected by what you know.*

Excerpt	How Historical Context Aids Understanding
1. "The Seafarer": "This tale is true, and mine. It tells/How the sea took me, swept me back/ And forth in sorrow and fear and pain,/Showed me suffering in a thousand ships, . . ."	**1.**
2. "The Wanderer": "'So have I also, often in wretchedness/Fettered my feelings, far from my kin,/Homeless and hapless, since days of old,/When the dark earth covered my dear lord's face,/And I sailed away with sorrowful heart,/Over wintry seas, seeking a gold-lord . . .'"	**2.**
3. "The Wife's Lament": "I must far and near/ bear the anger of my beloved./The man sent me out to live in the woods/under an oak tree in this den in the earth./Ancient this earth hall./I am all longing."	**3.**

© Pearson Education, Inc., publishing as Pearson Prentice Hall. All rights reserved.

"The Seafarer," translated by Burton Raffel
"The Wanderer," translated by Charles Kennedy
"The Wife's Lament," translated by Ann Stanford
Vocabulary Builder

Using the Suffix *-ness*

A. DIRECTIONS: *Answer each of the following questions, changing the underlined word to a word with the suffix -ness.*

1. Why did she think the cake was too <u>sweet</u>? _____
2. How did the <u>bright</u> light affect you? _____
3. Did you think Ryan was <u>eager</u> enough to convince Mrs. Malone that he should be in the band? _____
4. What do you think the teacher thought when Alan was so <u>helpful</u> on Thursday? _____

Using the Word List

admonish	rapture	compassionate	fervent	blithe
rancor	sentinel	redress	grievous	winsomeness

B. DIRECTIONS: *On the line, write the letter of the definition for each word in the right column.*

___ 1. fervent   **A.** ill-will
___ 2. compassionate   **B.** advise; caution
___ 3. sentinel   **C.** expression of joy
___ 4. admonish   **D.** someone who guards
___ 5. grievous   **E.** cheerful
___ 6. rancor   **F.** having great feeling
___ 7. redress   **G.** sympathizing; pitying
___ 8. blithe   **H.** causing sorrow; hard to bear
___ 9. rapture   **I.** compensation, as for a wrong
___10. winsomeness   **J.** charm; appeal

C. DIRECTIONS: *Circle the letter of the word that best completes each sentence.*

1. James was kind and caring; he was a _____ person.
   A. flippant   **B.** apathetic   **C.** blithe   **D.** compassionate
2. It was the queen's _____ hope that her subjects respected her just rule.
   A. grievous   **B.** fervent   **C.** blithe   **D.** important
3. The _____ kept watch over the sleeping troops.
   A. elegy   **B.** sentinel   **C.** tradition   **D.** exile

© Pearson Education, Inc., publishing as Pearson Prentice Hall. All rights reserved.

"The Seafarer," translated by Burton Raffel
"The Wanderer," translated by Charles Kennedy
"The Wife's Lament," translated by Ann Stanford

Grammar and Style: Compound Predicates

A **compound predicate** consists of two or more verbs having the same subject. The complete compound predicate includes the verbs; their modifiers, objects, and complements; and conjunctions.

A. PRACTICE: *In each passage, underline the compound predicate, and circle the subject.*

1. . . . and my soul/Called me eagerly out, sent me over/The horizon

2. The world's honor ages and shrinks, . . .

3. I grieved each dawn/wondered where my lord my first on earth might be.

4. . . . the sea took me, swept me back/and forth in sorrow and fear and pain,/showed me suffering. . . .

5. . . . and day by day/All this earth ages and droops into death.

B. Writing Application: *Rewrite each sentence so that it has a compound predicate.*

1. Hardship groaned around my heart.

   _____

   _____

2. The weakest survives.

   _____

   _____

3. Lonely and wretched, I wailed my woe.

   _____

   _____

4. Ever I know the dark of my exile.

   _____

   _____

5. I must far and near bear the anger of my beloved.

   _____

   _____

© Pearson Education, Inc., publishing as Pearson Prentice Hall. All rights reserved.

Name _____ Date _____

"The Seafarer," translated by Burton Raffel
"The Wanderer," translated by Charles Kennedy
"The Wife's Lament," translated by Ann Stanford
Support for Writing

Use the chart below to record images and details about feelings that relate to the theme of exile in each poem.

Poem	Feelings and Images
"The Seafarer"	
"The Wanderer"	
"The Wife's Lament"	

On a separate page, write a draft of an essay that explores the theme of exile in each poem. Use examples that show the richness of imagery and powerful feelings in the poems.

© Pearson Education, Inc., publishing as Pearson Prentice Hall. All rights reserved.

Name _____ Date _____

From the Translator's Desk
Burton Raffel Introduces *Beowulf*

DIRECTIONS: *Use the space provided to answer the questions.*

1. According to Burton Raffel, who or what drives the plot of *Beowulf*?

   _____

   _____

2. What are two magical qualities that the hero Beowulf possesses?

   _____

   _____

3. What are three ways that Beowulf's name tells us that he is no mere human being?

   _____

   _____

   _____

4. According to Raffel, how does the author of *Beowulf* create suspense at the start of the poem?

   _____

   _____

   _____

   _____

5. Why does Grendel's mother enter the narrative?

   _____

6. According to Raffel, how does the fire-breathing dragon contrast with a good king like Beowulf?

   _____

   _____

7. What arguments does Raffel use to support his claim that *Beowulf* is "very much an Old Testament poem"? Do you find these arguments persuasive? Why or why not?

   _____

   _____

   _____

   _____

   _____

© Pearson Education, Inc., publishing as Pearson Prentice Hall. All rights reserved.

Burton Raffel
Listening and Viewing

Segment 1: Meet Burton Raffel
• What does Burton Raffel attempt to do to a poem that he translates?
• When discussing translation, Raffel quotes Ezra Pound: "You don't translate what a man says; you translate what a man means." Do you agree or disagree with Pound? Explain.

_____

_____

_____

_____

Segment 2: Burton Raffel on Beowulf
• Why is *Beowulf* a culturally significant poem that we still read today?

_____

_____

_____

_____

Segment 3: The Writing Process
• What are the steps that Burton Raffel goes through while translating a text into English?
• Why do you think it is important to follow such a rigorous method when translating?

_____

_____

_____

_____

Segment 4: The Rewards of Writing
• According to Burton Raffel, why are translations important to society?
• What do you think you could learn from translated literature?

_____

_____

_____

_____

© Pearson Education, Inc., publishing as Pearson Prentice Hall. All rights reserved.

from **Beowulf**, translated by Burton Raffel
Literary Analysis: The Epic

The **epic** *Beowulf* is a long narrative poem that recounts the exploits of the legendary warrior Beowulf. Like other epic heros, Beowulf represents good and earns glory by struggling against the forces of evil represented by several monstrous creatures. He represents the values of his nation, culture, and religion. *Beowulf* is a typical epic poem in its serious tone and elevated language, which portrays characters, action, and setting in terms larger and grander than life. The use of **kennings,** two-word metaphorical names for familiar things, is also a particular characteristic of Anglo-Saxon poetry.

DIRECTIONS: *Read each passage from* Beowulf. *Then list the characteristics of epic poetry represented in it.*

1. So mankind's enemy continued his crimes, / Killing as often as he could, coming / Alone, bloodthirsty and horrible. Though he lived / In Herot, when the night hid him, he never / Dared to touch king Hrothgar's glorious / Throne, protected by God—God, / Whose love Grendel could not know. . . .

   _____

   _____

   _____

   _____

2. "Hail Hrothgar! / Higlac is my cousin and my king; the days / Of my youth have been filled with glory. Now Grendel's / Name has echoed in our land: sailors / Have brought us stories of Herot, the best / Of all mead-halls, deserted and useless when the moon / Hangs in skies the sun had lit, / Light and life fleeing together. / My people have said, the wisest, most knowing / And best of them, that my duty was to go to the Danes' / Great king. They have seen my strength for themselves, / Have watched me rise from the darkness of war. . . ."

   _____

   _____

   _____

   _____

3. "Grant me, then, / Lord and protector of this noble place, / A single request! I have come so far, / O shelterer of warriors and your people's loved friend, / That this one favor you should not refuse me— / That I, alone and with the help of my men, / May purge all evil from this hall."

   _____

   _____

   _____

   _____

© Pearson Education, Inc., publishing as Pearson Prentice Hall. All rights reserved.

translated by Burton Raffel

rategy: Paraphrase

Long sentences and difficult language can make a piece of writing hard to follow. Don't be discouraged when you come across passages that give you trouble. Instead, use paraphrasing to make sure that you're getting the point of these passages. When you **paraphrase,** you identify the key ideas in a passage and restate them in your own words. Look at this example:

Passage from *Beowulf*	Paraphrased
"I've never known fear, as a youth I fought In endless battles. I am old, now, But I will fight again, seek fame still, If the dragon hiding in his tower dares To face me."	I have been fearless throughout life and will continue to fight if the dragon dares to face me.

DIRECTIONS: *Use this graphic organizer to help you paraphrase difficult passages in* Beowulf. *Each time you come across a difficult passage, write it in the column labeled "Passage from Beowulf." Then write any difficult words from that passage in the appropriate column. Define each difficult word, either by using the words surrounding it to piece together its meaning or by looking it up in the dictionary. Next, determine the key ideas in the passage, and jot these down in the appropriate column. Finally, use the key ideas, along with your understanding of the difficult words, to paraphrase the passage. One passage has already been paraphrased for you.*

Passage from **Beowulf**	Difficult Words	Key Ideas	Paraphrase
No one waited for reparation from his plundering claws: That shadow of death hunted in the darkness, . . .	reparation (making up for wrong or injury) plundering (taking by force, theft, or fraud)	No one expected to be repaid for what Grendel took in his claws. Grendel was a shadow hunting in the darkness.	No one expected to be repaid for what Grendel took. He hunted in the darkness.

© Pearson Education, Inc., publishing as Pearson Prentice Hall. All rights reserved.

from **Beowulf**, translated by Burton Raffel
Vocabulary Builder

Using the Root *-sol-*

The root *-sol-* comes from the Latin *solari*, meaning "to comfort."

A. DIRECTIONS: *Explain how the root -sol- influences the meaning of the underlined word in each sentence.*

1. Before Beowulf arrived, Hrothgar and his Danes were <u>disconsolate</u> over the deeds of Grendel.

   _____

2. He <u>consoled</u> his little daughter for the loss of her goldfish by promising to buy her a new one.

   _____

3. The Geats grieved <u>inconsolably</u> when the dragon killed their once mighty king, Beowulf.

   _____

4. Although she won the <u>consolation</u> tournament, Allison was disappointed in her performance.

   _____

Using the Word List

reparation	solace	purge
writhing	massive	loathsome

B. DIRECTIONS: *For each underlined word, substitute a word or phrase with the same meaning. Write it in the blank following the sentence.*

1. Only a hero of Beowulf's strength could hope to lift the <u>massive</u> sword in Grendel's battle hall.

   _____

2. The third monster, most <u>loathsome</u> of all, had eight eyes on stalks and was covered with slime.

   _____

3. Most epic heroes strive to <u>purge</u> the world of wicked beings.

   _____

4. Snakes can move rapidly with their <u>writhing</u> form of locomotion.

   _____

5. The badly defeated warrior found <u>solace</u> in the affection of his family.

   _____

6. The captured bandits were ordered to give gold to their victims as <u>reparation</u>.

   _____

© Pearson Education, Inc., publishing as Pearson Prentice Hall. All rights reserved.

from **Beowulf,** translated by Burton Raffel
Grammar and Style: Appositives and Appositive Phrases

Appositives are words that are placed next to nouns or pronouns to explain the nouns or pronouns more fully. When an appositive is accompanied by modifiers, it is called an **appositive phrase.** Look at these appositive phrases from *Beowulf*:

"Hrothgar, *their lord,* sat joyless / in Herot."

". . . he came riding down, / *Hrothgar's lieutenant,* spurring his horse. . ."

In the first example, the appositive phrase immediately follows the noun *Hrothgar* and provides more information: *Hrothgar* was their lord. The appositive phrase in the second example is separated from the pronoun to which it refers, but it also provides more information: *he* was Hrothgar's lieutenant. These phrases do not change the meaning of the noun or pronoun they refer to; they merely add more information.

A. PRACTICE: *In these lines from* Beowulf, *underline each appositive phrase and circle the noun or pronoun to which it refers.*

1. He was spawned in that slime,
   Conceived by a pair of those monsters born
   of Cain, murderous creatures banished
   By God, punished forever for the crime
   Of Abel's death.

2. . . . so Herot
   Stood empty, and stayed deserted for years,
   Twelve winters of grief for Hrothgar. . .

3. Soon, fourteen Geats arrived
   At the hall, bold and warlike, and with Beowulf,
   Their lord and leader, they walked on the meadhall . . .

4. In his far-off home Beowulf, Higlac's
   Follower and the strongest of the Geats—

5. Grendel's mother
   Is hidden in her terrible home, in a place
   You've not seen.

B. Writing Application: *Combine each pair of sentences by turning one into an appositive or an appositive phrase. Set off the appositives with commas.*

1. Fourteen men went with Beowulf. Beowulf was their fearless leader.

   _____

2. They sailed in a mighty vessel. Their ship was the master of the sea.

   _____

3. Hrothgar welcomed Beowulf and his men to Herot. Herot was the strongest hall ever built.

   _____

© Pearson Education, Inc., publishing as Pearson Prentice Hall. All rights reserved.

from **Beowulf,** translated by Burton Raffel
Support for Writing

Use the chart below to take notes on passages in *Beowulf* that either show an insight into people or that show a lack of insight. Pay attention to characters' actions and why they take these actions. Write the page number for each passage so you can go back to reread it later as you draft your response.

Page numbers	How character's action shows insight	How character's action shows lack of insight

On a separate page, draft a brief essay that agrees or disagrees with translator Burton Raffel's comment that one of the most satisfying aspects of *Beowulf* is "the poet's insight into people." Use your notes to support your essay.

Unit 1 Resources: From Legend to History
© Pearson Education, Inc., publishing as Pearson Prentice Hall. All rights reserved.

Name _____ Date _____

from **A History of the English Church and People** by Bede
from **The Anglo-Saxon Chronicle,** translated by Anne Savage
Literary Analysis: Historical Writing

A **historical writing** is a factual narrative or record of past events, gathered through observation and outside, or secondary, sources. In the excerpts from *The History of the English Church and People* and *The Anglo-Saxon Chronicle,* the authors do not reveal their sources, but most probably they used their own observations, documents in court or monastic libraries, and stories they heard from others (many probably handed down orally for generations).

DIRECTIONS: *On the lines following each quotation, write what source or sources the authors might have used to gather information. Comment on the probable accuracy of the quotation.*

1. "The original inhabitants of the island were the Britons, from whom it takes its name, and who, according to tradition, crossed into Britain from Armorica. . . ."

   _____

   _____

   _____

2. ". . . it is said that some Picts from Scythia put to sea in a few long ships and were driven by storms around the coasts of Britain, arriving at length on the north coast of Ireland. Here they found the nation of the Scots, from whom they asked permission to settle, but their request was refused."

   _____

   _____

   _____

3. In agreeing to allow the Picts to take Scottish wives, the Scots said that ". . . they (Picts) should choose a king from the female (Scottish) royal line rather than the male."

   _____

   _____

   _____

4. "They got away because the other ships ran aground. They were very awkwardly aground: three were stranded on the same side of the deep water as the Danish ships, and the others all on the other side."

   _____

   _____

   _____

5. "In the same year, Aethelred passed away, who was an ealdorman in Devon, four weeks before king Alfred."

   _____

   _____

   _____

© Pearson Education, Inc., publishing as Pearson Prentice Hall. All rights reserved.

from **A History of the English Church and People** by Bede
from **The Anglo-Saxon Chronicle,** translated by Anne Savage
Reading Strategy: Break Down Sentences

Long sentences and complex language can make a piece of writing very difficult to follow. One strategy for reading this type of material is to **break down complicated sentences** by finding their key parts and their clarifying details. When you have identified the key parts, you will find it much easier to understand the complete sentence. The best way to break down sentences is to ask yourself questions.

Look at this example from Bede's *A History of the English Church and People.*

Having no women with them, these Picts asked wives of the Scots, who consented on condition that, when any dispute arose, they should choose a king from the female royal line rather than the male.

A. DIRECTIONS: *Answer each of the following questions, using the sentence above.*

1. What is the main action of the sentence? _____

_____

2. Why? _____

3. What happened next? _____

_____

4. Why? _____

B. DIRECTIONS: *Use a graphic organizer like the one here to help you break down difficult sentences in* A History of the English Church and People *and* The Anglo-Saxon Chronicle. *When you come across a long, complicated sentence, write it in the column labeled "Difficult Sentence." Then look for the most important ideas in the sentence or its main action. Write these in the column labeled "Key Ideas." Then look for key details or information that explains the main action. Write those details in the column labeled "Why? What else?" One sentence from* The Anglo-Saxon Chronicle *has been broken down for you as an example.*

Difficult Sentence	Key Ideas	Why? What else?
He was king over all the English, except for that part which was under Danish rule; and he held that kingdom for one and a half years less than thirty.	He was king over all the English. He held that kingdom for one and a half years less than thirty (or twenty-eight and one-half years).	except for that part which was under Danish rule

© Pearson Education, Inc., publishing as Pearson Prentice Hall. All rights reserved.

from **A History of the English Church and People** by Bede
from **The Anglo-Saxon Chronicle,** translated by Anne Savage
Vocabulary Builder

Using the Suffix -*ade*

A. DIRECTIONS: *Match each word in the list to a definition and use the word in a sentence.*

ambuscade   1. To block the way _____

barricade   2. A disguise, as a mask _____

masquerade   3. An ambush, or trap _____

promenade   4. From the Latin *prominare*, meaning "to drive forward" _____

_____

Using the Word List

promontories	innumerable	stranded	barricaded	ravaged

B. DIRECTIONS: *Write the word from the Word List that best completes each sentence.*

1. _____ people lined up to shake the king's hand.
2. The ship was _____ just off the coast.
3. Lookouts were posted at all the _____.
4. They tried to enter, but the door had been _____.
5. The enemy burned and _____ the town.

C. DIRECTIONS: *Put a check mark in the blank next to the synonym for the underlined word or phrase in the sentence.*

1. According to Bede there were <u>a vast number of</u> wonderful things in Ireland.
   ____ A. hallowed   ____ B. ravaged   ____ C. innumerable   ____ D. stranded

2. The king wanted to help the townspeople who had been <u>left helpless</u> at the crossroads.
   ____ A. barricaded   ____ B. innumerable   ____ C. hallowed   ____ D. stranded

3. The lighthouses were perched along the <u>cliffs above the ocean</u>.
   ____ A. promontories   ____ B. furlongs   ____ C. cockles   ____ D. barricades

4. The enemy had <u>blocked</u> all the exits and set fire to the building.
   ____ A. stranded   ____ B. barricaded   ____ C. confounded   ____ D. achieved

© Pearson Education, Inc., publishing as Pearson Prentice Hall. All rights reserved.

Name _____ Date _____

from **A History of the English Church and People** by Bede
from **The Anglo-Saxon Chronicle,** translated by Anne Savage

Grammar and Style: Compound Sentences

A **compound sentence** contains two or more independent clauses (groups of words, with subjects and predicates, that can stand alone as sentences). In a compound sentence, the clauses can be joined by *and, or, but,* or a semicolon.

The following sentence from Bede's *A History of the English Church and People* is broken into two parts; its independent clauses are underlined.

<u>Consequently both summer days and winter nights are long</u>

and

<u>when the sun withdraws southwards, the winter nights last eighteen hours.</u>

A. PRACTICE: *The following sentences are from* The Anglo-Saxon Chronicle. *Decide whether each is a compound sentence. Underline the independent clauses within each compound sentence.*

1. Then King Alfred commanded longships to be built against the ash-ships.

2. They were nearly twice as long as the others; some had sixty oars, some more.

3. The Danes went out with three ships against them, and three stood higher up the river's mouth, beached on dry land; the men from them had gone inland.

4. Then he stole himself away under the cover of night, and sought the force in Northumbria.

5. Alfred died, who was town reeve at Bath; and in the same year the peace was fastened at Tiddingford, just as King Edward advised, both with the East Anglians and the Northumbrians.

B. Writing Application: *Rewrite each group of simple sentences as a compound sentence. Remember that each compound sentence must have at least two independent clauses joined by a conjunction or a semicolon. Use pronouns as necessary.*

1. Ireland is broader than Britain. Ireland's climate is superior.

   _____

2. There are no reptiles there. No snake can exist there.

   _____

3. The island abounds with milk and honey. There is no lack of vines, fish, and birds. Deer and goats are widely hunted.

   _____

4. In these latitudes the sun does not remain long below the horizon. Consequently both summer days and winter nights are long.

   _____

5. Britain is rich in grain and timber. It has good pasturage. Vines are cultivated.

   _____

© Pearson Education, Inc., publishing as Pearson Prentice Hall. All rights reserved.

from **A History of the English Church and People** by Bede
from **The Anglo-Saxon Chronicle**, translated by Anne Savage

Support for Writing

Use the graphic organizers below to gather information on aspects of the national identity of Britain that are covered in *A History of the English Church and People* and *The Anglo-Saxon Chronicles.* Find information about geography, customs, events, and one other aspect that contributes to national identity. Then jot down details for each category.

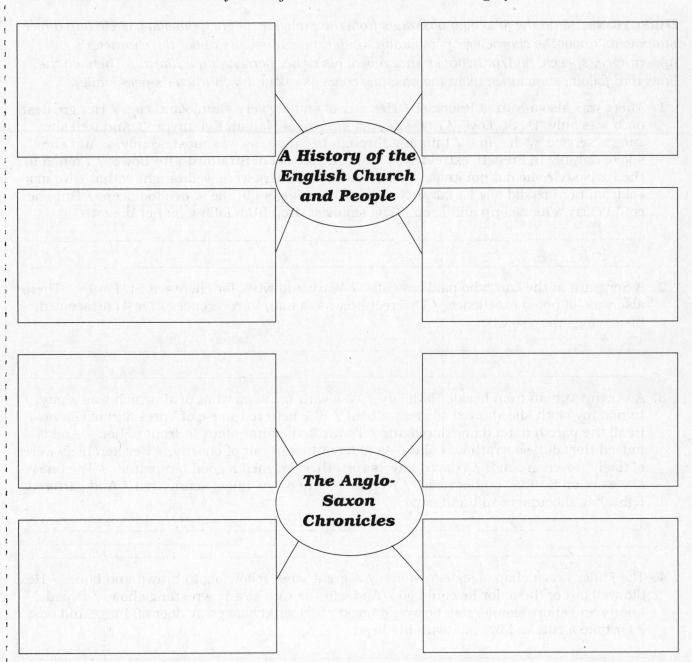

Use a separate page to draft an essay that analyzes the vision of national identity in each work. Begin by asking questions that your essay will answer. Develop your points in a logical order.

© Pearson Education, Inc., publishing as Pearson Prentice Hall. All rights reserved.

The Prologue *from* **The Canterbury Tales** by Geoffrey Chaucer
Literary Analysis: Characterization

   Characterization is the writer's act of creating and developing the personality traits of a character. Chaucer uses both **direct characterization**—that is, stating facts about a personality directly—and **indirect characterization**—that is, revealing personality through details of appearance, thoughts, speech, and/or actions—to develop the vivid personalities of the pilgrims in *The Canterbury Tales*.

DIRECTIONS: *Read the following passages from the Prologue. In each passage, circle any direct statements about the character's personality. Underline statements about the character's appearance, speech, and/or behavior that reveal his or her personality indirectly. Then, on the lines that follow, summarize what the passage conveys about the character's personality.*

1. There was also a Nun, a Prioress, / Her way of smiling very simple and coy. / Her greatest oath was only "By St. Loy!" / And she was known as Madam Eglantyne. / And well she sang a service, with a fine / Intoning through her nose, as was most seemly, / And she spoke daintily in French, extremely, / After the school of Stratford-atte-Bowe; / French in the Paris style she did not know. / At meat her manners were well taught withal / No morsel from her lips did she let fall, / Nor dipped her fingers in the sauce too deep; / But she could carry a morsel up and keep / The smallest drop from falling on her breast.

    _____

    _____

2. A Sergeant at the Law who paid his calls, / Wary and wise, for clients at St. Paul's / There also was, of noted excellence. / Discreet he was, a man to reverence, / Or so he seemed, his sayings were so wise.

    _____

    _____

3. A worthy woman from beside Bath city / Was with us, somewhat deaf, which was a pity. / In making cloth she showed so great a bent / She bettered those of Ypres and of Ghent. / In all the parish not a dame dared stir / Towards the altar steps in front of her. / And if indeed they did, so wrath was she / As to be quite put out of charity. / Her kerchiefs were of finely woven ground; / I dared have sworn they weighed a good ten pound, / The ones she wore on Sunday on her head. / Her hose were of the finest scarlet red / And gartered tight; her shoes were soft and new.

    _____

    _____

4. The Miller was a chap of sixteen stone. / A great stout fellow big in brawn and bone. / He did well out of them, for he could go / And win the ram at any wrestling show. / Broad, knotty and short-shouldered, he would boast / He could heave any door off hinge and post, / Or take a run and break it with his head.

    _____

    _____

© Pearson Education, Inc., publishing as Pearson Prentice Hall. All rights reserved.
18

The Prologue *from* The Canterbury Tales by Geoffrey Chaucer
Reading Strategy: Analyze Difficult Sentences

When you encounter long or involved sentences that seem too difficult to understand, asking yourself *who, what, when, where, why,* and *how* questions can help you figure out their meaning.

DIRECTIONS: *Read the following sentences from the Prologue. Then, answer the* who, what, *when, where, why,* and/or how *questions following them to decode their meaning.*

He knew the taverns well in every town / And every innkeeper and barmaid too / Better than lepers, beggars and that crew, / For in so eminent a man as he / It was not fitting with the dignity / Of his position, dealing with a scum / of wretched lepers; nothing good can come / Of dealings with the slum-and-gutter dwellers, / But only with the rich and victual-sellers.

1. What and whom did he know well? _____

2. Whom didn't he know as well? Why? _____

   _____

If, when he fought, the enemy vessel sank, / He sent his prisoners home; they walked the plank.

3. What did he do? _____

4. How did he do this? _____

They had a Cook with them who stood alone / For boiling chicken with a marrow-bone, / Sharp flavoring-powder and a spice for savor.

5. Who "stood alone"? _____

6. For what did he stand alone? _____

A Doctor too emerged as we proceeded; No one alive could talk as well as he did / On points of medicine and of surgery, / For, being grounded in astronomy, / He watched his patient's favorable star / And, by his Natural Magic, knew what are / The lucky hours and planetary degrees / For making charms and magic effigies.

7. Whom is this about? _____

8. What can he do? _____

9. How does he treat his patients? _____

   _____

But best of all he sang an Offertory, / For well he knew that when that song was sung / He'd have to preach and tune his honey-tongue / And (well he could) win silver from the crowd, / That's why he sang so merrily and loud.

10. What does he do best? _____

11. What does he know he'll have to do when he's done singing? _____

   _____

12. Why does he sing so merrily and loud? _____

© Pearson Education, Inc., publishing as Pearson Prentice Hall. All rights reserved.

Name _____ Date _____

The Prologue *from* The Canterbury Tales by Geoffrey Chaucer
Vocabulary Builder

Using the Suffix *-tion*

A. DIRECTIONS: *Change each verb into a noun with the suffix -tion. Then, fill in each blank in the sentences with the appropriate noun.*

contribute _____   navigate _____

recreate _____   decorate _____

1. The Knight has in his possession fine horses but wears clothes lacking _____.
2. The Monk prefers hunting for _____ to poring over books and tilling the soil.
3. The Friar gives absolution and an easy penance to those who accompany their confessions with a large financial _____.
4. When it comes to getting a boat from one destination to another, apparently none can compare with the Skipper at _____.

Using the Word List

solicitous	garnished	absolution	commission
sanguine	avouches	prevarication	

B. DIRECTIONS: *Write the word from the Word List that best completes each of the following sentences.*

1. The Franklin is probably most _____ when he is dining, since eating well gives him tremendous pleasure.
2. The Friar believes that _____ should come at a price so that people experience painful consequences for their sinful actions.
3. The Miller _____ that just by feeling grain with his thumb he can tell how much it is worth, which is a fairly bold assertion.
4. The Knight's son's garments are _____ with embroidery.
5. The innkeeper is a _____ host, doing all he can to make sure his guests are comfortable and happy.
6. A Pardoner given to _____ ought to be afraid of excommunication.
7. The Friar claims to have a _____ from the Pope to hear confessions.

© Pearson Education, Inc., publishing as Pearson Prentice Hall. All rights reserved.

The Prologue *from* The Canterbury Tales by Geoffrey Chaucer

Grammar and Style: Past and Past Perfect Tenses

Tenses of verbs indicate when events happen. Writers use the **past tense** to show that an action or a condition began and ended at a particular time in the past. They use the **past perfect tense** to clarify that an action or a condition ended before another past action began. The past tense is formed by adding *-ed* or *-d* to the base form of the verb. The past perfect tense uses the helping verb *had* before the past participle of the main verb. This passage from the Prologue contains both the past tense and past perfect tense.

He had his son with him, a fine young Squire,

A lover and cadet, a lad of fire

With locks as curly as if they <u>had been pressed</u>.   **past perfect tense**

He was some twenty years of age, <u>I guessed</u>.   **past tense**

A. PRACTICE: *Read the following sentences. On the line that follows each sentence, list each verb and identify its tense as* past *or* past perfect.

1. The Knight had followed the chivalric code and had achieved success in many battles.

   _____

2. The Yeoman had burnished his hunting horn clean before he dangled it from a baldric of bright green.

   _____

3. According to the narrator, the Nun had learned fine table manners and so never dipped her fingers in the sauce too deep.

   _____

4. The Oxford Cleric had found no preferment in the church or more worldly employment but, instead, just lived off loans from his friends.

   _____

B. Writing Application: *Read each sentence. On the line that follows it, rewrite it, using the correct form of the verb that appears in brackets.*

1. Chaucer [intend] to write 124 tales, but [complete] only 24 by the time he died.

   _____

2. The narrator [decide] to go to Canterbury before he met the other pilgrims but [agree] to travel with them once he made their acquaintance.

   _____

3. The narrator [want] to write down what he [observe] of each pilgrim while he still had the time and space to do so.

   _____

© Pearson Education, Inc., publishing as Pearson Prentice Hall. All rights reserved.

The Prologue *from* **The Canterbury Tales** by Geoffrey Chaucer
Support for Extend Your Learning

Writing

Use the chart to gather details for a **critical response** about whether you agree or disagree with the idea that Chaucer's characters apply to people today. Choose characters from the Prologue. Then, write words that describe each character's personality.

Characters	Words that Show Character's Personality

On a separate page, draft a critical response to the poet William Blake, who believed that Chaucer's characters represented "all ages and nations." Use the details in your chart to help you agree or disagree with Blake.

Listening and Speaking

Use the graphic organizer below to gather ideas about the character you will play. Then, perform a **dialogue** with your partners that includes your ideas.

Why are you going on the pilgrimage?	What do you think of the arrangement with the Host?

Your character: _____

What do you think of your companions?	What story will you tell?

Unit 1 Resources: From Legend to History
© Pearson Education, Inc., publishing as Pearson Prentice Hall. All rights reserved.

Name _____ Date _____

"The Pardoner's Tale" *from* The Canterbury Tales by Geoffrey Chaucer
Literary Analysis: Allegory

An **allegory** is a narrative that has both a literal meaning and a deeper, symbolic meaning. On the literal level, it tells a story. On the symbolic level, many or all of its characters, events, settings, and objects symbolize, or represent, abstract ideas and work to teach a moral message. For example, a character who represents faith may use a hammer (representing hard work) to build a homeless shelter (representing good deeds). Later, that character enters a beautiful, peaceful mansion (representing heaven). The moral of the allegory might be: Those who are faithful and work hard to perform good deeds will be rewarded with heaven in the afterlife.

Sometimes, allegories actually name the people, places, and things in a way that indicates what they symbolize. In the allegory summarized above, for example, the allegory might tell of a character named Faith who uses the Hammer of Hard Work to build the Good-Deed Homeless Shelter and later enters the Heavenly Mansion.

"The Pardoner's Tale" is a type of allegory called an **exemplum,** the Latin word for "example." An exemplum is used as part of a sermon to offer an example of the point that the sermon is trying to make.

A. DIRECTIONS: *Answer these questions about "The Pardoner's Tale."*

1. What vices do the rioters seem to represent? _____

2. What might the old man represent? _____

3. Which character has a name indicating the abstract idea he represents? _____

4. What might the gold florins represent? _____

5. Consider the events near the end of the tale. What might the revelers' actions toward one another represent? _____

6. What is the moral message that the Pardoner's allegory attempts to teach? _____
_____

B. DIRECTIONS: *On the lines below or on a separate sheet, write your ideas for a modern allegory illustrating the same message as "The Pardoner's Tale" or another moral message.*

_____

_____

_____

_____

_____

_____

_____

© Pearson Education, Inc., publishing as Pearson Prentice Hall. All rights reserved.

Name _____ Date _____

"The Pardoner's Tale" *from* The Canterbury Tales by Geoffrey Chaucer
Reading Strategy: Reread for Clarification

Rereading can often help clarify characters' identities and relationships, the sequence or cause of events, unfamiliar language, and other puzzling information. Often, earlier passages provide the key to understanding the puzzling information. Study this example:

> ### Passage
> They made their bargain, swore with appetite,
> These three, to live and die for one another
> As brother-born might swear to his born brother.

> ### Puzzling Detail
> What bargain did the three men make?

> ### Reread Earlier Passage
> Hold up your hands, like me, and we'll be brothers
> In this affair, and each defend the others,
> And we kill this this traitor Death, I say!

> ### Clarification
> They made a bargain to kill Death.

DIRECTIONS: *For each item below, reread earlier passages of "The Pardoner's Tale" to clarify the possibly puzzling information about which the question asks. On the lines provided, write the details that clarify the information.*

1. In line 102, the publican tells the rioters, "Be on your guard with such an adversary." What adversary is he talking about?

   _____

2. In lines 174–175, one rioter tells the old man, "I heard you mention, just a moment gone, / A certain traitor Death. . . ." What did the old man say earlier about Death?

   _____

3. In line 213, one of the rioters says that they must bring the gold back at night. What reason did he give earlier for doing this?

   _____

4. In lines 260–262, the Pardoner tells us that the youngest rioter "Kept turning over, rolling up and down / Within his heart the beauty of those bright / New florins. . . ." Does the rioter have any florins with him? If not, what does this passage mean?

   _____

5. In lines 304–305, the Pardoner tells us, "Exactly in the way they'd planned his death/They fell on him and slew him. . . ." What was the plan?

   _____

© Pearson Education, Inc., publishing as Pearson Prentice Hall. All rights reserved.
24

Name _____ Date _____

"The Pardoner's Tale" *from* The Canterbury Tales by Geoffrey Chaucer
Vocabulary Builder

Using the Root *-cap-* and the Prefix *apo-*

A. DIRECTIONS: *In each sentence, underline the word that contains the root -cap- or the prefix apo-. Then, use your knowledge of the root or prefix to define the word you underlined.*

1. The captain turned off the "Fasten Your Seatbelts" sign.

   _____

2. As the waves grew higher, we all grew concerned that the boat might capsize.

   _____

3. The audience had filled the auditorium to capacity.

   _____

4. After insulting the group of businessmen, the engineer apologized.

   _____

5. The apothegm the gambler used when he lost was: "You win some, you lose some."

   _____

Using the Word List

tarry	apothecary	pallor	hoary	prating

B. DIRECTIONS: *Read each series of words. Write the word from the Word List that best fits with the other words in the series.*

1. linger, hang behind _____

2. pharmacist, medical person _____

3. chattering, talking foolishly _____

4. paleness, white skin, deathly hue _____

5. ancient, gray, white _____

© Pearson Education, Inc., publishing as Pearson Prentice Hall. All rights reserved.

"The Pardoner's Tale" *from* **The Canterbury Tales** by Geoffrey Chaucer

Grammar and Style: Clauses With *who* and *whom*

A clause is a group of words that contain a subject and a verb. Relative pronouns connect one idea in a sentence to another part of the sentence. In **clauses with *who* and *whom*,** the relative pronoun *who* acts as the subject of the clause; *whom* acts as a direct object, an indirect object, or the object of a preposition within the clause.

The apothecary is the one who gave the younger rioter the poison.

The old man was the one to whom the three rioters spoke on the road.

A. PRACTICE: *Circle the relative pronoun in each sentence, underline the clause it introduces, and draw an arrow from the clause to the word it modifies.*

1. There came a privy thief, they call him Death, / Who kills us round here . . .

2. A certain traitor who singles out / And kills the fine young fellows hereabout.

3. The one who draws the longest, lucky man, / Shall run to town as quickly as he can . . .

4. . . . away he ran / Into a neighboring street, and found a man / Who lent him three large bottles.

B. Writing Application: *Rewrite each pair of sentences. Combine them using a clause with* who *or* whom. *Use the relative pronoun that appears in brackets.*

1. The rioters did not know the old man. They spoke to the old man. [whom]

   _____

   _____

2. The two rioters planned to attack the young rioter. The young rioter had gone to town. [who]

   _____

   _____

3. The two rioters plotted against their companion. They sent him to town. [whom]

   _____

   _____

4. The young rioter planned to poison the men. They were his friends. [who]

   _____

   _____

© Pearson Education, Inc., publishing as Pearson Prentice Hall. All rights reserved.

"The Pardoner's Tale" *from* **The Canterbury Tales** by Geoffrey Chaucer

Support for Extend Your Learning

Research and Technology

Use the chart to help you prepare for a **multimedia report** on the plague known as the Black Death. Take notes about social issues and list ideas for maps and other images that can be used to illustrate and explain the events.

Social Issues and the Black Death	Ideas for Images
1. _____ _____	1. _____ _____
2. _____ _____	2. _____ _____
3. _____ _____	3. _____ _____

Writing

To prepare for writing a summary of "The Pardoner's Tale," use the lines below to jot down notes about important ideas. Include any supporting details.

Important idea: _____

Details: 1. _____

       2. _____

       3. _____

Important idea: _____

Details: 1. _____

       2. _____

       3. _____

Important idea: _____

Details: 1. _____

       2. _____

       3. _____

On a separate page, write a summary of "The Pardoner's Tale." Review your version of the story to make sure it includes all of the important ideas and supporting details.

© Pearson Education, Inc., publishing as Pearson Prentice Hall. All rights reserved.

Name _____ Date _____

"The Wife of Bath's Tale" *from* **The Canterbury Tales** by Geoffrey Chaucer
Literary Analysis: Frame

A **frame** is a story in which one or more other stories unfolds. The frame usually introduces a set of characters in a particular situation that prompts one or more of these characters to tell a **story-within-the-story.** For example, in the *Decameron*, a famous story collection by Giovanni Boccaccio (boh KAH chee oh), the frame tells of ten characters who go to the country to escape a plague sweeping Florence, Italy. To pass the time during their temporary exile, the characters entertain one another by telling stories. The stories-within-the-story are the stories that these characters tell. The premise in the frame allows Boccaccio to tie together a group of otherwise unrelated stories that he drew from a wide variety of sources. Completed in about 1350, the *Decameron* helped inspire Chaucer to write *The Canterbury Tales.*

A. DIRECTIONS: *On the lines provided, answer these questions about the frame of* The Canterbury Tales *and its relationship to "The Wife of Bath's Tale."*

1. What is the main frame for the stories in *The Canterbury Tale?*

   _____

2. What premise does Chaucer supply in the frame to explain his story collection?

   _____

3. How does Chaucer's premise make reading the different stories more interesting?

   _____

   _____

4. In addition to the main story about the knight, what other story does the Wife of Bath tell in part in "The Wife of Bath's Tale"?

   _____

   _____

5. Consider the characterization of the Wife of Bath in the General Prologue to the Canterbury Tales. How does the story she tells suit her personality and background?

   _____

   _____

B. DIRECTIONS: *What premise would you use in a frame that would bring together a group of contemporary storytellers? Jot down your ideas for a modern frame on the lines below.*

_____

_____

_____

_____

© Pearson Education, Inc., publishing as Pearson Prentice Hall. All rights reserved.

"The Wife of Bath's Tale" *from* **The Canterbury Tales** by Geoffrey Chaucer
Reading Strategy: Use Context Clues

You can often figure out the meaning of an unfamiliar word if you examine its **context,** or surroundings, for clues to its meaning. The following list shows common types of context clues and examples in which they appear. In the examples, the possibly unfamiliar words are underlined, and the context clues are in italics.

- **Synonym or Definition:** a word or words that mean the same as the unfamiliar word
  She dined in a bistro, *a small French restaurant.*

- **Antonym or Contrast:** a word or words that mean the opposite of the unfamiliar word or tell you what the unfamiliar word is not
  The race will *begin* at 6 o'clock and terminate three hours later.

- **Explanation:** words that give more information about an unfamiliar word
  Ocelots are *like leopards, only smaller.*

- **Example:** a word or words that illustrate the unfamiliar word, or a word or words that tell what the unfamiliar word illustrates
  Rodents include *rats, mice, and squirrels.*

- **Sentence Role:** hints about the word's meaning based on its use in a sentence. For example, in this sentence, you can tell that a *bistro* is a noun and that it is not abstract, since it can be entered.
  Example: The couple entered the bistro.

DIRECTIONS: *Answer these questions about words in "The Wife of Bath's Tale."*

1. What synonym in line 72 helps you know the meaning of *jollity?* _____

2. What two examples in lines 78–80 help clarify the meaning of *flattery?* _____
_____

3. In lines 82–84, what does the contrast suggest that *reprove* means? _____
_____

4. What nearby synonym helps clarify the meaning of *maim* in line 278? _____

5. From the explanation in lines 303–304, what do you think *churl* means? _____
_____

© Pearson Education, Inc., publishing as Pearson Prentice Hall. All rights reserved.

"The Wife of Bath's Tale" *from* **The Canterbury Tales** by Geoffrey Chaucer
Vocabulary Builder

Using Multiple-Meaning Words

A. DIRECTIONS: *The italicized words in these lines from "The Wife of Bath's Tale" each can have more than one meaning. Use the context to determine which of the two possible meanings applies to the lines from the selection, and circle that meaning. Then, on the line provided, write a sentence illustrating the other meaning of the word.*

1. Ovid *relates* that under his long hair / The unhappy Midas grew a splendid pair / Of ass's ears.

   Possible Meanings: shows a connection   narrates

   _____

2. He begged her not to tell a living creature / That he possessed so horrible a *feature:*

   Possible Meanings: any part of the face   a special newspaper or magazine story

   _____

3. There wasn't a living creature to be seen / Save on old woman sitting on the *green*

   Possible Meanings: a color blending yellow and blue   an expanse of grass or plants

   _____

4. It was such torture that his wife looked *foul.*

   Possible Meanings: disgusting   hit out of bounds

   _____

Using the Word List

implored	misalliance	bequeath	esteemed
relates	contemptuous	prowess	rebuke

B. DIRECTIONS: *Use your knowledge of the Word List to decide whether each statement below is true or false. Then, on the line before the statement, write T if it is true and F if it is false.*

____ 1. Someone who skates with *prowess* often falls flat on her face.

____ 2. A smile is a *contemptuous* expression.

____ 3. A storyteller *relates* a story.

____ 4. People sometimes *bequeath* property to their heirs.

____ 5. Most people enjoy having someone *rebuke* them.

____ 6. The king and queen will be overjoyed if their son makes a *misalliance.*

____ 7. If someone *implored* you to leave, they would not want you to move.

____ 8. People often stand up when an *esteemed* figure enters the room.

© Pearson Education, Inc., publishing as Pearson Prentice Hall. All rights reserved.

"The Wife of Bath's Tale" *from* **The Canterbury Tales** by Geoffrey Chaucer

Grammar and Style: Correcting Run-On Sentences

An **independent,** or main, clause is one that can stand alone as a sentence. A **run-on sentence** improperly joins or punctuates two or more independent clauses. One kind of run-on sentence runs two independent clauses together with no punctuation:

The knight committed a foul crime the queen showed him mercy.

Another kind incorrectly uses just a comma to separate the independent clauses:

The knight committed a foul crime, the queen showed him mercy.

There are many ways to correct run-on sentences. However, if the two independent clauses are closely related, a good way to correct the problem is to use a semicolon:

The knight committed a foul crime; the queen showed him mercy.

Sometimes, the relationship of the two causes will be clearer if, in addition to the semicolon, a conjunctive adverb is added. Notice how the conjunctive adverb nevertheless clarifies the contrast between the two clauses. Notice, too, that when a conjunctive adverb is added, it is followed by a comma.

The knight committed a foul crime; **nevertheless,** the queen showed him mercy.

Here are some conjunctive adverbs you might use when correcting run-on sentences:

> additionally, besides, consequently, furthermore, however, indeed, instead, moreover, nevertheless, nonetheless, otherwise, therefore, thus

DIRECTIONS: *Correct these run-on sentences by rewriting them on the lines provided. Use a semicolon followed by a conjunctive adverb.*

1. The knight's execution was postponed the queen sent him on a quest.

   _____

   _____

2. The knight sought the answer to a question, there was a time limit of just one year.

   _____

   _____

3. A correct answer could save him, he looked high and low for it.

   _____

   _____

4. The old woman offered the answer the knight had to marry her to get it.

   _____

   _____

5. He did not want an old woman as his bride, he agreed to marry her.

   _____

Unit 1 Resources: From Legend to History

© Pearson Education, Inc., publishing as Pearson Prentice Hall. All rights reserved.

"The Wife of Bath's Tale" *from* **The Canterbury Tales** by Geoffrey Chaucer
Support for Writing

Use the organizer to gather ideas for your allegory. Write your moral or theme in the large circle. Then identify characters and their qualities. Exaggerate their qualities.

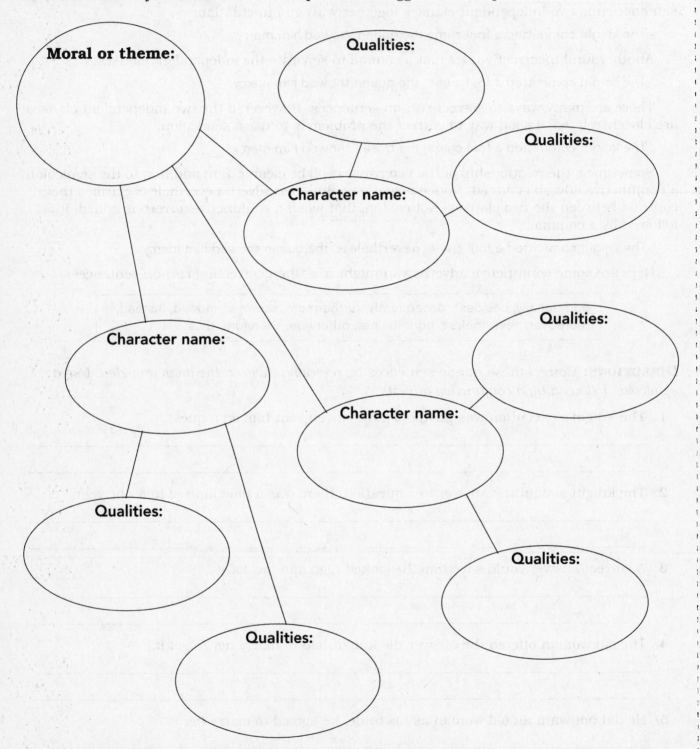

On a separate page, draft your allegory. Make sure that each character's personality reflects the moral of the allegory. Give them colorful names.

Unit 1 Resources: From Legend to History

© Pearson Education, Inc., publishing as Pearson Prentice Hall. All rights reserved.

Name _____ Date _____

from **Sir Gawain and the Green Knight,** translated by Marie Borroff
from **Morte d'Arthur** by Sir Thomas Mallory
Literary Analysis: Medieval Romance

Medieval romances were the popular adventure stories of the Middle Ages. Originally cast in verse, they were later sometimes told in prose. In England, the best known of the medieval romances involve King Arthur and his knights.

DIRECTIONS: *Following is a series of characteristics of medieval romances. On the lines below each characteristic, cite at least two details from* Sir Gawain and the Green Knight *and* Morte d' Arthur *that illustrate the characteristic.*

1. Medieval romances convey a sense of the supernatural.

   Sir Gawain and the Green Knight: _____

   _____

   Morte d' Arthur: _____

   _____

2. Medieval romances give a glamorous portrayal of castle life.

   Sir Gawain and the Green Knight: _____

   _____

   Morte d' Arthur: _____

   _____

3. Chivalric ideals—bravery, honor, courtesy, fairness to enemies, respect for women—guide the characters.

   Sir Gawain and the Green Knight: _____

   _____

   Morte d' Arthur: _____

   _____

4. Medieval romances are imbued with adventure.

   Sir Gawain and the Green Knight: _____

   _____

   Morte d' Arthur: _____

   _____

© Pearson Education, Inc., publishing as Pearson Prentice Hall. All rights reserved.

Name _____ Date _____

from Sir Gawain and the Green Knight, translated by Marie Borroff
from Morte d'Arthur by Sir Thomas Mallory
Reading Strategy: Summarize

Summarizing is one way to check your understanding of what you have read. A summary briefly states the main point and key details in your own words. A summary is always much shorter than the original, but it must reflect the original accurately. Look at this example from *Morte d'Arthur.*

Passage	Key Ideas and Events	Summary
King Arthur smote Sir Mordred under the shield, with a thrust of his spear, throughout the body more than a fathom. And when Sir Mordred felt that he had his death's wound, he thrust himself with the might that he had up to the burr of King Arthur's spear, and right so he smote his father King Arthur with his sword holden in both his hands, upon the side of the head, that the sword pierced the helmet and the casing of the brain.	King Arthur speared Sir Mordred. Sir Mordred felt that he was dying from the wound, but he forced himself to hit King Arthur in the head.	Sir Mordred and King Arthur fought a terrible battle. Sir Mordred was killed and King Arthur was wounded in the head.

DIRECTIONS: *Use this graphic organizer to summarize this excerpt.*

Passage	Key Ideas and Events	Summary
. . . Sir Lucan departed, for he was grievously wounded in many places. And so as he walked he saw and harkened by the moonlight how that pillagers and robbers were come into the field to pill and to rob many a full noble knight of brooches and bracelets and of many a good ring and many a rich jewel. And who that were not dead all out there they slew them for their harness and their riches. When Sir Lucan understood this work, he came to the King as soon as he might and told him all what he had heard and seen.		

© Pearson Education, Inc., publishing as Pearson Prentice Hall. All rights reserved.

from Sir Gawain and the Green Knight, translated by Marie Borroff
from Morte d'Arthur by Sir Thomas Mallory
Vocabulary Builder

Using the Root -droit-

A. DIRECTIONS: *The word root -droit- means "right." In the following sentences, decide whether the italicized word is used properly. If it is, write "correct." If it is not, rewrite the sentence using the correct form of a word with the root -droit-.*

1. Because of his *adroitness* with a football, Charley was unable to make the football team.
   _____

2. Amber was very *adroit* at gymnastics, so she knew she would never go to the Olympics.
   _____

3. Marla is no longer *maladroit* in her movements now that she takes ballet lessons.
   _____

4. Tad prides himself on his *maladroitness*, having never broken a leg in all his years as a skier.
   _____

Using the Word List

assay	adjure	feigned	adroitly	largesse
righteous	entreated	peril	interred	

B. DIRECTIONS: *Each excerpt below is from one of the poems. Choose the word from the Word List that best matches the meaning of the italicized word or phrase.*

1. If there be one so willful my words to *prove*, Let him leap hither lightly. . . .
   _____

2. He proffered, with good grace, His bare neck to the blade, And *pretended* a cheerful face. . . . _____

3. . . . those that I did battle for in *just* quarrels, _____

4. First I ask and *appeal* to you, how you are called
   That you tell me true. . . . _____

5. Sir Mordred did his devoir that day and put himself in great *danger.* _____

6. . . . Withdrew the ax *skillfully* before it did damage. _____

7. . . . and there they *pleaded with* Sir Mordred . . . _____

8. . . . contrary both to *noble spirit* and loyalty belonging to the knights . . .
   _____

9. "What man is there here *buried* that you pray so fast for?" _____

© Pearson Education, Inc., publishing as Pearson Prentice Hall. All rights reserved.

from **Sir Gawain and the Green Knight,** translated by Marie Borroff
from **Morte d'Arthur** by Sir Thomas Mallory

Grammar and Style: Comparative and Superlative Forms

The **comparative form** of an adjective or adverb compares two things. The **superlative form** of an adjective or adverb compares more than two things to the highest degree.

    Comparative: . . . Grow green as the grass and *greener,* it seemed . . .

    Superlative: . . . *Worthiest* of their works the wide world over . . .

A. PRACTICE: *Identify which form of adjective is used in each sentence.*

1. Aparna sold a larger amount of her jewelry at the art fair this year than she did last year.
   _____

2. The early recording was finer than the new one. _____

3. Jordan holds the record for the largest number of cans collected during a food drive.
   _____

4. This painting is even more beautiful than the last one. _____

5. Monday was the coldest day of the month. _____

B. Writing Application: *Rewrite the following sentences, using the appropriate comparative or superlative form of the adjective or adverb in parentheses.*

1. Marcie is the (compassionate) person I know.

   _____

   _____

2. Katrusha will be (happy) working outdoors than in an office this summer.

   _____

   _____

3. Fresh fruit and a bagel makes a (nutritious) breakfast than coffee and a donut.

   _____

   _____

4. Angelo explained to his grandfather that writing a letter is (easy) with a computer than with a pen and paper. _____

   _____

5. Up in the hills, it's always (chilly) in the morning before the sun comes up.

   _____

   _____

© Pearson Education, Inc., publishing as Pearson Prentice Hall. All rights reserved.

Name _____ Date _____

from Sir Gawain and the Green Knight, translated by Marie Borroff
from Morte d'Arthur by Sir Thomas Mallory
Support for Writing

Use the graphic organizers below to help you think of ideas. Choose an event or situation that Sir Gawain would react to that could become an interior monologue.

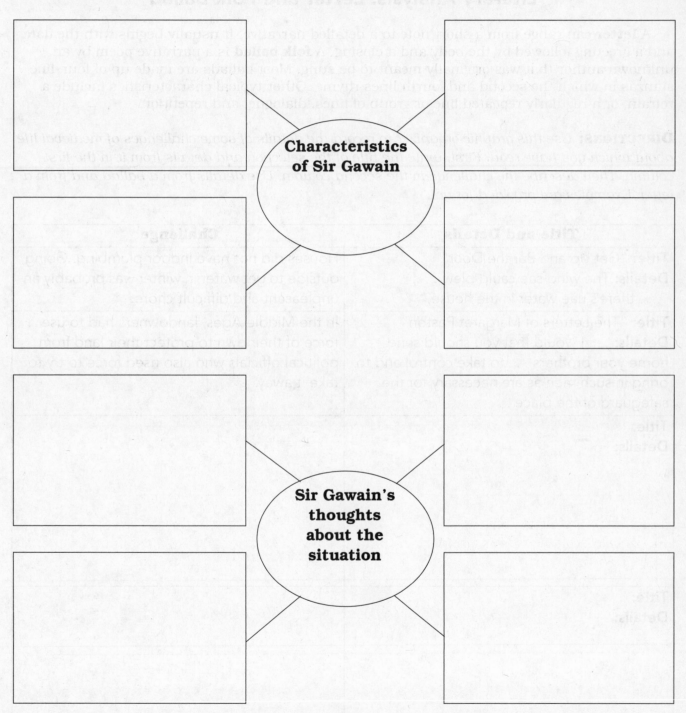

Use a separate page to draft Sir Gawain's interior monologue. Write in the first person as though you are Gawain, talking to himself.

Unit 1 Resources: From Legend to History
© Pearson Education, Inc., publishing as Pearson Prentice Hall. All rights reserved.

Letters of Margaret Paston by Margaret Paston
"The Twa Corbies" Anonymous
"Lord Randall" Anonymous
"Get Up and Bar the Door" Anonymous
"Barbara Allan" Anonymous

Literary Analysis: Letter and Folk Ballad

A **letter** can range from a short note to a detailed narrative. It usually begins with the date and a greeting followed by the body and a closing. A **folk ballad** is a narrative poem by an unknown author that was originally meant to be sung. Most ballads are made up of four-line stanzas in which the second and fourth lines rhyme. Other typical characteristics include a refrain, or a regularly repeated line or group of lines, dialogue, and repetition.

DIRECTIONS: *Use this graphic organizer to record the details of some challenges of medieval life about which you have read. First, write the title of the selection and details from it in the first column. Then describe the challenge in the second column. Use details from a ballad and from a letter. Examples are provided for you.*

Title and Details	Challenge
Title: "Get Up and Bar the Door" **Details:** The wind sae cauld blew . . .; ". . . there's nae water in the house,"	Houses did not have indoor plumbing. Going outside to get water in winter was probably an unpleasant and difficult chore.
Title: "The Letters of Margaret Paston" **Details:** . . . I would that you should send home your brothers . . . to take control and to bring in such men as are necessary for the safeguard of the place . . .	In the Middle Ages, landowners had to use force of their own to protect their land from political officials who also used force to try to take it away.
Title: **Details:**	
Title: **Details:**	

© Pearson Education, Inc., publishing as Pearson Prentice Hall. All rights reserved.

Letters of Margaret Paston by Margaret Paston
"The Twa Corbies" Anonymous
"Lord Randall" Anonymous
"Get Up and Bar the Door" Anonymous
"Barbara Allan" Anonymous

Reading Strategy: Understand Dialect

Dialect is the form of a language spoken by people in a particular region or group. Poetry and prose written in dialect can be difficult to understand because the vocabulary and the pronunciation of certain words are unfamiliar. You can understand what you are reading by translating the dialect to modern English. Following are some strategies you can use to do this.

1. Use footnotes to find the meaning of words no longer used in modern English.
2. Use the context of the sentence to figure out what a word or phrase means.
3. Read the word aloud to figure out if it sounds like a word in modern English.

In this line from "The Twa Corbies," the two instances of Scottish-English dialect are italicized: "'And I'll *pike* out his bonny blue *e'en*;'" **1. e'en:** Eyes.

The footnote explains the meaning of *e'en*. You can use context and the sound of the word *pike* to figure out that it means "poke." Now the sense of the line is clear: "And I'll poke out his bonny blue eyes."

DIRECTIONS: *Read the stanzas from "The Twa Corbies" and underline all instances of dialect in them. Then rewrite the stanzas, using modern English in place of the dialect.*

As I was walking all alane,

I heard twa corbies[1] making a mane.[2]

The tane unto the tither did say,

"Whar sall we gang and dine the day?"

   1. twa corbies: two ravens

   2. mane: moan

"In behint yon auld fail dyke,[3]

I wot[4] there lies a new-slain knight;

And naebody kens[5] that he lies there

But his hawk, his hound, and his lady fair."

   3. fail dyke: bank of earth

   4. wot: know

   5. kens: knows

_____

_____

_____

_____

_____

_____

_____

_____

Unit 1 Resources: From Legend to History
© Pearson Education, Inc., publishing as Pearson Prentice Hall. All rights reserved.

Name _____ Date _____

Letters of Margaret Paston by Margaret Paston
"The Twa Corbies" Anonymous
"Lord Randall" Anonymous
"Get Up and Bar the Door" Anonymous
"Barbara Allan" Anonymous
Vocabulary Builder

Using the Root -cert-

A. DIRECTIONS: *Use context and the meaning of the word root -cert- to write a definition of the italicized word in each sentence below.*

1. Margaret Paston was *certain* her son would defend Caister.

   _____

2. The ringing of the church bells was like a death *certificate* for Sir John Graeme.

   _____

3. With *certitude*, the man and his wife determined neither would bar the door.

   _____

Using the Word List

alderman	enquiry	succor	certify
remnant	ransacked	asunder	assault

B. DIRECTIONS: *On each line, write the word from the Word List that has the same meaning as the italicized word or phrase in the sentence.*

1. Two thieves broke into a house and *pillaged* every room in search of valuables.

   _____

2. The *official* voted against a proposal to raise parking meter rates in her district.

   _____

3. The only *remainder* of the delicious meal was a spoonful of mashed potatoes.

   _____

4. After I knocked on the door, I heard the *question* "Who's there?" from behind it.

   _____

5. The pirates planned to *violently attack* the trade ship and steal any cargo on board.

   _____

6. Nurse Florence Nightingale offered *aid* to wounded soldiers during the Crimean War.

   _____

7. The explosives expert recommended using dynamite to blow the boulder *into pieces*.

   _____

8. Only an anthropologist will be able to *verify* whether the artifact is authentic.

   _____

© Pearson Education, Inc., publishing as Pearson Prentice Hall. All rights reserved.

Letters of Margaret Paston by Margaret Paston
"The Twa Corbies" Anonymous
"Lord Randall" Anonymous
"Get Up and Bar the Door" Anonymous
"Barbara Allan" Anonymous
Grammar and Style: Direct Address

Direct address refers to the way a character in a story or poem speaks to someone or something. A character who uses direct address is speaking directly to a person or a thing, and not simply speaking about it. The person or thing being addressed is referred to by a name, a title, or a descriptive phrase, which is always set off by commas in writing.

The italicized words in these lines from "Get Up and Bar the Door" and "Lord Randall" are examples of direct address.

"'My hand is in my hussyfskap, *Goodman,* as ye may see;'"

"'O yes, I am poison'd; *mother,* make my bed soon,'"

A. PRACTICE: *This stanza is from "Lord Randall." Circle the examples of direct address.*

"Where gat ye your dinner, Lord Randall, my son?

Where gat ye your dinner, my handsome young man?"

"I dined wi' my true-love; mother, make my bed soon,

For I'm weary wi' hunting, and fain wald lie down."

B. Writing Application: *In this ballad, underline any line that contains an example of direct address and add the correct punctuation to it.*

"Are you hungry Lord Randall for there's plenty to eat,

and I'll spread it all out on the table.

Eat hearty my love of the bread and the broth.

Fill up as much as you are able."

"Now surely my darling there's room in you still.

Won't you try some more delicate eel?

'Twas a pleasure dear man to cook you this food.

It's as good as the love I feel."

"Be off stupid hounds there's no scraps for you!

They are all for my love to keep strong.

Now go home gentle knight you've eaten quite well,

and your sleep will be deep and long."

© Pearson Education, Inc., publishing as Pearson Prentice Hall. All rights reserved.

Letters of Margaret Paston by Margaret Paston
"The Twa Corbies" Anonymous
"Lord Randall" Anonymous
"Get Up and Bar the Door" Anonymous
"Barbara Allan" Anonymous

Support for Writing

Use the graphic organizer below to collect information for your investigative report on the accuracy and value of Paston's letters.

Conclusion #1: _____	Sources to support conclusion: 1. _____ 2. _____	Facts to support conclusion: 1. _____ 2. _____
Conclusion #2: _____	Sources to support conclusion: 1. _____ 2. _____	Facts to support conclusion: 1. _____ 2. _____
Conclusion #3: _____	Sources to support conclusion: 1. _____ 2. _____	Facts to support conclusion: 1. _____ 2. _____

On a separate page, draft your report on Margaret Paston's letters. Begin with background on the letters. Then introduce your conclusions and support them with your sources and facts.

© Pearson Education, Inc., publishing as Pearson Prentice Hall. All rights reserved.

Name _____ Date _____

Sonnets 1, 35, and 75 by Edmund Spenser
Sonnets 31 and 39 by Sir Philip Sidney
Literary Analysis: The Sonnet

A **sonnet,** a lyric poem of fourteen lines, originated in Italy. The Italian, or **Petrarchan,** sonnet is divided into two parts. The first eight lines form the *octave* and the next six lines the *sestet*. While the Italian sonnet had a fairly strict rhyme scheme, English poets took many liberties with the sonnet form. Sir Philip Sidney used an *abab abab* rhyme scheme in addition to the Italian *abba abba* rhyme scheme for the octave. In the sestet, Sidney's rhyme schemes were *cdcdee, cddcee,* or *ccdeed*. The **Spenserian** sonnet, named for Edmund Spenser, uses the *abab, bcbc, cdcd, ee* rhyme scheme.

Recognizing the Sonnet Form

A. DIRECTIONS: *In this sonnet by Spenser, bracket and label the stanzas and rhyme schemes.*

Lyke as a ship that through the ocean wyde,
By conduct of some star doth make her way,
Whenas a storme hath dimd her trusty guyde,
Out of her course doth wander far astray.
[5] So I whose star, that wont with her bright ray,
Me to direct, with cloudes is overcast,
Doe wander now in darknesse and dismay,
Through hidden perils round about me plast.
Yet hope I well, that when this storme is past
[10] My Helice the lodestar of my lyfe
Will shine again, and looke on me at last,
With lovely light to cleare my cloudy grief.
Till then I wander carefull comfortlesse,
In secret sorrow and sad pensivenesse.

Sonnet Sequence

B. DIRECTIONS: *A **sonnet sequence** is a group of sonnets linked by subject matter or theme, and following certain conventions. Compare two of the sonnets from the sonnet sequence* Astrophel and Stella *by Sir Philip Sidney by answering the following questions about Sonnets 31 and 39.*

1. To what inanimate object is each sonnet addressed?
   A. Sonnet 31 is addressed to the _____.
   B. Sonnet 39 is addressed to _____.
2. The speaker in each sonnet desires something from the one addressed.
   A. In Sonnet 31, he wants _____.
   B. In Sonnet 39, he wants _____.
3. Both poems are lyric and reflect the speaker's feelings.
   A. In Sonnet 31, he feels _____ about the way women treat men.
   B. In Sonnet 39, he feels a _____ for peace.

© Pearson Education, Inc., publishing as Pearson Prentice Hall. All rights reserved.

Sonnets 1, 35, and 75 by Edmund Spenser
Sonnets 31 and 39 by Sir Philip Sidney
Reading Strategy: Paraphrase

Poetic language often uses condensed imagery to convey the poet's ideas. **Paraphrasing,** or restating passages in your own words, can help you understand and explore a poem's meaning. When paraphrasing poetry, look for the main ideas within the imagery. Think about what the images might be representing and how those images convey a bigger theme.

Spenser, Sonnet 1, lines 1–3:	"Happy ye leaves when as those lily hands, / which hold my life in their dead doing might, / Shall handle you and hold in love's soft bands, . . . "
Paraphrase:	The pages of a book are happy when held in the beautiful, soft hands of my beloved, hands that also hold me in their power.

DIRECTIONS: *In the chart below, paraphrase one of Spenser's sonnets and one of Sidney's sonnets.*

Try these tips as you paraphrase a sonnet:

- Break down the sonnet into parts (octaves, quatrains, sestets, or couplets).
- Paraphrase parts, not every line.
- Focus on complete thoughts.

Sonnet	Paraphrase

Name _____ Date _____

Sonnets 1, 35, and 75 by Edmund Spenser
Sonnets 31 and 39 by Sir Philip Sidney
Vocabulary Builder

Using Forms of *Languished*

A. DIRECTIONS: *Fill in the blanks in the following sentences with the appropriate form of the word* languished: languish *(verb)*, languid *(adjective), or* languor *(noun).*

1. Maria's _____ caused her mother to worry.

2. The _____ breeze offered little relief from the sweltering heat.

3. Jamie's severe depression causes him to grow more _____ daily.

4. Keats continued to _____ from the effects of tuberculosis.

5. As I watched the dreamy _____ of the slow-moving river, I could feel my eyelids grow heavy.

Using the Word List

deign	assay	devise
wan	languished	balm

B. DIRECTIONS: *Match each word in the left column with its definition in the right column. Write the letter of the definition on the line next to the word it defines.*

___ 1. balm   **A.** try or attempt

___ 2. wan   **B.** weak

___ 3. assay   **C.** lower oneself

___ 4. deign   **D.** grew weak

___ 5. devise   **E.** something that heals

___ 6. languished   **F.** plan

C. DIRECTIONS: *On the lines that follow, write a paragraph describing the thoughts of a lover who is longing for his beloved. Use each word in the Word List at least once in your paragraph.*

_____

_____

_____

_____

_____

_____

© Pearson Education, Inc., publishing as Pearson Prentice Hall. All rights reserved.

Sonnets 1, 35, and 75 by Edmund Spenser
Sonnets 31 and 39 by Sir Philip Sidney
Grammar and Style: Capitalization of Proper Nouns

A noun that names a specific person or thing is a **proper noun** and should be **capitalized.** Some writers, especially poets, give the names of some things a human quality by treating them as if they are proper nouns. Sir Philip Sidney addresses the moon as if it were a person, for example, and emphasizes his intention by capitalizing *Moon.*

A. PRACTICE: *Capitalize any proper noun or other word requiring capitalization in the sentences below.*

1. When my mother was in the hospital, kate Chapman sent her a beautiful plant.

2. Oh, dawn, why must you arrive so soon?

3. My brother tom will start at southridge high school next year.

B. Writing Application: *Write two sentences for each of the following words. The first sentence should use the word as a noun in a way that should be capitalized. In the second sentence, use the word as a noun in a way that should NOT be capitalized. Sentences using the first word have been done as an example.*

nightingale	wind	bill
carpenter	cook	street

1. Florence Nightingale was the founder of modern nursing.
    The nightingale sang throughout the night.

2. _____
    _____

3. _____
    _____

4. _____
    _____

5. _____
    _____

6. _____
    _____

© Pearson Education, Inc., publishing as Pearson Prentice Hall. All rights reserved.

Name _____ Date _____

Support for Writing

Use these two graphic organizers to collect information for your introduction.

Sonnet: _____

Section	Lines	Summary
Beginning		
Middle		
End		

Sonnet: _____

Section	Lines	Summary
Beginning		
Middle		
End		

© Pearson Education, Inc., publishing as Pearson Prentice Hall. All rights reserved.

"The Passionate Shepherd to His Love" by Christopher Marlowe
"The Nymph's Reply to the Shepherd" by Sir Walter Raleigh
Literary Analysis: Pastoral

A **pastoral** is a poem or another work that celebrates the pleasures of a simple life in the country. The term comes from the Latin word *pastor,* which means "shepherd." Pastoral poems generally display some or all of these features:

- The speaker is a shepherd, or herder of sheep.
- The shepherd describes the simple joys of country living.
- The shepherd usually addresses or describes a shepherdess whom he loves.
- The shepherd uses much more sophisticated vocabulary and imagery than would be expected from the simple rural fellow he pretends to be.
- The picture of rural life is highly idealized, ignoring the hardships of living close to the land, and instead, making such an existence seem carefree.
- The actual audience for the poem is an educated urban reader or member of court seeking to escape the complexities of his or her life by reading about what he or she imagines to be the free and untroubled existence of ordinary country folk.

A. DIRECTIONS: *On the lines provided, answer these questions about "The Passionate Shepherd to His Love."*

1. Who is the speaker in Marlowe's poem, and whom does he address?

   _____

2. What basic request does the speaker make of the person he addresses?

   _____

3. How would you describe the portrait the speaker paints of country living?

   _____

4. Identify three instances in which the speaker exaggerates the joys of country life.

   _____

   _____

   _____

5. Cite three examples of sophisticated language and imagery in Marlowe's poem.

   _____

   _____

   _____

B. DIRECTIONS: *On the lines below, explain why Sir Walter Raleigh's poem is not a traditional pastoral.*

   _____

   _____

   _____

© Pearson Education, Inc., publishing as Pearson Prentice Hall. All rights reserved.

Name _____ Date _____

"The Passionate Shepherd to His Love" by Christopher Marlowe
"The Nymph's Reply to the Shepherd" by Sir Walter Raleigh
Reading Strategy: Identify with the Speaker of a Poem

You can often better appreciate a poem if you **identify with the poem's speaker.** To do this, put yourself in the speaker's place and try to understand his or her feelings, thoughts, and motives. Once you can understand those feelings, thoughts, and motives, you are more likely to understand the poem's theme, or central message.

To identify with the poem's speaker, you might find it helpful to use this checklist of questions:

- Do I have an idea of the speaker's name, age, and/or gender? If so, what are they?
- What is the speaker's profession or situation in life?
- Is the speaker addressing anyone or anything in particular? If so, whom or what, and what does the speaker seem to feel about this person or thing?
- What seems to be the speaker's general purpose or goal in speaking the poem?
- What seems to be the speaker's mood or attitude?
- How would you describe the speaker's general outlook on the world?
- What do I have in common with the speaker?
- Based on my understanding of the speaker, what would I state is the central theme or message of the poem?

DIRECTIONS: *Now, apply the checklist of questions to either of the two poems in this grouping. Write your answers on the lines provided.*

1. Do I have an idea of the speaker's name, age, and/or gender? If so, what are they?

    _____

2. What is the speaker's profession or situation in life?

    _____

3. Is the speaker addressing anyone or anything in particular? If so, whom or what, and what does the speaker seem to feel about this person or thing?

    _____

    _____

4. What seems to be the speaker's general purpose or goal in speaking the poem?

    _____

5. What seems to be the speaker's mood or attitude?

    _____

6. How would you describe the speaker's general outlook on the world?

    _____

7. What do I have in common with the speaker? _____

    _____

8. Based on my understanding of the speaker, what would I state as the central theme or message of the poem? _____

© Pearson Education, Inc., publishing as Pearson Prentice Hall. All rights reserved.

"The Passionate Shepherd to His Love" by Christopher Marlowe
"The Nymph's Reply to the Shepherd" by Sir Walter Raleigh
Vocabulary Builder

Using Word Origins: *wither*

A. DIRECTIONS: *Based on what you have learned about the origin and meaning of the word* wither, *circle the letter of the best answer to each item below.*

1. Based on the word's origin, which of these might cause something to *wither*?
   A. a loud noise   B. the sun's rays   C. a clock's chime   D. dirt

2. Which of these words most likely has the same origin as *wither*?
   A. *weather*, meaning "wear away"
   B. *widen*, meaning "make broader"
   C. *widow*, meaning "woman whose husband died"
   D. *willow*, meaning "a type of tree"

3. Which sentence uses the word *wither* correctly?
   A. Exercise caused my muscles to *wither*.
   B. Use the vegetable scraper to *wither* the carrot.
   C. His harsh words made my love for him *wither*.
   D. *Wither* you go, I will go.

Using the Word List

madrigals	melodious	move	reckoning	wither

B. DIRECTIONS: *For each item below, write* T *if the statement is true. Write* F *if it is false.*

____ 1. Elizabethan women wore *madrigals* in their hair.

____ 2. A screeching voice is very *melodious*.

____ 3. A politician tries to *move* you to vote for him or her.

____ 4. At the end of a meal, a waiter or waitress brings the *reckoning*.

____ 5. Illness might cause someone's skin to *wither*.

C. DIRECTIONS: *Circle the letter of the choice with the same meaning as the word in CAPITAL LETTERS.*

1. MOVE:	A. convince	B. prevent	C. praise	D. insult
2. WITHER:	A. question	B. repel	C. shrivel	D. increase
3. RECKONING:	A. covering	B. forgetting	C. waiting	D. accounting
4. MELODIOUS:	A. noisy	B. tuneful	C. quiet	D. holy
5. MADRIGALS:	A. wigs	B. cradles	C. verbs	D. songs

© Pearson Education, Inc., publishing as Pearson Prentice Hall. All rights reserved.

"The Passionate Shepherd to His Love" by Christopher Marlowe
"The Nymph's Reply to the Shepherd" by Sir Walter Raleigh
Grammar and Style: Adjective and Adverb Phrases

A **prepositional phrase** consists of a preposition, its object, and any words that modify the object. The entire phrase serves as an adjective or an adverb. An **adjective phrase** is a prepositional phrase that modifies a noun or a pronoun. An **adverb phrase** is a prepositional phrase that modifies a verb, an adjective, or another adverb.

Adjective Phrase: I will make you a cap *of flowers.* [modifies the noun *cap*]

Adverb Phrase: Come live *with me.* [modifies the verb *live*]

Identifying Adjective and Adverb Phrases

A. DIRECTIONS: *Circle the adverb or adjective phrase in each sentence, and draw an arrow to the word it modifies. On the line before the sentence, write* ADJ *if the phrase is an adjective phrase. Write* ADV *if it is an adverb phrase.*

_____ 1. The shepherd spoke to the shepherdess.

_____ 2. He invited her into his home.

_____ 3. Their life in the country would be very pleasant.

_____ 4. His words of love did not persuade her.

_____ 5. She would not live with him.

Using Adjective and Adverb Phrases

B. DIRECTIONS: *Expand these sentences by adding an adjective or adverb phrase to each one. Write the new sentences on the lines provided.*

1. I can picture our wedding.

_____

2. You will wear a long gown.

_____

3. You will carry a bouquet.

_____

4. Your shoes will have buckles.

_____

5. Organ music will echo loudly.

_____

© Pearson Education, Inc., publishing as Pearson Prentice Hall. All rights reserved.

Name _____ Date _____

"The Passionate Shepherd to His Love" by Christopher Marlowe
"The Nymph's Reply to the Shepherd" by Sir Walter Raleigh
Support for Writing

Use the chart below to take notes for your **comparison-and-contrast essay.** Review the poems, writing notes and citing examples that show how the speakers' views are alike and different.

	"The Passionate Shepherd to His Love"	**"The Nymph's Reply to the Shepherd"**
Love		
Nature		
Time		
Material World		

© Pearson Education, Inc., publishing as Pearson Prentice Hall. All rights reserved.

Sonnets 29, 106, 116, and 130 by William Shakespeare
Literary Analysis: Shakespearean Sonnet

Read the following sonnet by Michael Drayton (1563–1631). First indicate the rhyme scheme by writing the appropriate letters on the lines at the right. Then answer the questions that follow the poem.

Calling to mind since first my love began _____

Th'incertain times oft varying in their course. _____

How things still unexpectedly have run, _____

As please the Fates, by their resistless force, _____

[5] Lastly, mine eyes amazedly have seen _____

Essex great fall, Tyrone his peace to gain. _____

The quiet end of that long-living Queen, _____

This King's fair entrance, and our peace with Spain, _____

We and the Dutch at length ourselves to sever. _____

[10] Thus the world doth, and evermore shall reel, _____

Yet to my goddess am I constant ever, _____

Howe'er blind Fortune turn her giddy wheel. _____

Though heaven and earth prove both to me untrue, _____

Yet am I still inviolate to you. _____

Lines 7–10 refer to the failure of the Earl of Essex (Robert Devereux) to conquer the Earl of Tyrone (Hugh O'Neill), to the death of Elizabeth I, who was succeeded by James I, and to other historical events.

1. According to the rhyme scheme, is Drayton's sonnet an example of Shakespearean form or of Petrarchan form? _____

2. What is the premise stated in the poem? _____

_____

3. What is the conclusion stated in the poem? _____

_____

4. In what way is Drayton's philosophy similar to Shakespeare's? _____

_____

© Pearson Education, Inc., publishing as Pearson Prentice Hall. All rights reserved.

Name _____ Date _____

Sonnets 29, 106, 116, and 130 by William Shakespeare
Reading Strategy: Relate Structure to Theme

Readers **relate structure to theme** in literature by looking at how the form of a work influences what is being said. The form of the sonnet—its three quatrains and ending couplet—molds its contents. An idea, situation, or problem is usually presented in the first eight or twelve lines. This means that thoughts must be shaped to fit three quatrains, while the final couplet provides a succinct conclusion in a burst of rhyme. For example, Sonnet 130 examines the features of the speaker's beloved one by one, each time making a case against overstating her worth. The descriptions are beautifully suited to the concise format of the quatrain as each line builds on the last, leading to the surprising conclusion in the couplet.

DIRECTIONS: *Use this graphic organizer to help you understand the relationship of structure and theme in Shakespeare's sonnets. As you read each sonnet, use the middle column to summarize in a sentence or two what the initial idea, situation, or problem is. Then, in the last column, briefly describe what you think the concluding couplet is saying.*

Sonnet	Idea, Situation, or Problem	Conclusion
Sonnet 29		
Sonnet 106		
Sonnet 116		
Sonnet 130		

© Pearson Education, Inc., publishing as Pearson Prentice Hall. All rights reserved.

Name _____ Date _____

Sonnets 29, 106, 116, and 130 by William Shakespeare
Vocabulary Builder

Using the Root -chron-

A. DIRECTIONS: *The root -chron- comes from the Greek word* khronos, *meaning "time."*
Complete the following paragraph using the -chron- based words provided.

synchronize	chronic	chronologer
synchronicity	chronicle	chronology

    Mr. Khronos has suffered from anxiety all his life. Some say he's a _____
worrier. His problem is that he's always watching the clock. He has to—it's his job. As a
_____ of geological history, he measures time in terms of fixed periods and
events. When not at work, Mr. Khronos collects clocks and keeps a _____ of his
purchases. Once, a friend bought him a Felix the Cat clock at the very same moment he was
picking one out for himself at another store. Talk about _____! Not
surprisingly, he has managed to _____ all the timepieces in his house to
Greenwich Mean Time. At some time in the future, someone will probably write the
_____ of the life and times of Mr. Khronos.

Using the Word List

scope	sullen	chronicle
prefiguring	impediments	alters

B. DIRECTIONS: *Write the word from the Word List that best matches each situation that follows.*

1. She was imagining her future life as his wife. _____
2. The father of the bride did all he could to stop the wedding. _____
3. The groom oversaw the extent of the crisis. _____
4. He kept a careful account of the key events in their relationship. _____
5. Her mother's wedding dress fit the bride nearly perfectly, but some pieces of old lace
   needed replacing. _____
6. After her father put a stop to the wedding, she fell silent for weeks. _____

Sonnets 29, 106, 116, and 130 by William Shakespeare
Grammar and Style: Participles as Adjectives

Participles are verb forms that often end in *-ing* or *-ed*. They can sometimes be used as adjectives to modify nouns or pronouns. When a participle functions as an adjective, it must appear near the noun or pronoun it modifies. Shakespeare's descriptive writing is enhanced by the skillful use of participles as adjectives:

O, no! It is an *ever-fixed* mark / That looks on tempests and is never shaken. (Sonnet 116)

Yet well I know / That music hath a far more *pleasing* sound. (Sonnet 130)

A. PRACTICE: *Shakespeare's Sonnet 128, which is not in your text, appears below. Underline participles used as adjectives. Circle the noun or pronoun each participle modifies.*

How oft, when thou, my music, music play'st
Upon that blessèd wood whose motion sounds
With thy sweet fingers when thou gently sway'st
The wiry concord that mine ear confounds,
Do I envy those jacks that nimble leap
To kiss the tender inward of thy hand,
Whilst my poor lips, which should that harvest reap,
At the wood's boldness by thee blushing stand.
To be so tickled they would change their state
And situation with those dancing chips
O'er whom thy fingers walk with gentle gait,
Making dead wood more blest than living lips.
Since saucy jacks so happy are in this,
Give them thy fingers, me thy lips to kiss.

B. Writing Application: *Make each of these sentences more descriptive by adding a participle used as an adjective to modify the noun or pronoun shown in italics.*

1. During his time, Shakespeare had a public reputation as a *playwright*.
   _____

2. Shakespeare's plays were performed at the *Globe Theater*. _____

3. In 1593, a *plague* broke out in London, forcing the city's theaters to close.
   _____

4. Shakespeare's sonnets have a *variety* of themes. _____

© Pearson Education, Inc., publishing as Pearson Prentice Hall. All rights reserved.

Name _____ Date _____

Sonnets 29, 106, 116, and 130 by William Shakespeare
Support for Writing

After you have analyzed the individual images in the sonnet you have chosen, describe each one and note the main idea it expresses. Then, summarize these main ideas into the main idea of the sonnet.

Image 1: _____

_____

Main idea of image 1: _____

_____

_____

Image 2: _____

_____

Main idea of image 2: _____

_____

_____

Image 3: _____

_____

Main idea of image 3: _____

_____

_____

Summary: Main idea of the sonnet

_____

_____

_____

_____

© Pearson Education, Inc., publishing as Pearson Prentice Hall. All rights reserved.

Name _____ Date _____

from **Utopia** by Sir Thomas More
Elizabeth's Speech Before Her Troops by Queen Elizabeth I
Literary Analysis: Theme—The Monarch as Hero

Both the fiction and nonfiction of the English Renaissance portray **monarchs as heroes.**
These men and women are often drawn as superhuman archetypes: they forfeit their lives for
the sake of their kingdoms; their power and generosity know no bounds; they are perfect,
larger-than-life human beings. Some of these characterizations are realistic, while others are
the exaggerations of an adoring public or high-minded leader. Notice Queen Elizabeth's personal
sense of heroism in this excerpt from "Speech Before Defeating the Spanish Armada":

> And therefore I am come amongst you at this time, not as for my creation or sport, but being
> resolved, in the midst and heat of the battle, to live or die amongst you all. . . .

The people under the monarchies during the English Renaissance had great expectations of
their rulers, as the rulers often did of themselves. Generosity, courage, and intelligence are
among the qualities monarchs were expected to possess.

DIRECTIONS: *Answer the following questions on the lines provided.*

1. Look back over the selections by Sir Thomas More and Queen Elizabeth I to find individual
   words or phrases that you think characterize the monarch as hero. Use some of these
   words in a brief description of a heroic Elizabethan monarch.

   _____

   _____

   _____

   _____

2. How do heroic characteristics help monarchs rule? Use examples from More's speech to
   support your answer.

   _____

   _____

   _____

   _____

3. Do you think heroism, as opposed to simple trustworthiness and solid character, was a
   necessary quality in the monarchs of the time? Why or why not?

   _____

   _____

   _____

   _____

© Pearson Education, Inc., publishing as Pearson Prentice Hall. All rights reserved.

Name _____ Date _____

from **Utopia** by Sir Thomas More
Elizabeth's Speech Before Her Troops by Queen Elizabeth I
Reading Strategy: Summarize

Long, complex passages can make a piece of writing difficult to follow. **Summarizing** these passages by briefly restating the main idea can help you in your reading. Look at this example from Queen Elizabeth's "Speech Before Defeating the Spanish Armada."

Let tyrants fear; I have always so behaved myself that, under God, I have placed my chiefest strength and safeguard in the loyal hearts and good will of my subjects.

Summary: The Queen has every faith in her subjects' loyalty.

DIRECTIONS: *Use the graphic organizer below to help you summarize the difficult passages in the speeches of Sir Thomas More and Queen Elizabeth I. As you read, write any difficult passages in the first column of the chart. In the next column, jot down the main idea of the passage. Note the supporting ideas, and record these in the third column. Finally, summarize the main idea of the passage in your own words. One example has already been done for you.*

Passage	Main Idea	Supporting Ideas	Summary
And that therefore a prince ought to take more care of his people's happiness than of his own, as a shepherd ought to take care of his flock than of himself.	A prince should put his people's happiness before his own.	A shepherd must look after his sheep before he cares for himself.	A prince should be more concerned with his subjects' welfare than with his own.

© Pearson Education, Inc., publishing as Pearson Prentice Hall. All rights reserved.

from **Utopia** by Sir Thomas More
Elizabeth's Speech Before Her Troops by Queen Elizabeth I
Vocabulary Builder

Using the Root -*sequent*-

A. DIRECTIONS: *The word root* -sequent- *means "following in time or order." On a separate sheet of paper, rewrite each sentence by replacing the underlined word or phrase with one of the following words.*

consequence	sequentially	non sequitur	sequel	inconsequential

1. His outrageous behavior appeared to be a <u>result</u> of the tragedy.
2. Following the death of the queen, his everyday troubles seemed <u>trivial</u>.
3. These crucial events, from earliest to latest, do indeed flow in <u>order by time</u>.
4. I saw "Young Emperor," the original episode, but missed "Old Emperor," which is the <u>following episode</u>.
5. After making her first point, she delivered a <u>remark that had no bearing on what she had just said</u>.

Using the Word List

confiscation	sloth	subsequently	abrogated
forfeited	fraudulent	treachery	stead

B. DIRECTIONS: *Complete each sentence with an appropriate word from the Word List.*

1. The monarch's _____ of property was like death to his people.
2. He was a detestable man, displaying his _____ as a soldier displays a medal.
3. The king requested the lieutenant general escort the queen in his _____, for he trusted him like a brother.
4. The ruler's _____ promises were revealed by his heir to the throne.
5. When she _____ the death penalty, the once-doomed prisoners cheered like exhilarated school boys.
6. Noble monarchs, who live to serve their people, know nothing of _____.
7. Because the jester was as entertaining as a stone, he _____ his turn to cheer up the queen.
8. The king unwittingly consumed a vial of poison; _____ he died.

© Pearson Education, Inc., publishing as Pearson Prentice Hall. All rights reserved.

from **Utopia** by Sir Thomas More
Elizabeth's Speech Before Her Troops by Queen Elizabeth I
Grammar and Style: Complex Sentences

Complex sentences contain a main clause and one or more subordinate clauses relating to that clause. The main clause, which can appear anywhere in the sentence, can stand by itself. However, the subordinate clauses are dependent on the main clause. Complex sentences are useful for showing relationships between ideas, such as time, logic, or cause and effect. In the following complex sentence from *Utopia*, note the position of the main clause, which is italicized.

He ought to shake off either his sloth or his pride, for the people's hatred and scorn arise from these faults in him.

A. PRACTICE: *In the space provided, combine each pair of simple sentences to make a complex sentence. Use connecting words (subordinate conjunctions) like* but, because, when, although, *and* who.

1. The royals loved their jester. He never failed to make them laugh.

   _____

2. The general worshipped his queen. He was still forced to fight against her.

   _____

3. The king called for an end to taxes. His subjects cried for joy.

   _____

B. Writing Application: *Revise the following paragraph by making some of the simple sentences into complex sentences. Use connecting words such as* because, although, when, after, before, until, *and* if.

The queen enjoyed her morning ritual. She drank her tea. She read the paper. Then, she watered the plants in her room. She didn't trust her staff with such delicate specimens. Her Majesty ate a delicious royal breakfast. She strolled the grounds of the main house. The groundskeeper spoke with her about landscaping matters. The resident rabbit was scared off by their voices. The queen extended her stroll. It was a sure sign that her mood had soured. She continued on a long walk. The dignitaries from France arrived. It seemed she might be cross. The queen still looked cheerful.

_____

_____

_____

_____

_____

_____

_____

_____

© Pearson Education, Inc., publishing as Pearson Prentice Hall. All rights reserved.

from **Utopia** by Sir Thomas More
Elizabeth's Speech Before Her Troops by Queen Elizabeth I
Support for Writing

Use the chart below to compare the leadership qualities of Sir Thomas More and Queen Elizabeth with those of a modern leader. List each leadership quality of More and Elizabeth in the left column. In the right column, list actions or words the modern leader has done or said that relate to each quality. Then, write your conclusion below.

Modern Leader: _____

Ideas of Leadership	Characteristics of Modern Leader in Actions and Words

Conclusion:

_____

_____

_____

_____

_____

© Pearson Education, Inc., publishing as Pearson Prentice Hall. All rights reserved.

Name _____ Date _____

Psalms, sermons, and parables are literary forms found in the Bible. A **psalm** is a lyric poem or a sacred song praising God. A psalm usually contains figurative language. Many psalms were originally written to be sung. A **sermon** is a speech with a moral or religious message, usually spoken by one person to a group. A **parable** is a short story that conveys a moral or religious lesson. Parables have simple plots and often contain dialogue.

DIRECTIONS: *Read each passage and answer the questions that follow.*

1. And he arose, and came to his father. But when he was yet a great way off, his father saw him, and had compassion, and ran, and fell on his neck, and kissed him.

   And the son said unto him. Father, I have sinned against heaven, and in thy sight, and am no more worthy to be called thy son.

   But the father said to his servants, Bring forth the best robe, and put it on him; and put a ring on his hand, and shoes on his feet.

   What elements in this passage are characteristic of parables? _____

   _____

2. Behold the fowls of the air: for they sow not, neither do they reap, nor gather into barns; yet your heavenly Father feedeth them. Are ye not much better than they?

   A. What is the religious message in the passage? _____

   _____

   B. Is this a psalm, sermon, or parable? _____

   _____

3. He maketh me to lie down in green pastures; he leadeth me beside the still waters.
   He restoreth my soul: he leadeth me in the paths of righteousness for his name's sake.

   A. What figures of speech are used in this passage? _____

   _____

   B. To whom does *He* refer? _____

   _____

   C. What elements in this passage are characteristic of psalms? _____

   _____

© Pearson Education, Inc., publishing as Pearson Prentice Hall. All rights reserved.

Name _____   Date _____

from **The King James Bible**
Reading Strategy: Infer Meaning

Some passages from the Bible include difficult language and images that require you to **make inferences,** or draw conclusions, about the meaning of the passage. You can **infer meaning** by using the following strategy. First, ask yourself what you already know about the words or images in the passage. Second, look for context clues that help you understand the meaning. Look at this example from Psalm 23 showing how you can infer meaning.

Biblical Passage	What I Know	Context Clues
Thou preparest a table before me in the presence of mine enemies; thou anointest my head with oil; my cup runneth over.	I know that he's speaking to God and that he is using metaphors.	The psalm begins with the phrase "The shepherd," which means God is taking care of him; anointing with oil is probably a sign of honor; a cup that runs over must refer to having more than enough.

From these clues, the reader can infer that God is protecting the poet from his enemies, honoring him, and providing him with all that he needs.

DIRECTIONS: *Use this chart to help you infer the meaning of difficult passages in* The King James Bible. *Each time you come across a difficult passage, write it in the column labeled Biblical Passage. In the next column, write what you know about the words or ideas in the passage. Then write clues to the meaning that you find in the context. Finally, combining what you know together with the context clues, write what you think the passage means.*

Biblical Passage	What I Know	Context Clues	Meaning

© Pearson Education, Inc., publishing as Pearson Prentice Hall. All rights reserved.
64

from **The King James Bible**
Vocabulary Builder

Using the Root -stat-

A. DIRECTIONS: *Combine the word root -stat-, which means "to stand," with each prefix or suffix listed below to make a word. Then use that word in a sentence.*

1. Suffix *-ic* Word: _____

   Sentence: _____

2. Prefix *thermo-* Word: _____

   Sentence: _____

3. Suffix *-ion* Word: _____

   Sentence: _____

4. Suffix *-us* Word: _____

   Sentence: _____

Using the Word List

righteousness	stature	prodigal
entreated	transgressed	

B. DIRECTIONS: *The questions below consist of a related pair of words in CAPITAL LETTERS followed by four lettered pairs of words. Choose the pair that best expresses a relationship similar to that in the pair in capital letters.*

____ 1. RIGHTEOUSNESS : INJUSTICE ::
   - **A.** pleasure : pain
   - **B.** accurate : correct
   - **C.** anger : emotion
   - **D.** rule : control

____ 2. TRANSGRESS : DISOBEY ::
   - **A.** break : rule
   - **B.** shade : tree
   - **C.** argue : quarrel
   - **D.** hope : future

____ 3. ENTREAT : FORGIVENESS ::
   - **A.** ask : favor
   - **B.** answer : deny
   - **C.** work : achieve
   - **D.** deny : admit

____ 4. PRODIGAL : FORTUNE ::
   - **A.** careful : careless
   - **B.** glass : windows
   - **C.** height : mountain
   - **D.** wasteful : possessions

____ 5. STATURE : MAN ::
   - **A.** archer : skill
   - **B.** inches : feet
   - **C.** agility : dancer
   - **D.** speaker : listener

© Pearson Education, Inc., publishing as Pearson Prentice Hall. All rights reserved.

Name _____ Date _____

from **The King James Bible**
Grammar and Style: Infinitive Phrases

Infinitive phrases are made up of the word *to* followed by the base form of a verb (*to run, to sing*) plus its complements (*to run swiftly, to sing loudly*) and/or its objects (*to run swiftly home*) and its modifiers (*to sing loudly in the shower*). An infinitive phrase can function as a noun, an adjective, or an adverb.

Noun:	*To praise God* was David's intention. (subject)
	All his life he had loved *to sing psalms of praise.* (direct object)
Adjective:	He believed that God had the power *to supply all his needs.* (modifies *power*)
Adverb:	He was a devout man, quick *to turn to God for help.* (modifies *quick*)

A. PRACTICE: *Underline the infinitive phrases in the sentences. Then indicate whether each phrase functions as a noun, an adjective, or an adverb by writing N, ADJ, or ADV on the line following the sentence, and tell how the phrase functions in the sentence.*

1. Reginald is afraid to raise his hand in class. _____

2. Mary Ann refused to answer the question. _____

3. The store is looking for someone to work evenings. _____

B. Writing Application: *Fill in the blank in each sentence with an infinitive phrase. Then write N, ADV, or ADJ to indicate whether the infinitive functions as a noun, an adverb, or an adjective.*

1. _____ a doctor's most important responsibility. _____

2. We'll be ready when you give the signal _____. _____

3. The whole class stopped _____. _____

4. Andrew is working _____. _____

5. People do not have the right _____. _____

6. Michael always loved _____. _____

© Pearson Education, Inc., publishing as Pearson Prentice Hall. All rights reserved.

from The King James Bible
Support for Writing

A parable is organized like a story. It is built around a problem that one or more characters try to solve. Various events occur as the characters try to solve the problem. Eventually, a solution is found, and the parable comes to an end. In the process of telling the plot, a moral is taught. Use the lines below to organize your ideas for a parable that supports a moral in which you believe.

Who are the characters, and what do readers need to know about them?

_____

_____

_____

What is the problem that sets events in motion?

_____

_____

What happens as the characters try to solve the problem?

1. _____

2. _____

3. _____

4. _____

5. _____

How is the problem solved?

_____

_____

_____

_____

The Moral:

_____

_____

_____

© Pearson Education, Inc., publishing as Pearson Prentice Hall. All rights reserved.

Name _____ Date _____

Frank Kermode Introduces *Macbeth* by William Shakespeare

DIRECTIONS: *Use the space provided to answer the questions.*

1. Identify two liberties that Shakespeare takes with history in *Macbeth*.

   _____

   _____

2. According to Kermode, why did Shakespeare portray Banquo in a favorable light?

   _____

   _____

3. In the passage shown from Act I and discussed by Frank Kermode, what conflict does Macbeth experience?

   _____

   _____

4. What are three reasons that Macbeth should *not* kill King Duncan?

   _____

   _____

   _____

5. Why is Macbeth's soliloquy so famous, according to Kermode? Do you agree or disagree with Kermode here? Briefly explain your answer.

   _____

   _____

   _____

   _____

   _____

6. What factor does Kermode single out in order to explain the extraordinary range and flexibility of Shakespeare's language in *Macbeth*?

   _____

   _____

7. How does *Macbeth* comply with native ethical traditions, according to Kermode?

   _____

   _____

© Pearson Education, Inc., publishing as Pearson Prentice Hall. All rights reserved.

Frank Kermode
Listening and Viewing

Segment 1: Meet Frank Kermode
- What is the job of a literary critic?
- Why do you think literary criticism is important to society?

_____

_____

_____

Segment 2: Frank Kermode Introduces Shakespeare
- Why do you think Shakespeare has become a cultural icon?
- What do sports and theater have in common, according to Frank Kermode?

_____

_____

_____

Segment 3: The Writing Process
- When Frank Kermode writes, what does he assume about his audience?
- How do you think this shapes his writing?

_____

_____

_____

_____

Segment 4: The Rewards of Writing
- According to Frank Kermode, why is it important to learn how to read well?
- Why do you think it is important to learn to read difficult texts, such as the works of Shakespeare?

_____

_____

_____

_____

Name _____ Date _____

The Tragedy of Macbeth, *Act I,* by William Shakespeare
Literary Analysis: Elizabethan Drama

In the years before Elizabeth I came to power in England, troupes of actors traveled the English countryside performing religious plays. They performed wherever they could: in the courtyards of inns, in town squares, and in open areas on the outskirts of villages. Many of the plays they presented were based on biblical stories.

During the Elizabethan period, the style of English drama changed radically. Permanent theaters were built, giving actors not only an artistic home, but also the luxury of perfecting certain aspects of presentation. Plays began to veer away from religious themes. Instead, audiences found themselves watching plays about familiar problems and events. Playwrights used poetic language and rich imagery to tell a wide variety of stories—from dramas about tragic figures to comedies about hapless lovers. This kind of theater, with its nonreligious entertainment value, became very popular. Audiences loved watching plays about characters with motivations and feelings they could understand.

DIRECTIONS: *Answer the following questions about Act I of* The Tragedy of Macbeth.

1. What might the three witches represent to an audience used to watching plays with religious themes?

   _____

   _____

2. In what ways might the content of the following speech be said to echo the religious sentiments of Shakespeare's audience?

   . . . But I have spoke
   With one that saw him die, who did report
   That very frankly he confessed his treasons,
   Implored your Highness' pardon and set forth
   A deep repentance . . .

   _____

   _____

3. In the following speech, what is Lady Macbeth saying about her husband's character? How might such sentiments about Macbeth win an audience's sympathy?

   Glamis thou art, and Cawdor, and shalt be
   What thou art promised. Yet do I fear thy nature;
   It is too full o' the milk of human kindness
   To catch the nearest way. Thou wouldst be great,
   Art not without ambition, but without
   The illness should attend it. . . .

   _____

   _____

© Pearson Education, Inc., publishing as Pearson Prentice Hall. All rights reserved.

The Tragedy of Macbeth, *Act I,* by William Shakespeare
Reading Strategy: Use Text Aids

Playwrights use stage directions to help readers, actors, and directors understand how a play should look when it is staged. Stage directions can give readers hints about mood, setting, movement, and characters' intentions. Look at these opening stage directions.

An open place.

[*Thunder and lightning. Enter* THREE WITCHES.]

With very few words William Shakespeare has told you a great deal about the play.

1. Where does the scene take place?

    In "An open place," a place where there are no trees, hills, or houses.

2. What is going on at this place?

    "Thunder and lightning." The weather is bad, and the mood is a little frightening.

3. Who is in the scene?

    "Three witches enter." Right away, the reader can tell that something strange is about to happen.

DIRECTIONS: *Stage directions can guide the reader to a better understanding of a play's action. Use a graphic organizer like this one to help you pick up hints from the stage directions.*

Act/Scene	Characters	Setting	Specific Action
Act I, Scene i	Three witches	An open place	Thunder and lightning. Three witches enter.

Notes in the margin of *The Tragedy of Macbeth* and other plays provide another useful tool. To get more from what you read, see if you can figure out an annotated term or expression before you look at the margin note. Usually the context of the play provides clues. Look at these lines from *The Tragedy of Macbeth:*

MALCOLM. . . . He died

As one that had been studied[3] in his death,

To throw away the dearest thing he owed[4]

As 'twere a careless[5] trifle.

The lines may seem confusing, but if you look at the context, you will find hints about the meaning. The context makes it clear that Malcolm is praising the Thane of Cawdor for the noble way in which he died. According to Malcolm, the Thane's death turned out to be his greatest achievement. Knowing this, when you read "He died / As one that had been studied in his death," you might be able to guess that *studied* means "prepared for" or "rehearsed." Then, to check your interpretation, look at the margin note.

The Tragedy of Macbeth, *Act I,* by William Shakespeare
Vocabulary Builder

Using Words About Power

A. DIRECTIONS: The Tragedy of Macbeth *is a play about the misuse of political and personal power. There are many words in the English language that have political associations. Here are a few such words you will find in Shakespeare's play: thane, earl lord, king, traitor. Think of other words that might apply to political situations and relationships in the United States. For example, in the United States there are no lords or kings but there is a president. On the lines below, write as many words having to do with American political relationships as you can think of.*

_____   _____   _____

_____   _____   _____

Using the Word List

imperial	liege	sovereign	treasons	valor

B. DIRECTIONS: *Fill in each blank with the word from the Word List that best completes the sentence.*

1. Macbeth's _____ in battle was unsurpassed.

2. "Acts of betrayal against the king are _____!" cried the general.

3. "I bring news of the battle, my _____," the messenger whispered to the king.

4. King Duncan is the _____ ruler of Scotland.

5. Macbeth's _____ virtues have impressed the king.

C. DIRECTIONS: *In each sentence that follows there is a word in italics. Choose the lettered word or phrase that is closest in meaning to the word in italics, and write the letter of your choice in the blank.*

____ 1. The military leader wanted to preserve his *sovereign* power.
  A. economic   B. meager   C. supreme   D. brave

____ 2. *Valor* is a trait that is associated with heroism in battle.
  A. lightning   B. courage   C. beauty   D. ferocity

____ 3. The rebels attempted to strip the queen of her *imperial power.*
  A. supreme authority   C. army
  B. religious beliefs   D. court

____ 4. The subject bowed before his *liege.*
  A. royal personage   C. witch
  B. high-ranking general   D. doctor

© Pearson Education, Inc., publishing as Pearson Prentice Hall. All rights reserved.

Name _____ Date _____

The Tragedy of Macbeth, *Act I,* by William Shakespeare
Grammar and Style: Action Verbs and Linking Verbs

Action verbs express physical or mental action. **Linking verbs** connect the subject of a sentence with a complement that either renames or modifies the subject. Linking verbs include forms of *be, seem, taste, sound, look, become, appear, feel,* and *smell.*

Action verbs: "Who was the thane *lives* yet,

But under heavy judgment *bears* that life

Which he *deserves* to lose."

Linking verbs: "The rest *is* labor, which is not used for you.

I'*ll be* myself the harbinger, . . . "

A. PRACTICE: *Each of the quotations below is from* The Tragedy of Macbeth. *Underline the action verbs and circle the linking verbs.*

1. But in a sieve I'll thither sail,
   And like a rat without a tail
   I'll do, I'll do, I'll do.

2. Hover through the fog and filthy air.

3. Live you, or are you aught
   That man may question?

4. Speak if you can: what are you?

5. . . . He bade me, from him, call thee Thane of Cawdor;
   In which addition, hail, most worthy Thane!
   For it is thine.

6. The sin of my ingratitude even now
   Was heavy on me: thou art so far before,
   That swiftest wing of recompense is slow
   To overtake thee.

7. The King comes here tonight.

B. Writing Application: *If the underlined verb in each sentence is an action verb, rewrite the sentence using a linking verb. If the underlined verb is a linking verb, rewrite the sentence using an action verb.*

Example: Macbeth <u>speaks</u> of his unhappiness. (action verb)
Rewritten: Macbeth seems unhappy *or* Macbeth is unhappy.

1. Lady Macbeth <u>sees</u> a way to make her husband king.

   _____

2. The witches <u>are</u> evil.

   _____

3. King Duncan <u>trusts</u> Macbeth completely.

   _____

4. Duncan's sons <u>look</u> guilty.

   _____

© Pearson Education, Inc., publishing as Pearson Prentice Hall. All rights reserved.

Name _____ Date _____

The Tragedy of Macbeth, *Act I,* by William Shakespeare
Support for Extend Your Learning

Writing
Use the lines below to gather and organize your ideas for your speech of welcome.

Opening: _____

_____

Body: _____

_____

_____

_____

Conclusion: _____

_____

_____

Research and Technology
Use the chart below to compare how different film actresses have portrayed Lady Macbeth in Act I. Write how they are alike in the left column and how they are different in the right column. Use the information to help organize ideas for your oral report.

The actresses: _____

How they are alike:	How they are different:

© Pearson Education, Inc., publishing as Pearson Prentice Hall. All rights reserved.

The Tragedy of Macbeth, *Act II,* by William Shakespeare
Literary Analysis: Blank Verse

Blank verse consists of lines of poetry written in iambic pentameter. Each line contains five poetic feet of stressed and unstressed syllables. The form is flexible and versatile and can produce the effect of smooth, natural speech in a way that other metrical patterns cannot. For this reason, Shakespeare relied primarily on blank verse throughout his plays. However, Shakespeare occasionally used prose, especially for the speech of characters from lower stations in life. He also employed occasional rhymes when it seemed appropriate to a particular character: The witches in *The Tragedy of MacBeth,* for example, often speak in rhymes. Finally, like most dramatists of the English Renaissance, Shakespeare often used one or more rhymed lines of dialogue to signal that a scene had ended or that new players must make their entrances, in this way alerting offstage players or other members of the company.

Following is a series of passages from *The Tragedy of Macbeth.* On the line below each passage, identify it as "prose," "rhyme," or "blank verse." Then scan the lines that are in blank verse by marking the stressed and unstressed syllables.

1. **SECOND WITCH.** When the hurlyburly's done.
   When the battle's lost and won.

   _____

2. **ROSS.** I'll see it done.
   KING. What he hath lost, noble Macbeth hath won.

   _____

3. **ROSS.** The King hath happily received, Macbeth,
   The news of thy success. And when he reads
   Thy personal venture in the rebel's fight,
   His wonders and his praises do contend
   Which should be thine or his.

   _____

4. **LADY MACBETH (Reads).** They met me in the day of success; and I have learned by the per-fect'st report they have more in them than mortal knowledge. When I burned in desire to question them further, they made themselves air, into which they vanished.

   _____

© Pearson Education, Inc., publishing as Pearson Prentice Hall. All rights reserved.

The Tragedy of Macbeth, *Act II*, by William Shakespeare
Reading Strategy: Read Verse for Meaning

Some readers see that a text is written in verse and automatically assume they will have a difficult time understanding it. Verse texts can indeed seem more complicated than prose. However, there are many tools a reader can use to break verse down into manageable and understandable ideas. A good strategy is to read verse passages for the ideas that they present rather than simply as individual lines of poetry. One way to do this is to read the lines aloud in order to better follow complete sentences or thoughts. If you stop at the end of each line, rather than reading all the way to the end of the thought, you will probably become confused. Pay close attention to punctuation to note where a sentence ends. If you reach the end of the thought in a passage and you don't understand what you've read, go back through the passage slowly, paraphrasing as you go. Look at this example from Act II of *The Tragedy of Macbeth*.

> **MALCOLM.** This murderous shaft that's shot
> Hath not yet lighted, and our safest way
> Is to avoid the aim. Therefore to horse;
> And let us not be dainty of leave-taking,
> But shift away. There's warrant in that theft
> Which steals itself when there's no mercy left.

1. How many sentences are there in this passage?

   _____

2. Paraphrase the first sentence.

   _____

   _____

3. Paraphrase the next two sentences.

   _____

   _____

   _____

4. What is the basic thrust of the passage?

   _____

   _____

As you continue reading *The Tragedy of Macbeth*, break long passages down into individual sentences and restate the sentences in your own words.

© Pearson Education, Inc., publishing as Pearson Prentice Hall. All rights reserved.

The Tragedy of Macbeth, *Act II*, by William Shakespeare
Vocabulary Builder

Using the Root -*voc*-

A. DIRECTIONS: *The word root -voc- means "voice" or "calling." Read each definition and then choose the word that best completes each sentence.*

evocative (adj.), calling forth an emotional response
provocative (adj.), serving to provoke or stimulate
vocation (n.), a summons or strong inclination to a particular state or course of action; the work at which a person is regularly employed
vociferously (adv.), marked by or given to insistent outcry
vocalize (adj.), to give voice to

1. The witches speak to Macbeth _____; they will not be quieted.
2. Macbeth finds the witches' predictions very _____.
3. The setting of the first scene in *Macbeth* is _____ of loneliness.
4. Macbeth's _____ at the beginning of the play might be said to be that of a warrior.

Using the Word List

augment	palpable	stealthy
multitudinous	equivocate	predominance

B. DIRECTIONS: *Each question below consists of a pair of words in CAPITAL LETTERS followed by four lettered pairs of words. Choose the pair that best expresses a relationship similar to that expressed in the pair in capital letters.*

____ 1. MULTITUDINOUS : MANY ::
   A. gigantic : large
   B. some : few
   C. up : down
   D. survive : prosper

____ 2. AUGMENT : PREVENT ::
   A. terrify : frighten
   B. beg : plead
   C. hollow : empty
   D. help : hinder

____ 3. STEALTHY : OBVIOUS ::
   A. quiet : healthful
   B. adventuresome : timid
   C. fat : heavy
   D. polluted : filthy

____ 4. PALPABLE : TANGIBLE ::
   A. stealthy : furtive
   B. shy : outgoing
   C. few : multitudinous
   D. ambitious : lazy

____ 5. EQUIVOCATE : DECEPTION ::
   A. whine : exhibit
   B. beautiful : attractive
   C. death : die
   D. sing : song

____ 6. PREDOMINANCE : WEAKNESS ::
   A. valor : courage
   B. success : failure
   C. happiness : gladness
   D. selfishness : miserliness

© Pearson Education, Inc., publishing as Pearson Prentice Hall. All rights reserved.

Name _____ Date _____

The Tragedy of Macbeth, *Act II*, by William Shakespeare
Grammar and Style: Commonly Confused Words: *Lie* and *Lay*

A few rules can help you distinguish between *lie* and *lay*.

Lie means "to lie down or recline." *Lay* means "to place."

Example: I'm going to *lie* down before dinner. **Example:** *Lay* the king's robe over the chair.

The past tense of *lie* is *lay*; the past participle is *lain*.

Example: Macbeth devised his plot while the king *lay* sleeping; the king had *lain* in his bed scarcely two hours when he was murdered.

The past tense of *lay* is *laid*; the past participle is *laid*.

Example: Lady Macbeth *laid* the king's robe aside; the robe had been *laid* in the king's blood after the murder.

A. PRACTICE: *If the underlined verb form in each sentence is correct, write* OK *in the blank. If it is incorrect, write the correct verb form on the blank.*

_____ 1. Morning came but still the revelers <u>lay</u> in their beds.

_____ 2. Lady Macbeth <u>laid</u> the daggers down by the sleeping guards.

_____ 3. Foul deeds <u>lie</u> heavily upon the conscience.

_____ 4. The porter had already gone to <u>lay</u> down when Macduff arrived.

B. Writing Application: *Follow the directions to write sentences using* lie *and* lay *correctly.*

1. Use *lie* to tell about taking a nap.

   _____

2. Use *laid* in reference to putting away some clothes.

   _____

3. Use *lain* to describe the dust on an old piece of furniture.

   _____

4. Use *lay* to describe a sleeping cat.

   _____

5. Use *lying* to describe someone who is sleeping in the next room at the moment.

   _____

6. Use *laying* to describe a hen producing an egg.

   _____

© Pearson Education, Inc., publishing as Pearson Prentice Hall. All rights reserved.

The Tragedy of Macbeth, *Act II,* by William Shakespeare
Support for Extend Your Learning

Listening and Speaking

Use the chart below to organize your arguments for and against the **debate** proposition. On the left side of the chart, write arguments to prove that Ross is a self-seeking flatterer, not a loyal Scot. On the right side, write arguments against this proposition. Include quotations and other details from Act II that support each position.

Proposition: Ross is a self-seeking flatterer, not a loyal Scot.	
Arguments for the proposition	**Arguments against the proposition**

Writing

Use the lines below to record clues and testimony that will help you create an **investigational journal** regarding the murder of King Duncan.

Clues: _____

_____

_____

Testimony: _____

_____

_____

_____

_____

© Pearson Education, Inc., publishing as Pearson Prentice Hall. All rights reserved.

The Tragedy of Macbeth, *Act III,* by William Shakespeare
Literary Analysis: Conflict

In literature, as in life, **conflict** is a struggle between two opposing forces. It is an essential dramatic element; it builds tension and holds the reader's interest. Without conflict there can be no drama. There are many conflicts within Shakespeare's *The Tragedy of Macbeth.* Some of them are external conflicts that take place between characters with opposing goals. Others are internal conflicts that take place within the consciousness of certain characters. Often conflict begins in one scene and escalates throughout a number of scenes that follow. For example, the fact that Banquo is with Macbeth when the witches make their prophesies in Act I leads to conflict between the two men in later scenes.

DIRECTIONS: *Answer the following questions, and then find a quotation from Act III of* The Tragedy of Macbeth *that supports your answer.*

1. In Scene i, what is the conflict between the murderers and Banquo?

   _____

   _____

   _____

   Quotation: _____

2. Why is Banquo in conflict with Macbeth?

   _____

   _____

   _____

   Quotation: _____

3. Why does Macbeth experience an internal conflict at the state dinner?

   _____

   _____

   _____

   Quotation: _____

4. Why is Lady Macbeth in conflict with Macbeth during the state dinner?

   _____

   _____

   _____

   Quotation: _____

© Pearson Education, Inc., publishing as Pearson Prentice Hall. All rights reserved.

Name _____ Date _____

The Tragedy of Macbeth, *Act III,* by William Shakespeare
Reading Strategy: Read Between the Lines

Often *what* a character in a play says is not as important as *why* he or she says it. For example, shortly after the beginning of Act III, Banquo speaks to Macbeth:

BANQUO. Let your Highness
Command upon me, to the which my duties
Are with a most indissoluble tie
For ever knit.

If you were to take Banquo's words at face value, you would think that he is a most loyal subject to King Macbeth. However, in a speech just before Macbeth enters the scene, Banquo voices not only his suspicions about what criminal acts Macbeth might have committed in order to achieve the throne, but also his own hopes for the future regarding the throne. Therefore, you must assume that Banquo has a very good reason for not confronting Macbeth. With this thought in mind, you can begin to see how the character of Banquo, like that of Macbeth, serves as more positive embodiment of the play's themes of deception and the quest for power. Such "reading between the lines" can help you understand more than simply what the words say.

DIRECTIONS: *Use the following questions to help you analyze and read between the lines of Act III of* The Tragedy of Macbeth. *As you continue through the play, remember to look for the intentions behind each character's words by asking yourself similar questions.*

MACBETH. Both of you
Know Banquo was your enemy.
BOTH MURDERERS. True, my lord.
MACBETH. So is he mine, and in such bloody distance
That every minute of his being thrusts
Against my near'st of life. . . .

1. What is Macbeth telling the murderers about his relationship to Banquo?

_____

2. Why does he tell them this?

_____

MACBETH. [to MURDERER] Thou art the best o' th' cutthroats.
Yet he's good that did the like for Fleance;
If thou didst it, thou art the nonpareil.

3. What is Macbeth saying about the murderer's deeds?

_____

4. Why is he saying this?

_____

© Pearson Education, Inc., publishing as Pearson Prentice Hall. All rights reserved.

Name _____ Date _____

The Tragedy of Macbeth, *Act III,* by William Shakespeare
Vocabulary Builder

Using the Prefix *mal-*

A. DIRECTIONS: *The prefix* mal- *means "bad or badly," or "poor or poorly." Rewrite each sentence, replacing the underlined word or words with a word that contains the prefix* mal-.

1. The airplane engine continued to <u>function poorly</u> during a routine inspection.

   _____

2. Sheri was <u>poorly adjusted</u> to her new school environment.

   _____

3. The doctor said my problem with digesting proteins came from <u>improper absorption</u> of certain nutrients.

   _____

4. Every time Tomas comes for a visit, I remember that he is a <u>person who is not content.</u>

   _____

Using the Word List

indissoluble	dauntless	jocund
infirmity	malevolence	

B. DIRECTIONS: *For each item, choose the lettered word or phrase that is most nearly* opposite *in meaning to the numbered word. Write the letter of your choice in the blank.*

____ 1. infirmity
    A. bad mood   **C.** sickness
    B. good cheer   **D.** good health

____ 2. jocund
    A. grumpy   **C.** elderly
    B. sickly   **D.** sleepy

____ 3. indissoluble
    A. easily undone   **C.** often repeated
    B. not to go forward   **D.** not to be heard

____ 4. dauntless
    A. agreeable   **C.** hapless
    B. humorless   **D.** fearful

____ 5. malevolence
    A. happiness   **C.** good will
    B. ill feelings   **D.** desire

© Pearson Education, Inc., publishing as Pearson Prentice Hall. All rights reserved.

Name _____ Date _____

The Tragedy of Macbeth, *Act III,* by William Shakespeare
Grammar and Style: Subject-Verb Agreement

The **subject and verb** in a sentence must **agree,** or be the same in number. That means that a singular subject takes a singular verb and a plural subject takes a plural verb.

Singular subject and singular verb: Macbeth murders Duncan.

Plural subject and plural verb: The witches predict that Macbeth will become king.

Determining whether to use a singular or plural verb can be difficult when there are other words or phrases between the subject and its verb.

Example: Macbeth, despite his pangs of conscience, (*does, do*) kill King Duncan.

The subject of the sentence is *Macbeth*, not *pangs*, so the verb form is singular: *does*.

A. PRACTICE: *Underline the correct form of the verb in each sentence.*

1. ". . . Command upon me, to the which my duties / (*Is, Are*) with a most indissoluble tie / For ever knit."

2. "Your spirits (*shines, shine*) through you."

3. The three murderers (*attempts, attempt*) to do away with Banquo and Fleance.

4. Of the two, only Banquo (*is, are*) killed.

5. (*Has, Have*) Macbeth and his wife gotten away with murder?

B. Writing Application: *Look at each of the following sentences and decide whether its subject and verb agree. If the sentence is correct, write* OK *on the line. If the sentence is incorrect, rewrite it, replacing each italicized word with one that agrees with its subject or verb.*

1. The three murderers who were hired by Macbeth *is* upset when Fleance *escape*.

_____

2. Macbeth is shocked that no one else *see* the ghost of Banquo.

_____

3. The other dinner guests *are* appalled at Macbeth's behavior.

_____

4. Lady Macbeth *become* alarmed when she sees that Macbeth is out of control.

_____

5. She *tell* the dinner guests that Macbeth is prone to this kind of fit.

_____

© Pearson Education, Inc., publishing as Pearson Prentice Hall. All rights reserved.

Name _____ Date _____

Support for Extend Your Learning

Writing

Use the chart below to organize your ideas for your **diary entry.** On the left side, list the strange events you will write about. On the right side, list vivid words and phrases that convey a tone of shock, outrage, and bewilderment about each of the events.

Strange Events	Vivid Language

Research and Technology

Use the chart below to gather information for your **annotated bibliography.**

Sources	Summary of Information

© Pearson Education, Inc., publishing as Pearson Prentice Hall. All rights reserved.

The Tragedy of Macbeth, *Act IV*, by William Shakespeare
Literary Analysis: Imagery

Imagery can create responses from any of the reader's senses: sight, hearing, touch, smell, or taste. Written images can illuminate for the reader the meaning of both individual moments and patterns of meaning that run throughout the text. Look at this imagery-laden quotation from the First Witch in *The Tragedy of Macbeth*, Act IV.

"Pour in sow's blood, that hath eaten

Her nine farrow, grease that's sweaten

From the murderer's gibbet throw into the flame."

This passage contains visual imagery: "sow's blood"; a mother pig eating her nine young. It also contains imagery of touch: "grease" from the noose that hangs a murderer; grease added to a "flame."

Paying attention to imagery can guide you to a deeper understanding of the text. As you read, be on the lookout for repeated imagery; for example, think about the image of blood that runs throughout the entire text of *The Tragedy of Macbeth*. Blood as an image can mean many different things: loyalty, guilt, revenge, death, brotherhood, parent-child relationship, royalty, and so on. Think about the significance of each of these ideas within the plot of the play.

DIRECTIONS: *Read the following passages from* The Tragedy of Macbeth *and identify the imagery in each. Then write the connection, or what the image makes you think of.*

1. "When shall we three meet again? / In thunder, lightning, or in rain?"

   Imagery: _____

   Connection: _____

2. "Stars, hide your fires; / Let not light see my black and deep desires . . ."

   _____

3. "I have no spur / To prick the sides of my intent, but only / Vaulting ambition, which o'er-leaps itself / And falls on th' other . . ."

   Imagery: _____

   Connection: _____

4. "But now I am cabined, cribbed, confined, bound in / To saucy doubts and fears . . ."

   Imagery: _____

   Connection: _____

© Pearson Education, Inc., publishing as Pearson Prentice Hall. All rights reserved.

Name _____ Date _____

Reading Strategy: Use Your Senses

In today's commercial theater environment, with its elaborate sets and extravagant special effects, it is difficult to imagine a time when a stage setting consisted of little more than a bare floor. Yet when Shakespeare was writing and producing his plays, theaters used almost nothing in the way of scenic design. Theatergoers depended on the words of the play to transport them to another time and place. Shakespeare was a master of poetic language. His plays contain rich, vivid imagery that allows audiences to experience dramatic moments through the senses of sight, hearing, smell, taste, and touch.

DIRECTIONS: *You will get more from what you read if you use your senses to try to see, hear, smell, taste, and feel the things Shakespeare's characters say. In the graphic organizer below, read each quotation from Act IV of* The Tragedy of Macbeth *and decide which of the senses it appeals to. Some quotations may appeal to more than one sense. Use the blank spaces in the graphic organizer to analyze other sensory images throughout the rest of the text.*

Quotation	Appeals to Sense(s) of
"This tyrant, whose sole name blisters our tongues / Was once thought honest . . ."	
". . . To offer up a week, poor, innocent lamb / T'appease an angry god."	
"Each new morn / New widows howl, new orphans cry . . ."	
"Double, double, toil and trouble; / Fire burn and caldron bubble."	
"Thy crown does sear mine eyelids."	

© Pearson Education, Inc., publishing as Pearson Prentice Hall. All rights reserved.
86

The Tragedy of Macbeth, *Act IV,* by William Shakespeare
Vocabulary Builder

Using the Root *-cred-*

A. DIRECTIONS: *Remember that the word root -cred- means "belief." Use the following words to complete the sentences.*

credibility	credence	credentials

1. The news reporter had to show his _____, or proof of his profession, to get into the crime scene.

2. The mayor's _____ was ruined when it was discovered that he had stolen funds from his office.

3. Those accusations are completely ridiculous; I give them no _____ whatsoever.

Using the Word List

pernicious	judicious	sundry
intemperance	avarice	credulous

B. DIRECTIONS: *Match each word in the left column with its definition in the right column. Write the letter of the definition on the blank next to the word it defines.*

___ 1. pernicious   A. lack of restraint
___ 2. judicious   B. greed
___ 3. sundry   C. tendency to believe readily
___ 4. intemperance   D. showing good judgment
___ 5. avarice   E. various
___ 6. credulous   F. highly injurious or destructive

C. DIRECTIONS: *Use words from the Word List to fill in the blanks.*

1. King Duncan was known as a wise and _____ ruler.

2. When it comes to power and fortune, Macbeth shows great _____.

3. Had Banquo been less _____ about Macbeth's evil intentions, he might have been able to save his own life.

4. Macbeth's control of Scotland had a _____ effect upon the country.

5. The murderers had committed _____ crimes before they killed Banquo.

6. Macbeth's _____ manifested itself when he had Banquo killed.

© Pearson Education, Inc., publishing as Pearson Prentice Hall. All rights reserved.

Name _____ Date _____

The Tragedy of Macbeth, *Act IV,* by William Shakespeare
Grammar and Style: Possessive Forms

You can write the **possessive form** of a singular noun by adding 's: *girl's, boy's, king's.* For the possessive of most plural forms, simply add an apostrophe: *creditors', goddesses', countries'.* However, some plural forms that do not already end in s do need an *'s: men's, women's, children's.* Remember that you don't add an apostrophe to make a word plural.

A. PRACTICE: *Decide which is the correct form of the noun in each sentence: the plural, the singular possessive, or the plural possessive. Circle your choice.*

1. The three (*witches/witch's/witches'*) stirred the bubbling cauldron.

2. Each (*glass's/glasses'/glasses*) stem was covered with dust.

3. Macbeth looked into the three weird (*sisters/sister's/sisters'*) cauldron.

4. (*Scotlands/Scotland's/Scotlands'*) future is in jeopardy.

5. These (*ladies'/lady's/ladys'*) opinions are good enough for me.

6. The (*Macbeths/Macbeth's/Macbeths'*) castle stands on a hill.

7. (*Rosses/Ross's/Rosses'*) warning can't save Lady Macduff from her fate.

B. Writing Application: *Use the possessive form of each underlined word or phrase to write a sentence based on* The Tragedy of Macbeth. *The first one has been done for you.*

1. The lives of the <u>characters</u>
   The characters' lives have been changed forever by the bloody deeds of Macbeth.

2. The eight <u>kings</u>

   _____

3. The escape of <u>Fleance</u>

   _____

4. The prophesies of the three <u>apparitions</u>

   _____

5. The words of the <u>messenger</u>

   _____

6. The deeds of the <u>murderers</u>

   _____

© Pearson Education, Inc., publishing as Pearson Prentice Hall. All rights reserved.

Name _____ Date _____

The Tragedy of Macbeth, *Act IV,* by William Shakespeare
Support for Extend Your Learning

Writing

On the lines below, list the reasons why young, working-class Englishmen should join the army. When you finish, number the reasons in the order you will list them on your **motivational flier.** You might begin with your second strongest reason followed by your weakest reason. Then build up to your strongest reason so that it appears last and makes the strongest impact.

Order	Reasons

Listening and Speaking

Use the chart below to develop questions and answers for your **interview.** For the response, write ideas rather than a word-for-word dialogue.

Questions	Response

© Pearson Education, Inc., publishing as Pearson Prentice Hall. All rights reserved.

The Tragedy of Macbeth, *Act V,* by William Shakespeare
Literary Analysis: Shakespearean Tragedy

Throughout the ages people have been fascinated by dramatic tragedy. One of the reasons for this is that tragedy allows readers to see themselves and their own potential for self-destruction. Each tragedy rests upon the premise that the tragic hero brings about his or her own downfall, often because of an inborn weakness in character or personality, a tragic flaw. This flaw can be any one of a number of things: pride, lust, greed, and so on. In a typical Elizabethan or Greek tragedy, the tragic hero begins the play as a respected, usually high-born, member of society. His or her virtues are described at length during the early scenes. In *The Tragedy of Macbeth,* for example, we first meet Macbeth as a hero in battle, a loyal supporter of King Duncan, a good husband, and an excellent friend. With all these wonderful qualities, what could Macbeth want that he does not already possess? What could possibly go wrong? The answer is, of course, human nature. With all the things Macbeth has, he wants most acutely that which he *doesn't* have. His ambition becomes his master, his tragic flaw.

DIRECTIONS: *Think about Macbeth's tragic flaw and answer the following questions.*

1. If Macbeth had never met the three witches, do you think the events of the play would have turned out the same way? Give reasons for your answer.

   _____

   _____

   _____

   _____

2. Is Macbeth aware of how ambitious he is? Find at least one quote from the text that supports your response.

   _____

   _____

   _____

   _____

3. Do you think Lady Macbeth is certain of her husband's ambition before Macbeth kills King Duncan? Find at least one quotation from the text that supports your response.

   _____

   _____

   _____

   _____

   _____

© Pearson Education, Inc., publishing as Pearson Prentice Hall. All rights reserved.

Name _____ Date _____

The Tragedy of Macbeth, *Act V,* by William Shakespeare
Reading Strategy: Infer Beliefs of the Period

The plays of William Shakespeare include many works of dramatic genius with much to say about the course of human events and history. In many ways these plays are universal; they transcend ethnic and cultural boundaries with their tales of fallen heroes, star-crossed lovers, and misguided nobles. But Shakespeare's plays also tell a reader quite a bit about the time period in which Shakespeare himself lived. The playwright applied many of the philosophies, beliefs, and superstitions of his day to illuminate the historical periods about which he wrote. As you look back over *The Tragedy of Macbeth*, ask yourself which ideas might be specific to the time period when William Shakespeare lived and which ones might be said to cross boundaries of time and place.

DIRECTIONS: *You can get more from what you read by analyzing a play or story for its historical perspectives. Use the graphic organizer below to find and keep track of places in the play that reveal something about the time in which the author lived. Two of the boxes are filled in for you. Fill in the rest with other examples from the text.*

Quotation	**Meaning**
THIRD WITCH: "All hail, Macbeth, that shalt be king hereafter!"	Macbeth seems to take this prophesy as the whole truth. People who lived in Shakespeare's time may have believed that certain individuals could read the future.

© Pearson Education, Inc., publishing as Pearson Prentice Hall. All rights reserved.

Name _____ Date _____

The Tragedy of Macbeth, *Act V,* by William Shakespeare
Vocabulary Builder

Using the Root *-turb-*

A. DIRECTIONS: *Knowing that the word root -turb- means "to disturb," create a sentence using each of the following italicized words.*

perturbed, adj., greatly disturbed in mind

turbine, n., a machine that changes the movement of a fluid into mechanical energy

turbojet, n., an airplane powered by turbines

turbid, adj., cloudy, muddy; mixed up or confused

1. _____

2. _____

3. _____

4. _____

Using the Word List

perturbation	pristine	clamorous	harbingers

B. DIRECTIONS: *Match each word in the left column with its definition in the right column. Write the letter of the definition on the line next to the word it defines.*

___ 1. perturbation   A. noisy

___ 2. pristine   B. forerunners

___ 3. clamorous   C. pure; untouched; unspoiled

___ 4. harbingers   D. disorder

C. DIRECTIONS: *Use words from the Word List to fill in the blanks in the sentences.*

1. Macbeth's honor, which was once _____, is now soiled with the blood of a murdered king.

2. The three witches are _____ of Macbeth's wretched fate.

3. The natural order of the heavens has experienced severe _____.

4. The people have become _____; they are insistent that the king should be dethroned.

© Pearson Education, Inc., publishing as Pearson Prentice Hall. All rights reserved.

The Tragedy of Macbeth, *Act V,* by William Shakespeare
Grammar and Style: Pronouns and Antecedents

Pronouns are words that take the place of nouns to avoid awkward repetition. See the following example:

Macbeth was a great soldier, but Macbeth's ambition got the better of Macbeth. Macbeth's wife, Lady Macbeth, was just as ambitious as Macbeth. Together, Macbeth and Lady Macbeth devised a plot to kill King Duncan.

By using pronouns to avoid such repetition, the paragraph can read as follows:

Macbeth was a great soldier, but his ambition got the better of <u>him</u>. <u>His</u> wife, Lady Macbeth, was just as ambitious as <u>he</u>. Together, <u>they</u> devised a plot to kill King Duncan.

The second paragraph flows much better than the first because pronouns have been used in place of proper nouns. The word or group of words to which each pronoun refers is its **antecedent.** As you use pronouns in your own writing, make sure they agree with their antecedents in gender, number, and person.

A. PRACTICE: *Read the following sentences and write the correct pronoun in each blank.*

1. Macbeth becomes king of Scotland after _____ kills King Duncan.

2. Banquo, once Macbeth's good friend, later becomes _____ bitter enemy.

3. Lady Macduff and _____ children are killed.

4. Lady Macbeth imagines blood on _____ hands out of guilt.

5. Macduff and Malcolm lead an army against Macbeth, and Macduff later kills

   _____.

B. Writing Application: *Rewrite the following sentences using pronouns in place of the underlined names.*

1. When Macduff hears of the death of <u>Macduff's</u> children, <u>Macduff</u> determines to seek justice against Macbeth.

   _____

   _____

2. The three witches give Macbeth information that makes <u>Macbeth</u> feel <u>Macbeth</u> can't lose in battle against <u>Macbeth's</u> enemies.

   _____

   _____

3. Lady Macbeth spends several nights sleepwalking and washing <u>Lady Macbeth's</u> hands over and over again.

   _____

   _____

© Pearson Education, Inc., publishing as Pearson Prentice Hall. All rights reserved.

Name _____ Date _____

The Tragedy of Macbeth, *Act V,* by William Shakespeare
Support for Writing

Use the graphic organizer below to gather and organize ideas about each memorable scene. In the surrounding boxes, list details about the characters, the setting, and the events, whether they support or conflict with the quotation.

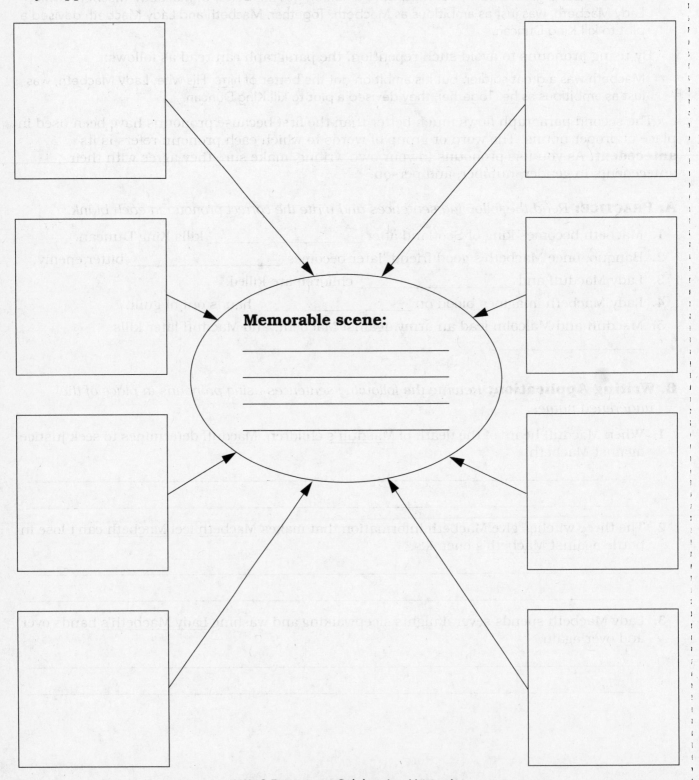

Memorable scene:

© Pearson Education, Inc., publishing as Pearson Prentice Hall. All rights reserved.

Name _____ Date _____

Works of John Donne
Literary Analysis: Metaphysical Poetry

Metaphysical poetry uses conceits and paradoxes as devices to convey the poet's message. A **metaphysical conceit** is an elaborate metaphor comparing very different ideas, images, or objects. The metaphysical poets used conceits that ranged from elaborate images developed over many lines to simple images presented in only a line or two.

DIRECTIONS: *On the lines following each excerpt, write what is being compared and explain the meaning of the conceit or metaphor expressed.*

1. Death be not proud, though some have called thee
   Mighty and dreadful, for thou art not so;
   For those whom thou think'st thou dost overthrow,
   Die not, poor death, nor yet canst thou kill me.
   From rest and sleep, which but thy pictures be,
   . . .
   One short sleep past, we wake eternally . . .

   _____

   _____

   _____

   _____

   _____

2. If they be two [souls], they are two so
   As stiff twin compasses are two;
   Thy soul, the fixed foot, makes no show
   To move, but doth, if th' other do.

   _____

   _____

   _____

   _____

   _____

© Pearson Education, Inc., publishing as Pearson Prentice Hall. All rights reserved.

Works of John Donne
Reading Strategy: Recognize the Speaker's Situation and Motivation

To understand a poem it may be helpful to **recognize the situation and motivation** for the speaker's words. What does the poem tell you about the speaker's circumstances? Are the words a cry of the heart? A song? A lament? As you read poetry, ask yourself about the speaker's motives for speaking, and identify the situation that gives rise to the speech.

DIRECTIONS: *The chart records some of the speaker's words from the poem "Song" in one column and an inference about the speaker's situation and motive for speaking in the second column. Continue adding the speaker's words and his possible motives as you read the poem.*

Speaker's Words	Motivation
"Sweetest love, I do not go, For weariness of thee."	He has to leave his beloved. He wants to reassure her that he still loves her and is not tired of her.

© Pearson Education, Inc., publishing as Pearson Prentice Hall. All rights reserved.

Works of John Donne
Vocabulary Builder

Using the Prefix *inter-*

A. DIRECTIONS: *Each of the following sentences includes an italicized word which contains the prefix* inter-, *meaning "between," "among," or "with each other." Using one of the three meanings, fill in each blank with a phrase that completes the sentence and reveals the meaning of the italicized word.*

1. An expert in *international* affairs understands the relations _____.

2. At the town's main *intersection*, two highways _____.

3. When a person *intercedes* between two disputing friends, she is _____.

4. *Intervals* in a series of events mean periods of time _____.

5. When a reporter and politician take part in an *interview*, they talk _____.

Using the Word List

contention	piety	intermit	coveteousness
profanation	laity	trepidation	breach

B. DIRECTIONS: *Write a word or words from the Word List to complete each sentence.*

1. Strong disagreement over the proper role of the congregation caused a _____ between the priests and the _____.

2. The active _____ over the family house did _____ briefly after the death of the grandfather.

3. The congregation approved of George's obvious _____ when he entered the cathedral because they believed it to be evidence of his _____.

4. The guide reminded the tourists to remove their shoes before entering the mosque, explaining that wearing shoes would be a _____.

5. The child gazed at the toy-shop display with undisguised _____.

© Pearson Education, Inc., publishing as Pearson Prentice Hall. All rights reserved.
97

Works of John Donne
Grammar and Style: Active and Passive Voice

When the subject of a sentence performs the action of the verb, the verb is in the **active voice.** When the subject receives the action of the verb, the verb is in the **passive voice.** This passage from "Meditation 17" shows how Donne uses both the active voice and the passive voice:

Active voice: And when she *buries* a man. . . .

Passive voice: . . . every chapter must *be* so *translated*.

A. PRACTICE: *Rewrite the passive sentences below in the active voice. Write "active" on the line if the sentence is already in the active voice. The first sentence has been done for you.*

1. Her eyes were cast up toward the sky.
   She cast her eyes up toward the sky. _____

2. God forgives us for coveting another's afflictions.
   _____

3. Death is enslaved by fate, chance, kings, and desperate men.
   _____

4. The two lovers are represented by the image of a drawing compass with two legs.
   _____

B. Writing Application: *Create a meaningful sentence from the nouns and verbs in each group. Use the voice identified in the parentheses, and add any necessary words. The first sentence has been done for you.*

1. boy, train, horse (passive voice)
   The horse was trained by the boy. _____

2. artist, draw, circle, compass (active voice)
   _____

3. lovers, separate, death (active voice)
   _____

4. earth, erode, sea (passive voice)
   _____

5. Donne, dismiss, employer (passive voice)
   _____

© Pearson Education, Inc., publishing as Pearson Prentice Hall. All rights reserved.

"Song," "A Valediction: Forbidding Mourning," "Holy Sonnet 10,"
and **"Meditation 17"** by John Donne

Support for Writing

Use the lines and chart below to develop ideas for your persuasive speech. First, choose one of Donne's works. Then, identify its situation, audience, and purpose. Next, complete the chart. In the left column, list images and comparisons that Donne uses to develop his arguments. In the right column, jot down ideas for images and comparisons you can use that will appeal to today's audience.

Title of Donne's work: _____

Speaker's situation: _____

Audience: _____

Persuasive purpose: _____

Donne's images and comparisons	Images and comparisons that would appeal to people today

On a separate page, write a draft of a speech delivered by Donne's speaker that uses images and comparisons that would appeal to an audience in today's times. Make your opening statement strong, and use vivid language.

© Pearson Education, Inc., publishing as Pearson Prentice Hall. All rights reserved.

"On My First Son," "Still to Be Neat," and **"Song: To Celia"** by Ben Jonson
Literary Analysis: Epigrams

An **epigram** is a short poem in which brevity, clarity, and permanence are emphasized. Short epigrams or lines from epigrams are often used as inscriptions on buildings or statues, or as an epitaph for a gravestone. For example, the lines "Rest in soft peace, and, asked, say here doth lie/Ben Jonson his best piece of poetry" is a good epitaph for Jonson's son. The English poet Samuel Taylor Coleridge wrote the following epigram to define epigrams:

What is an epigram? A dwarfish whole,
Its body brevity, and wit its soul.

A. DIRECTIONS: *Read each of the excerpts below and circle those that can be considered epigrammatic.*

1. Mary had a little lamb,
   Its fleece was white as snow.

2. Give me a look, give me a face,
   That makes simplicity a grace;

3. Drink to me only with thine eyes.

4. To err is human, to forgive divine.
   (Alexander Pope, *Essay on Criticism*)

5. What's in a name? That which we call a rose
   By any other name would smell as sweet.
   (Shakespeare, *Romeo and Juliet*)

B. DIRECTIONS: *On the lines below, write two short two- or four-line epigrams: one in praise of friendship and the other as an epitaph.*

_____

_____

_____

_____

_____

_____

_____

_____

_____

© Pearson Education, Inc., publishing as Pearson Prentice Hall. All rights reserved.

Name _____ Date _____

"On My First Son," "Still to Be Neat," and **"Song: To Celia"** by Ben Jonson
Reading Strategy: Hypothesize

Hypothesizing—making informed guesses about what you are reading based on information in the passage—and confirming your hypothesis helps you better understand what the writer is trying to say. You can hypothesize from the first line of a poem, and further reading may confirm or disprove your hypothesis. For example, in the first three lines of the poem "Still to Be Neat," Jonson says

> Still [always] to be neat, still to be dressed,
> As you were going to a feast;
> Still to be powdered, still perfumed;

You might hypothesize that the speaker does not appreciate a perfectly-groomed woman. Line 6 helps confirm that hypothesis: "All is not sweet, all is not sound." And lines 7 and 8, make clear his preference: "Give me a look, give me a face / That makes simplicity a grace."

DIRECTIONS: *Use the table below to help you hypothesize about passages in the poems and to confirm or disprove your hypotheses. In the left column, write the lines that lead to a hypothesis. Write your hypothesis in the second column. In the third column, write the phrases or lines that confirm (or disprove) your hypothesis. In the fourth column, confirm your hypothesis, or state a new hypothesis based on the additional information. The first row has been completed for you.*

Lines on Which Hypothesis is Based	Hypothesis	Lines Supporting or Disproving Hypothesis	Final Hypothesis
1. "Farewell, thou child of my right hand, and joy;" ("On My First Son," line 1)	Since the poet uses the term *farewell*, this poem is probably about a child who is dying or has died.	Line 3: "Seven years thou wert lent to me" Line 7: "To have so soon scaped world's and flesh's rage" Line 9: "Rest in soft peace"	These lines and phrases verify that the speaker's son has died.
2.			
3.			
4.			

© Pearson Education, Inc., publishing as Pearson Prentice Hall. All rights reserved.

"On My First Son," "Still to Be Neat," and **"Song: To Celia"** by Ben Jonson

Vocabulary Builder

Using Archaic Words

A. DIRECTIONS: *The following poem by Ben Jonson contains archaic words that are no longer used in modern English. Underline each archaic word and write an appropriate modern English word above it.*

How, best of kings, dost thou a scepter bear!
How, best of poets, dost thou laurel wear!
For such a poet, while thy days were green,
Thou wert, as chief of them are said t'have been.

("To King James" by Ben Jonson)

B. DIRECTIONS: *Use the clues below to fill in the crossword puzzle with the appropriate archaic words. Refer to the lines in Exercise A.*

Across

1. second-person singular form of *you*
3. second-person singular form of *do*
4. *your*

Down

1. *you do*
2. past-tense form of the verb *to be*

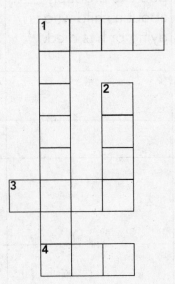

"On My First Son," "Still to Be Neat," and **"Song: To Celia"** by Ben Jonson
Grammar and Style: The Placement of *Only*

In the first line of Ben Jonson's "Song: To Celia" ("Drink to me only with thine eyes"), the placement of *only* conveys the meaning that the speaker wishes Celia to drink to him using just her eyes, not drinking from a cup. Placing the word *only* in a different position in the line conveys a different or an unclear meaning, as these examples show:

Drink only to me with thine eyes. ("Drink to me and no one else.")

Only drink to me with thine eyes. ("Just drink to me and do nothing else" or "Drink to me and no one else.")

A. PRACTICE: *The following sets of sentences contain the modifier* only *placed in two different ways. In the blank, write the letter of the lettered sentence that conveys the meaning of the underlined sentence.*

____ 1. <u>Mary Ann brought nothing but cookies.</u>
    A. Mary Ann brought only cookies.
    B. Only Mary Ann brought cookies.

____ 2. <u>Jeremy is the one person who can lead.</u>
    A. Jeremy can be only a leader.
    B. Only Jeremy can be a leader.

____ 3. <u>I have just one sister, whose hobby is taking long walks.</u>
    A. My sister's only hobby is taking long walks.
    B. My only sister's hobby is taking long walks.

B. Writing Application: *Rewrite each sentence inserting the modifier* only; *then explain the meaning of the sentence.*

1. We saw the dark forest through the window in the cabin.

_____

Meaning: _____

_____

2. I came to you for advice, not to borrow your radio.

_____

Meaning: _____

_____

3. Our day together was spent listening to the music we both loved—jazz.

_____

Meaning: _____

_____

© Pearson Education, Inc., publishing as Pearson Prentice Hall. All rights reserved.

Name _____ Date _____

"On My First Son," "Still to Be Neat," and "Song: To Celia" by Ben Jonson
Support for Writing

Use the chart below to take notes for your critical response. Review the poems, then write notes and cite examples that support or contradict Bush's defense of Jonson's style.

Clarity:

Unity:

". . . Jonson demanded . . . the ageless classical virtues of clarity, unity, symmetry, and proportion. . . ."

Symmetry:

Proportion:

On a separate page, write a draft of an essay that responds to Bush's ideas. Begin by summarizing both Bush's point and your position. Then, support your generalizations with quotations from Jonson.

© Pearson Education, Inc., publishing as Pearson Prentice Hall. All rights reserved.

Name _____ Date _____

"To His Coy Mistress" by Andrew Marvell
"To the Virgins, to Make Much of Time" by Robert Herrick
"Song" by Sir John Suckling
Literary Analysis: *Carpe Diem* Theme

Examples of the **theme** of *carpe diem,* which is Latin for "seize the day," can be found throughout world literature. Robert Herrick's poem "To the Virgins" contains lines that are frequently cited as an example of this theme.

Gather ye rosebuds while ye may,
Old time is still a-flying;
And this same flower that smiles today
Tomorrow will be dying.

The metaphor of the rosebuds is a particularly appropriate symbol for the *carpe diem* theme. The rose is one of the most beautiful of flowers, yet it lives only a short time.

DIRECTIONS: *Answer the following questions.*

1. In the opening lines of "To the Virgins, to Make Much of Time," Herrick uses the image of rosebuds as a symbol of the *carpe diem* theme. What other image does he use as a symbol in the poem?

   _____

   _____

2. In the opening lines from "To His Coy Mistress," the speaker implies that coyness is a crime. How does the speaker use the *carpe diem* theme to justify this implication?

   Had we but world enough, and time,
   This coyness lady were no crime.

   _____

   _____

3. What other lines from "To His Coy Mistress" reinforce the *carpe diem* theme? Give one example.

   _____

   _____

4. In "To His Coy Mistress," what is the speaker's purpose in trying to convince his listener that life is short? Use an example from the poem to support your statement.

   _____

   _____

© Pearson Education, Inc., publishing as Pearson Prentice Hall. All rights reserved.

Name _____ Date _____

"To His Coy Mistress" by Andrew Marvell
"To the Virgins, to Make Much of Time" by Robert Herrick
"Song" by Sir John Suckling

Reading Strategy: Infer the Speaker's Attitude

The tone and words in a poem can expresses the attitude of the speaker toward the poem's subject or person he or she is addressing. You can better understand the poem if you **infer,** or figure out, this attitude from what the speaker is saying. You'll find clues to the speaker's attitude in the poem's words, images, and rhythms. For example, look at the words used by the speaker in Robert Herrick's "To the Virgins, to Make Much of Time."

> Then be not coy, but use your time,
> And, while ye may, go marry;
> For, having lost but once your prime,
> You may forever tarry.

It can be inferred from the speaker's use of words like *coy, marry,* and *tarry* that the speaker's attitude is one of lighthearted earnestness. The words suggest both joyfulness and an urgent message. The rhythm of the lines is quick and full of energy, which seems to reinforce the speaker's enthusiasm for his subject.

DIRECTIONS: *Read the following examples from the poems. Then answer the questions.*

1. What is the image in these lines from "To the Virgins, to Make Much of Time" and what attitude does it express?

   And this same flower that smiles today
   Tomorrow will be dying.

   _____

   _____

2. What do the words "at my back" suggest about the speaker's attitude in "To His Coy Mistress" and what attitude does it imply?

   But at my back I always hear
   Time's wingè d chariot hurrying near:

   _____

   _____

© Pearson Education, Inc., publishing as Pearson Prentice Hall. All rights reserved.

"To His Coy Mistress" by Andrew Marvell
"To the Virgins, to Make Much of Time" by Robert Herrick
"Song" by Sir John Suckling
Vocabulary Builder

Using Related Forms of *prime*

A. DIRECTIONS: *Each of the following sentences includes an italicized form of the word* prime, *which means "first in importance" or "first in time." Write a second sentence that uses the same word and that demonstrates the word's meaning.*

1. The *primary* reason for going to the zoo was to observe the snow leopard.

   _____

2. Those young artists are *primarily* interested in improving their skills.

   _____

3. The *primacy* of the president is unquestioned.

   _____

4. They hoped to have a good voter turnout for the *primary*.

   _____

5. The runner was in her *prime* when she won the Olympic trials.

   _____

Using the Word List

coyness	amorous	languish	prime	wan

B. DIRECTIONS: *In each blank, write a word from the Word List to complete the sentence.*

1. At your age, you are just entering your _____.

2. His flirting showed his _____, since he never made a date.

3. She looked with _____ eyes at her new husband.

4. When she left him, he became _____ and went to bed.

5. When her husband left for the army, she began to _____ in despair.

© Pearson Education, Inc., publishing as Pearson Prentice Hall. All rights reserved.

Name _____ Date _____

"To His Coy Mistress" by Andrew Marvell
"To the Virgins, to Make Much of Time" by Robert Herrick
"Song" by Sir John Suckling

Grammar and Style: Irregular Forms of Adjectives

The comparative and superlative forms of most adjectives are created by adding the endings
-er and *-est* or *more* and *most* to the positive form. For example, the comparative form of the
adjective *cold* is *colder*; its superlative form is *coldest*. **Irregular** forms of comparative and
superlative adjectives are not created in this predictable way. This passage from "To His Coy
Mistress" contains the irregular adjective *last*, which here is a superlative form of *late*.

An age at least to every part,
And the *last* age should show your heart.

The table below contains examples of irregular adjectives in their positive, comparative, and
superlative forms.

Positive Form	Comparative	Superlative
late	later	last
many	more	most
little	less or lesser	least

A. PRACTICE: *Underline the irregular adjective in each sentence. Then identify its form by
writing* comparative *or* superlative *on the line.*

1. What is the best poem you have ever read? _____

2. Which do you think is the better poem, "To His Coy Mistress" or "Song"?
_____

3. The worst thing you can do when reading poetry is hurry through it. _____

4. Students spend less time studying Sir John Suckling than William Shakespeare.
_____

B. Writing Application: *Rewrite each sentence below, replacing the irregular adjective in
parentheses with its correct comparative or superlative form.*

1. It is (*good*) to read the poem now while you are not so tired rather than after you have
studied hard all day.

_____

2. Although they also studied Shakespeare and Milton, (*many*) students preferred the metaphysical poets.

_____

© Pearson Education, Inc., publishing as Pearson Prentice Hall. All rights reserved.

Name _____ Date _____

"To His Coy Mistress" by Andrew Marvell
"To the Virgins, to Make Much of Time" by Robert Herrick
"Song" by Sir John Suckling
Support for Writing

Use the graphic organizer below to develop poem ideas. Write your theme in the first box. Then, enter details, such as events or examples, in each box on the left. In the boxes on the right, list vivid words, images, and witty phrases to develop the details.

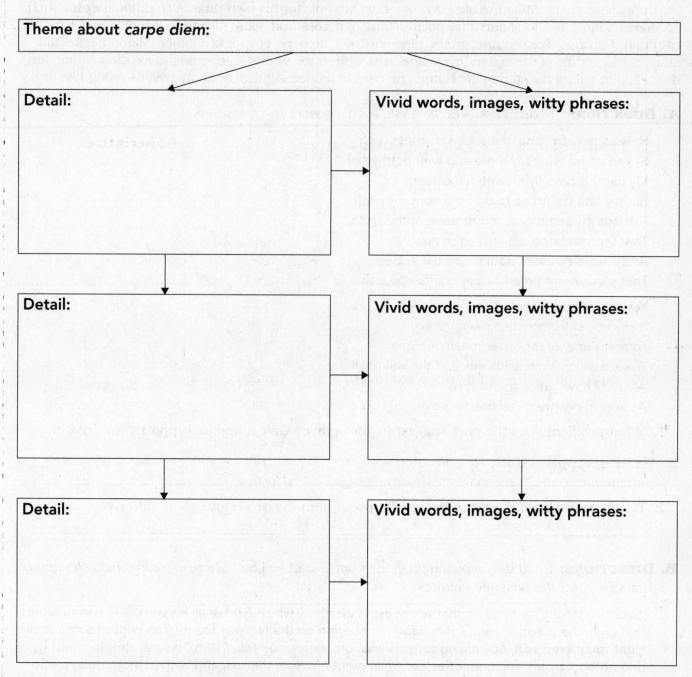

Theme about *carpe diem*:

Detail:

Vivid words, images, witty phrases:

Detail:

Vivid words, images, witty phrases:

Detail:

Vivid words, images, witty phrases:

On a separate page, write a poem that is persuasive and confident. Use puns and other forms of wordplay.

© Pearson Education, Inc., publishing as Pearson Prentice Hall. All rights reserved.

Poetry of John Milton
Literary Analysis: The Italian Sonnet; Epic Poetry

Desiring to become a great poet, the young Milton studied and imitated traditional poetry, including the **Italian sonnet,** a fourteen-line poem that follows the rhyme scheme *abbaabba cdecde* (or *cdedce*). The rhyme scheme naturally divides the poem into a group of eight lines, called the **octave,** and a group of six lines, called the **sestet.** In the octave, a poet may pose a problem, then answer or expand on it in the sestet.

In his later years, Milton wrote *Paradise Lost,* an epic for his own time. A traditional **epic,** such as Homer's *Iliad,* is a long narrative poem telling of heroes and gods. Although it builds on Christian tradition, *Paradise Lost* contains a few elements of a Homeric epic. Like Homer, Milton begins his story in the middle of the action (*in medias res*). Milton too writes an opening invocation calling for divine aid in telling his story. Like Homer, he uses extended similes, or comparisons using *like* or *as.*

A. DIRECTIONS: *Read Milton's Sonnet VII. Then, answer the questions.*

How soon hath Time, the subtle thief of youth,
Stolen on his wing my three and twentieth year!
My hasting days fly on with full career,
But my late spring no bud or blossom showeth.
Perhaps my semblance might deceive the truth,
That I to manhood am arrived so near,
And inward ripeness doth much less appear,
That some more timely-happy spirits endueth.

Yet be it less or more, or soon or slow,
It shall be still in strictest measure even
To that same lot, however mean or high,
Toward which Time leads me, and the will of Heaven;
All is, if I have grace to use it so,
As ever in my great Taskmaster's eye.

1. What problem does the poet suggest in the octave? Give a line to support your answer.

    _____

    _____

2. Briefly summarize the reassurance the poet offers in the sestet.

    _____

    _____

B. DIRECTIONS: *Read the following passage from* Paradise Lost. *Then, explain which element of Homeric epics the passage imitates.*

[Satan lay talking, as huge as] that sea beast / Leviathan, which God of all his works / Created hugest that swim the ocean stream: / Him haply slumbering on the Norway foam / The pilot of some small night-foundered skiff, / Deeming some island, oft, as seamen tell, / With fixed anchor in his scaly rind / Moors by his side under the lee, while night / Invests the sea, and wished morn delays: / So stretched out huge in length the Archfiend lay. . . .

    _____

    _____

© Pearson Education, Inc., publishing as Pearson Prentice Hall. All rights reserved.

Name _____ Date _____

Poetry of John Milton
Reading Strategy: Break Down Sentences

Milton's poetry is sometimes difficult to read and understand because of its long and complex sentence structure. Milton frequently shifts the order of the clauses to add emphasis to certain ideas. The main clause may appear in the middle or at the end of the sentence. One way to unravel the meaning of sentences that confuse you is to **break them down** into the main clause and supporting details.

DIRECTIONS: *Use the table below to help break down confusing sentences and decipher their meaning. The following passage has been used as a model.*

There the companions of his fall, o'erwhelmed
With floods and whirlwinds of tempestuous fire,
He soon discerns, and welt'ring by his side
One next himself in power, and next in crime,
Long after known in Palestine, and named Beelzebub. . . .

Main Clause	**Supporting Ideas**
1. "He soon discerns"	His companions are overwhelmed with floods and whirlwinds of fire. One of them is weltering by his side. Beelzebub is next to Satan in power and crime.
2.	
3.	
4.	

© Pearson Education, Inc., publishing as Pearson Prentice Hall. All rights reserved.

Name _____ Date _____

Poetry of John Milton
Vocabulary Builder

Using the Root *-lum-*

A. DIRECTIONS: *Each of the following sentences includes an italicized word that contains the word root -lum-, which comes from the Latin word meaning "light" or "lamp." Fill in each blank with a word or phrase that completes the sentence and reveals the meaning of the italicized word.*

1. When you flip the switch to *illuminate* the room, you _____.

2. When the physicist described the star's *luminance*, she was talking about its _____.

3. Because the face of the watch is *luminescent*, the hands and numbers are _____ enough to be read in the dark.

Using the Word List

semblance	illumine	transgress	transcendent	ignominy
guile	obdurate	tempestuous	suppliant	

B. DIRECTIONS: *Write the word from the Word List that best completes each analogy.*

1. *Trickery* is to _____ as *judgment* is to *wisdom*.

2. _____ is to *yielding* as *agitated* is to *peaceful*.

3. *Happiness* is to *joy* as *appearance* is to _____.

4. _____ is to *dishonor* as *pride* is to *conceit*.

5. *Ignorant* is to *educated* as _____ is to *calm*.

6. _____ is to *darken* as *love* is to *hate*.

7. *Obey* is to *comply* as *violate* is to _____.

8. *Imploring* is to _____ as *observant* is to *watchful*.

9. *Curious* is to *inquisitive* as _____ is to *exceeding*.

© Pearson Education, Inc., publishing as Pearson Prentice Hall. All rights reserved.

Poetry of John Milton
Grammar and Style: Correct Use of *Who* and *Whom*

Who and **Whom** are relative pronouns that refer to or relate to another word or idea in the sentence. *Who* is the subject of a verb; *whom* is the object of a verb or preposition. Milton uses *who* and *whom* correctly in these lines from *Paradise Lost*.

> . . . Be it so, since he
>
> *Who* now is sovereign can dispose and bid
>
> What shall be right: farthest from him is best,
>
> *Whom* reason hath equaled, force hath made supreme

In the second line, *who* is the subject of the verb "is." In the last line, *whom* is the object of the verb "hath equaled."

A. PRACTICE: *Read each sentence and decide whether* who *or* whom *has been used correctly. Circle those words that have been used incorrectly.*

1. John Milton, whom was born in 1608, was an English poet who attended Cambridge University.

2. Milton, who most people know as a poet, was also active in politics.

3. When King Charles I, who was Catholic, was overthrown, Oliver Cromwell, whom was Protestant, took over the reigns of government.

4. After Charles II gained the throne, Milton, whom had opposed Charles I, was imprisoned.

5. Andrew Marvell, with who Milton had long been friends, helped Milton regain his freedom.

B. Writing Application: *Rewrite each sentence, using* who *or* whom *correctly.*

1. (*Who, Whom*) has not read Milton's greatest work, *Paradise Lost?*

   _____

2. Milton, (*who, whom*) was totally blind by age forty-four, was a man for (*who, whom*) the loss of sight must have been especially tragic.

   _____

3. Milton, (*who, whom*) said he wanted to write something so important that later generations would not let it die, kept writing despite his blindness.

   _____

4. Many of those people (*who, whom*) know Milton's work best claim he is one of the greatest poets (*who, whom*) ever lived.

   _____

© Pearson Education, Inc., publishing as Pearson Prentice Hall. All rights reserved.

Sonnet VII ("How soon hath Time"), Sonnet XIX ("When I consider"),
and *from* Paradise Lost by Milton
Support for Writing

Use the graphic organizer below to develop ideas and write notes about villains from stories, books, and movies. Write at least two characteristics of each villain.

Villain's name:

Characteristics:

Villain's name:

Characteristics:

Villains

Villain's name:

Characteristics:

Villain's name:

Characteristics:

On a separate page, use your notes to draft an essay that explains why villains, such as Milton's Satan, are interesting to us as readers. Begin your draft by discussing why his character is engaging, and add your observations about the appeal of other villains.

© Pearson Education, Inc., publishing as Pearson Prentice Hall. All rights reserved.

Name _____ Date _____

from "Eve's Apology in Defense of Women" by Amelia Lanier
"To Lucasta, on Going to the Wars" and "To Althea, from Prison" by Richard Lovelace
Literary Analysis: Tradition and Reform

Tradition and **reform** go hand in hand. Political and social reformers usually propose ideas that are based on new readings of traditional stories familiar to most everyone in the culture. Bible episodes are often used to inspire reform. For example, Lanier reinterprets the story of Adam and Eve in support of her proposals to reform the treatment of women. Traditional stories, parables, fables, and books have always influenced reform because these stories help to form the basic beliefs of a culture.

DIRECTIONS: *Use the following excerpts from "Eve's Apology in Defense of Women" to answer each of the following questions. Give examples from the selection quoted as evidence to support your interpretation.*

1. In the following excerpt, when Lanier writes "Her fault though great, yet he was most to blame," what "fault" does she refer to? What does she say about the fault?

   But surely Adam can not be excused,
   Her fault though great, yet he was most to blame;
   What weakness offered, strength might have refused,
   Being lord of all, the greater was his shame. . . .

   _____

   _____

   _____

   _____

2. According to Lanier, what is the difference between Adam's guilt and Eve's guilt in the following excerpt? Whose is the greater?

   If Eve did err, it was for knowledge sake;
   The fruit being fair persuaded him to fall. . . .

   _____

   _____

   _____

   _____

© Pearson Education, Inc., publishing as Pearson Prentice Hall. All rights reserved.

from **"Eve's Apology in Defense of Women"** by Amelia Lanier
"To Lucasta, on Going to the Wars" and **"To Althea, from Prison"** by Richard Lovelace

Reading Strategy: Use Historical Context

The poems by Lanier and Lovelace were inspired by specific social and historical circumstances. Think about the **historical context** when you read these works by asking yourself whether the ideas, assumptions, and beliefs expressed are typical of the era in which the work was written. Ask also if these ideas are a response to events of the period.

Evidence of loyalty and ideas of honor can be found in both of Lovelace's poems. In "To Lucasta, on Going to the Wars," Lovelace says "I could not love thee, Dear, so much,/Loved I not honor more" (lines 11–12). In "To Althea, from Prison," the poet celebrates "The sweetness, mercy, majesty,/And glories of my King" (lines 19–20). By understanding the historical context, you can reach a deeper understanding of the poems and the poets.

DIRECTIONS: *Place the poems of Lanier and Lovelace into historical context using the chart below. Use the biographies and background on page 444 of the textbook to learn more about the poets and the events to which they were responding. As you read the poems, look for evidence of the events and circumstances of the era.*

Poem	Historical Event, Assumption, or Belief	Evidence of Historical Context Within Poem
"Eve's Apology in Defense of Women"		
"To Lucasta, on Going to the Wars"		
"To Althea, from Prison"		

© Pearson Education, Inc., publishing as Pearson Prentice Hall. All rights reserved.

Name _____ Date _____

from "Eve's Apology in Defense of Women" by Amelia Lanier
"To Lucasta, on Going to the Wars" and "To Althea, from Prison" by Richard Lovelace
Vocabulary Builder

Using Terms with *Breach*

Amelia Lanier uses the word *breach* in "Eve's Apology in Defense of Women." *Breach* means "breaking" and is often used in phrases related to the law, such as "breach of contract" or "breach of the peace."

A. DIRECTIONS: *Rewrite each of the following sentences to include the word* breach.

1. Richard said, "The owner of that car should be cited for disturbing the peace."

   _____

   _____

2. The subcontractor who failed to build the foundation on time was cited breaking the contract.

   _____

   _____

3. The knights finally broke through the town's defenses.

   _____

   _____

Using the Word List

> breach   discretion   inconstancy

B. DIRECTIONS: *The questions below consist of a related pair of words in CAPITAL LETTERS followed by four lettered pairs of words. Choose the pair that best expresses a relationship similar to that in the pair in capital letters.*

____ 1. BREACH : CONTRACT ::
    A. break : broken
    B. running : legs
    C. excavation : archaeological site
    D. engine : train

____ 2. INDISCRETION : DISCRETION ::
    A. indecisive : unsure
    B. fidelity : faithful
    C. love : loveless
    D. cowardice : courage

____ 3. INCONSTANCY : FICKLENESS ::
    A. true : faithful
    B. insolvency : solvent
    C. lightning : quickly
    D. hard : soft

© Pearson Education, Inc., publishing as Pearson Prentice Hall. All rights reserved.

Name _____ Date _____

from **"Eve's Apology in Defense of Women"** by Amelia Lanier
"To Lucasta, on Going to the Wars" and **"To Althea, from Prison"** by Richard Lovelace
Grammar and Style: Correlative Conjunctions

Correlative conjunctions are pairs of conjunctions that connect two words or groups of words. Stylistically, correlative conjunctions allow writers to link words clearly and elegantly. Examples of correlative conjunctions are *both . . . and, either . . . or, not so . . . as, neither . . . nor,* and *not only . . . but also.*

The following lines from "Eve's Apology in Defense of Women" shows two different uses of correlative conjunctions.

> Before poor Eve had *either* life *or* breath . . .
> Yea, having power to rule *both* Sea *and* Land . . .

A. PRACTICE: *Underline the correlative conjunctions in each of the following sentences.*

1. Lanier's poetry is both sincere and insightful.

2. The reader is forced to wonder whether Eve was justly punished or if Adam should have shared the blame.

3. Richard Lovelace was neither a Catholic nor a Puritan.

4. Lovelace was both arrested and imprisoned by anti-Royalists.

5. The poetry that Lovelace wrote while in prison was not only beautiful but also some of his finest.

B. Writing Application: *Use correlative conjunctions to combine the following pairs of sentences into one sentence.*

1. Lovelace's tone is coy in his poem about going to war. His tone is also quite serious.

   _____

   _____

2. The poem addressed to Althea is playful in its imagery. The poem addressed to Lucasta is less playful.

   _____

   _____

3. "To Althea, from Prison" is a poem about love. It is also a profound statement on the nature of freedom.

   _____

   _____

© Pearson Education, Inc., publishing as Pearson Prentice Hall. All rights reserved.

Name _____   Date _____

from "Eve's Apology in Defense of Women" by Amelia Lanier
"To Lucasta, on Going to the Wars" and "To Althea, from Prison" by Richard Lovelace
Support for Writing

Use the organizer below to take notes on personal experiences that have helped form your feelings and ideas about honor or freedom.

Experience:

Experience:

Conclusion about Honor or Freedom:

Experience:

Experience:

On a separate page, draft an essay based on your personal experience with honor or freedom. Begin by comparing your experiences to those of Richard Lovelace. Support your comparison by using quotations from Lovelace.

© Pearson Education, Inc., publishing as Pearson Prentice Hall. All rights reserved.

Name _____ Date _____

from **The Diary** by Samuel Pepys
from **A Journal of the Plague Year** by Daniel Defoe
Literary Analysis: Diaries and Journals

A **diary** or **journal** is a day-to-day description of the writer's experiences. Some diaries offer important insights into historical events or periods, and historians use diaries to research these events and eras. Reading historical diaries can also help a reader imagine what it would have been like to live through a particular event, because the diarist can give a first-person account usually not found in history texts.

A. DIRECTIONS: *As you read the following excerpt from* The Diary, *think like a historian—look for clues that might explain why the Great Fire of London caused so much damage. In the space below the excerpt, list at least four factors that might explain why the fire spread so far.*

Having stayed, and in an hour's time seen the fire rage every way . . . and the wind mighty high and driving it into the city; and everything, after so long a drought, proving combustible, even the very stones of churches. . . . So I was called for, and did tell the King and Duke of York what I saw, and that unless his Majesty did command houses to be pulled down nothing could stop the fire. They seemed much troubled, and the King commanded me to go to my Lord Mayor from him, and command him to spare no houses, but to pull down before the fire every way. . . . To the King's message he cried, like a fainting woman, "Lord! what can I do? I am spent: people will not obey me. I have been pulling down houses; but the fire overtakes us faster than we can do it." . . . So he left me, and I him, and walked home, seeing people all almost distracted, and no manner of means used to quench the fire. The houses, too, so very thick thereabouts, and full of matter for burning, as pitch and tar, in Thames Street, and warehouses of oil. . . .

1. _____

2. _____

3. _____

4. _____

B. DIRECTIONS: *Answer the following questions on the lines provided.*

1. Diaries and journals offer historians a unique view of the past. If you were to keep a detailed journal of daily activities, what type of information might a historian of the future learn from reading it?

_____

_____

2. Defoe's *Journal of the Plague Year* is actually a novel written in journal form. How would the effect of the novel on the reader be different if it were written as a regular narrative story?

_____

_____

_____

© Pearson Education, Inc., publishing as Pearson Prentice Hall. All rights reserved.

from **The Diary** by Samuel Pepys
from **A Journal of the Plague Year** by Daniel Defoe
Reading Strategy: Draw Conclusions

When reading a text, you can discover more than the writer is explicitly stating by using evidence to **draw conclusions**. In *The Diary,* for example, Pepys does not say he is afraid that he or his wife and family may get sick and die of the plague. However, you might draw that conclusion when he lists all the people he knows who have recently died and mentions how closely he interacted with them. Drawing conclusions is like solving a mystery. First, you look for clues the writer has left in the text, and then you use those clues to figure out what the writer is saying "between the lines."

DIRECTIONS: *Read the following excerpts from* The Diary *and* A Journal of the Plague Year. *Below each excerpt, write one conclusion that you can draw from it.*

From *The Diary* by Samuel Pepys

1. . . . Jane called us up . . . to tell us of a great fire they saw in the city. So I rose . . . but, being unused to such fires as followed, I thought it far enough off; and so went to bed again and to sleep. About seven rose again . . . and saw the fire not so much as it was and farther off. So to my closet to set things to rights after yesterday's cleaning.

   Conclusions: _____

   _____

   _____

   _____

From *A Journal of the Plague Year* by Daniel Defoe

2. I went all the first part of the time freely about the streets, though not so freely as to run myself into apparent danger. . . .

   Conclusions: _____

   _____

   _____

   _____

3. . . . people that were infected and near their end, and delirious also, would run to those pits, wrapped in blankets or rugs, and throw themselves in, and, as they said, bury themselves.

   Conclusions: _____

   _____

   _____

   _____

   _____

Name _____ Date _____

from **The Diary** by Samuel Pepys
from **A Journal of the Plague Year** by Daniel Defoe
Vocabulary Builder

Using the Prefix *dis-*

A. DIRECTIONS: *The prefix* dis- *can mean "apart," "not," "opposite of," or "absence of." The words below all contain the prefix dis-. The parentheses contain information about the word root for each word. Fill in each blank with a form of the word from the list.*

dispel (*pellere* = "to drive")

disgrace (*grazia* = "grace")

disinfect (*infecter* = "to infect")

distribute (*tribuere* = "to allot")

disheveling (*chevel* = "hair")

disgust (*gustus* = "a taste")

1. The wind blew fiercely, _____ Rob's neatly combed hair.

2. Anita groaned as her teacher began to _____ the test.

3. The first thing Albert did after moving into his new apartment was to clean and _____ the bathroom.

4. Gazing at his sister's messy room, Leroy could feel nothing but _____.

5. Because he had broken the law, the president resigned in _____.

6. Nancy posted a sign to _____ the rumors that school would be closed Friday.

Using the Word List

apprehensions	abated	lamentable	distemper	prodigious
combustible	malicious	discoursing	importuning	

B. DIRECTIONS: *Match each word in the left column with its definition in the right column. Write the letter of the definition on the line next to the word it defines.*

___ 1. apprehensions

___ 2. abated

___ 3. combustible

___ 4. lamentable

___ 5. malicious

___ 6. discoursing

___ 7. distemper

___ 8. importuning

___ 9. prodigious

A. huge

B. begging

C. flammable

D. distressing

E. disease

F. talking about

G. fears

H. deliberately harmful

I. lessened

© Pearson Education, Inc., publishing as Pearson Prentice Hall. All rights reserved.

Name _____ Date _____

from **The Diary** by Samuel Pepys
from **A Journal of the Plague Year** by Daniel Defoe
Grammar and Style: Gerunds

Gerunds are verb forms that end in *-ing* and function as nouns. Like nouns, gerunds can be preceded by articles. For example, in Defoe's phrase "nobody put on black or made a formal dress of mourning for their nearest friends," the word *mourning* is a gerund. Gerunds are often mistaken for present participles, which are also verbs ending with *-ing*. Present participles, however, function as verbs or as adjectives modifying nouns and pronouns.

A. PRACTICE: *For each phrase, write* gerund *if the word is a gerund. Write* not a gerund *if it is not.*

_____ 1. Some of our maids *sitting* up late last night . . .

_____ 2. and the *cracking* of houses at their ruin . . .

_____ 3. the voice of *mourning* was truly heard. . . .

_____ 4. the plague *raging* in a dreadful manner . . .

B. Writing Application: *Write a sentence using each of the following words as a gerund.*

1. summarizing

_____

_____

2. bicycling

_____

_____

3. farming

_____

_____

4. chewing

_____

_____

5. performing

_____

_____

© Pearson Education, Inc., publishing as Pearson Prentice Hall. All rights reserved.

from **The Diary** by Samuel Pepys
from **A Journal of the Plague Year** by Daniel Defoe

Support for Writing

Use the chart below to take notes for your response to Brian Fitzgerald's criticism that Defoe "used literature to express his views on social and other questions and only secondarily as a craftsman and artist."

Views on Social Conditions	Examples of craftsmanship (images, figures of speech, passages creating mood)

On a separate page, draft a response that agrees or disagrees with Fitzgerald's remark. Use details from your notes and Defoe's writing to support your thesis statement.

© Pearson Education, Inc., publishing as Pearson Prentice Hall. All rights reserved.

Name _____ Date _____

from **Gulliver's Travels** by Jonathan Swift
Literary Analysis: Satire

Satire uses wit and humor to ridicule vices, follies, and abuses. The intent, however, is rooted in a hope for reform: Satirists hope their work will open people's eyes to the real state of affairs in a society and do something about it. **Irony** and sarcasm are important tools of satirists, whose tone may be gentle and amused, or bitter and vicious. Jonathan Swift is one of the most famous and widely read satirists in English and *Gulliver's Travels* one of his most enduring works.

DIRECTIONS: *Plan a satire of your own by writing out the following steps:*

1. Name an institution or custom you believe merits criticism. It may be an organization or custom within your community, your state, the nation, or the world.

   _____

   _____

2. What aspect of this institution or custom deserves criticism? What vice or folly do you want to reveal?

   _____

   _____

3. Describe a setting that could be used in a satire about your subject. The setting can be the actual one, humorously disguised or, like Jonathan Swift's in *Gulliver's Travels,* it can be highly fanciful.

   _____

   _____

4. Name and briefly describe a character or two who will represent ordinary people who must deal with the institution or custom.

   _____

   _____

5. Practice using verbal irony. Describe the institution or custom you are satirizing, or have a character comment on it, making sure the comment says the opposite of what is really meant. Make a statement that seems to defend the institution or custom but actually reveals the institution's shortcomings.

   _____

   _____

   _____

   _____

© Pearson Education, Inc., publishing as Pearson Prentice Hall. All rights reserved.

Name _____ Date _____

from **Gulliver's Travels** by Jonathan Swift
Reading Strategy: Interpret

Good satire is packed with social and political references, but writers of satire are also concerned with telling a good story. They wrap their satirical observations inside the story to comment in a humorous way. To **interpret** satire, the reader needs to know the historical context of the time it was written.

Satirical works that survive their own historical time period, such as *Gulliver's Travels*, do so because they address questions of universal human interest. For example, Gulliver describes the effects of gunpowder to the king of Brobdingnag. To ingratiate himself with the king, Gulliver proudly tells him about the enormous destruction that can be perpetrated by mixing a few simple ingredients and discharging the mixture with the help of a small spark. To Gulliver's surprise, the king is horrified by this notion. In fact, the king becomes so upset by the "evil genius, enemy to mankind" who must have first conceived of gunpowder, that he tells Gulliver never to mention the subject again. Swift uses this discussion to point up the problem of unbridled violence and the need for pacifism in the world. Since violence continues to be a societal and political problem to this day, Swift's satirical commentary retains its relevance.

DIRECTIONS: *To interpret satirical works, you must look for the author's intended meaning. Use this graphic organizer to analyze and interpret material from* Gulliver's Travels. *One example has been completed for you.*

Quotation	Meaning	Relevance Today
1. "He observed, that among the diversions of our nobility and gentry I had mentioned gaming."	It is clear by the questions the king asks that Swift thinks of gambling as a disease and an addiction that ruins lives.	The problem of gambling addiction still exists today.
2.		
3.		
4.		

© Pearson Education, Inc., publishing as Pearson Prentice Hall. All rights reserved.

from **Gulliver's Travels** by Jonathan Swift
Vocabulary Builder

Using the Root *-jec-*

A. DIRECTIONS: *Each of the following sentences includes an italicized word that contains the word root -jec- meaning "throw." Fill in the blank with a word or phrase that completes the sentence and reveals the meaning of the italicized word.*

1. The criminal hung his head in *abject* misery; he looked completely _____.

2. The last time my grandmother had an *injection* was when she got _____.

3. My uncle liked to *interject* things into the conversation; he always had something to _____.

Using the Word List

conjecture	expostulate	schism
expedient	habituate	odious

B. DIRECTIONS: *The questions below consist of a related pair of words in CAPITAL LETTERS followed by four lettered pairs of words. Choose the pair that best expresses a relationship similar to that in the pair in capital letters.*

___ 1. SCHISM : GROUPS ::
    A. whole : pieces
    B. storm : clouds
    C. division : parts
    D. separation : separate

___ 2. ODIOUS : HATEFUL ::
    A. broken : fixed
    B. peaceful : calmer
    C. odium : vileness
    D. lovely : beautiful

___ 3. CONJECTURE : INFERENCE ::
    A. confer : talk
    B. speak : statement
    C. relate : relative
    D. go : leave

___ 4. EXPOSTULATE : EARNESTLY ::
    A. reason : incorrect
    B. apologize : sincerely
    C. vilify : villain
    D. swim : gladly

© Pearson Education, Inc., publishing as Pearson Prentice Hall. All rights reserved.

Name _____ Date _____

from **Gulliver's Travels** by Jonathan Swift
Grammar and Style: Correct Use of *Between* and *Among*

When you write, knowing how to use the prepositions *between* and *among* correctly can help you avoid making needless mistakes. Here are some rules to keep in mind:

Use *between* to refer to two items or two groups of items:

There is a special bond *between* the king of Brobdingnag and Gulliver.

Use *among* to refer to more than two items:

Many *among* us feel the same way Gulliver felt.

A. PRACTICE: *Fill in the blank using either* between *or* among.

1. The Lilliputians and the Blefuscudians had many disputes _____ them.

2. Of course, many Lilliputians probably bickered _____ themselves as well.

3. There were vast differences _____ Brobdingnag and England.

4. _____ the nobility of Brobdingnag, intelligence was rated very highly.

5. Gunpowder was the subject of a debate _____ Gulliver and the king.

B. Writing Application: *Write two sentences that use each of the following words, one sentence using* among *and one using* between.

argument

1. _____

2. _____

gossip

3. _____

4. _____

dispute

5. _____

6. _____

communication

7. _____

8. _____

© Pearson Education, Inc., publishing as Pearson Prentice Hall. All rights reserved.
128

Name _____ Date _____

from **Gulliver's Travels** by Jonathan Swift
Support for Writing

Use the chart below to generate ideas for your descriptive satire. First, write the behavior, trend, or attitude you want to satirize in the center circle. In the surrounding circles, list characteristics of that subject.

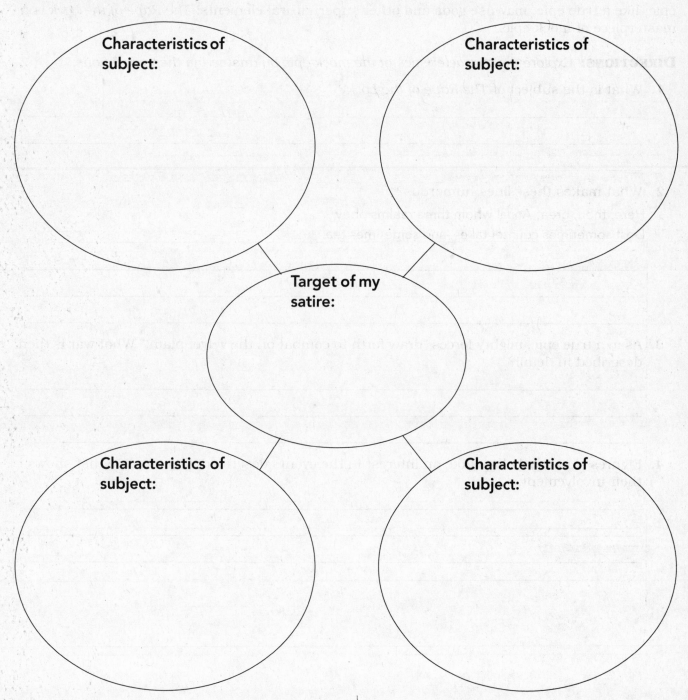

On a separate page, write a draft of your descriptive satire. Use the details you have collected on the target of your satire, and exaggerate each of the characteristics. Use the same presentation style that might be used by your subject.

© Pearson Education, Inc., publishing as Pearson Prentice Hall. All rights reserved.

Name _____ Date _____

from An Essay on Man and from The Rape of the Lock by Alexander Pope
Literary Analysis: Mock Epic

A **mock epic** uses the epic form for humorous effect. The key feature of a mock epic is its treatment of a trivial subject in an elevated style, thus showing how ridiculous it is. A mock epic tells a story of "heroes" doing "great deeds," but the heroes and deeds are actually petty. A mock epic, like a true epic, may use gods and other supernatural elements. *The Rape of the Lock* is a masterpiece of mock epic.

DIRECTIONS: *Explore the characteristics of the mock epic by answering these questions.*

1. What is the subject of *The Rape of the Lock*?

   _____

   _____

   _____

2. What makes these lines humorous?

   Here, thou, great Anna! whom three realms obey,
   Dost sometimes counsel take—and sometimes tea.

   _____

   _____

   _____

3. As in a true epic, mighty forces "draw forth to combat on the velvet plain." What war is then described in detail?

   _____

   _____

   _____

4. Figures from mythology take an interest in the events described. Quote a line that shows their involvement.

   _____

   _____

   _____

© Pearson Education, Inc., publishing as Pearson Prentice Hall. All rights reserved.

from **An Essay on Man** and *from* **The Rape of the Lock** by Alexander Pope
Reading Strategy: Recognize Author's Purpose

In *The Rape of the Lock*, Pope satirizes high society by focusing his wit and poetic talents on a petty incident that takes place among members of the wigged and powdered London upper-crust set. With elevated language and allusions to mythology, Pope deflates London society, exposing its silliness and shallowness. In the following passage, Pope appears to compliment the depth and grandeur of upper-class London society, but is really ridiculing such people by exposing their pettiness and the shallowness of their conversations.

> Hither the heroes and the nymphs resort,
> To taste awhile the pleasures of a court;
> In various talk th' instructive hours they passed,
> Who gave the ball, or paid the visit last;
> One speaks the glory of the British Queen,
> And one describes a charming Indian screen;
> A third interprets motions, looks, and eyes;
> At every word a reputation dies.

DIRECTIONS: *Use the chart below to interpret the author's purpose in examples from the* The Rape of the Lock. *The left column contains a quote from the poem. In the right column, interpret the meaning underlying the author's words. The first one has been done for you.*

Quotation	Author's Purpose
"To arms, to arms!" the fierce virago cries, / And swift as lightning to the combat flies. / All side in parties, and begin th' attack; / Fans clap, silks rustle, and tough whalebones crack . . .	1. Pope mocks the high-society ladies and gentlemen whose "arms" are fans, silk dresses and suits, and the whalebone stays of corsets.
Meanwhile, declining from the noon of day, / The sun obliquely shoots his burning ray; / The hungry judges soon the sentence sign, / And wretches hang that jurymen may dine; / The merchant from th' Exchange returns in peace, / And the long labors of the toilet cease.	2.
The skilful nymph reviews her force with care: / Let spades be trumps! she said, and trumps they were.	3.
The meeting points the sacred hair dissever / From the fair head, forever, and forever!	4.
When, after millions slain, yourself shall die; / When those fair suns shall set, as set they must, / And all those tresses shall be laid in dust, / This lock, the Muse shall consecrate to fame, / And midst the stars inscribe Belinda's name.	5.

© Pearson Education, Inc., publishing as Pearson Prentice Hall. All rights reserved.

from An Essay on Man and *from* The Rape of the Lock by Alexander Pope
Vocabulary Builder

Using Related Words: Words from Political Science

A. DIRECTIONS: *Read each of the lines from* The Rape of the Lock. *Describe the significance of the underlined word in upper-class British society during Alexander Pope's time. Use a dictionary if needed.*

1. To taste awhile the pleasures of a <u>court</u> . . .

   _____

2. Who gave the <u>ball</u>, or paid the visit last . . .

   _____

3. A third interprets motions, looks, and eyes;/At every word a <u>reputation</u> dies.

   _____

4. Now to the <u>baron</u> fate inclines the field.

   _____

Using the Word List

obliquely	plebeian	destitute
assignations	stoic	disabused

B. DIRECTIONS: *Write the word from the Word List that best completes each sentence.*

1. If Sir Plume thought he could get away with a lock of Belinda's hair, she certainly
   _____ him of that notion.

2. In Pope's time beggars lived on the street and were completely _____.

3. Sometimes ladies and gentlemen made secret _____ with one another.

4. If a person gives you a sidewise glance, he or she is looking at you _____.

5. The nobleman was considered by many to be haughty because he rarely spoke to those whom he considered _____, or lower class.

6. The _____ remained calm and collected while others reacted to the news emotionally.

© Pearson Education, Inc., publishing as Pearson Prentice Hall. All rights reserved.

Name _____ Date _____

from An Essay on Man and **from The Rape of the Lock** by Alexander Pope
Grammar and Style: Inverted Word Order

In his mock epic poem *The Rape of the Lock*, Alexander Pope often uses **inverted word order.** When poets invert word order, or change the normal word order of subject-verb-complement, they often do so to maintain a regular rhythm or to emphasize certain important words. Inverting words also frees the poet to use interesting words as end rhymes. Here is an example of inverted word order from *The Rape of the Lock*:

The rebel knave, <u>who dares his prince engage</u>,
Proves the just victim of his royal rage.

Here is the same excerpt written in normal English word order:

The rebel knave, <u>who dares engage his prince</u>,
Proves the just victim of his royal rage.

Inverting the word order in this case facilitates the end rhyme, *engage* and *rage*.

A. PRACTICE: *These lines from* The Rape of the Lock *contain inverted word order. On the lines, rewrite each line using normal English word order.*

1. His giant limbs in state unwieldy spread . . .

   _____

2. Clubs, diamonds, hearts in wild disorder seen . . .

   _____

3. The nymph exulting fills with shouts the sky. . . .

   _____

4. "Let wreaths of triumph now my temples twine. . . ."

   _____

B. Writing Application: *Write endings for each couplet below using inverted word order. Try to maintain the rhythm of the first line and use end rhymes. The first one has been done for you.*

1. But while my brother lies asleep in bed,
   His wife cold water pours upon his head.

2. When winter weather goes from bad to worse,

   _____

3. In springtime when the heart may turn to love

   _____

© Pearson Education, Inc., publishing as Pearson Prentice Hall. All rights reserved.

from An Essay on Man and **from The Rape of the Lock** by Alexander Pope
Support for Writing

Use the chart below to take notes for your **mock epic.** First, identify the conflict you will describe. Then, use the chart to jot down ideas for boasting speeches of your heroes and heroines, descriptions of warriors and their weapons, how gods and goddesses may enter the action, and epic similes you may use.

Conflict: _____

Epic Elements	
Boasts of heroes and heroines	
Descriptions of warriors and weapons	
Actions of gods and goddesses	
Elaborate comparisons (similes)	

Use a separate page to compose your mock epic. Remember to use devices, such as repetition of key words, antithesis (placing strong contrasts side-by-side), and parallel grammatical structures.

© Pearson Education, Inc., publishing as Pearson Prentice Hall. All rights reserved.

Name _____ Date _____

from The Preface to A Dictionary of the English Language and **from A Dictionary of the English Language** by Samuel Johnson
from The Life of Samuel Johnson by James Boswell

Literary Analysis: Dictionary

Samuel Johnson's *Dictionary* was not the first to attempt to include all the English words in one volume. However, it was the first dictionary to set a standard for how all English words should be used. Today's English dictionaries list and define words and provide information about their pronunciation, meanings, history, and usage. A modern dictionary entry may also contain a word's spelling, syllabication, pronunciation in phonetic symbols, part(s) of speech and the definitions for the word in each part of speech, illustrative sentences, synonyms, how to use the word correctly, and when to use it. Some entries contain a history of the word, correct grammatical usage of the word, illustrations, antonyms, idioms, and foreign words and phrases. Modern dictionaries may also contain roots and other combining forms, abbreviations, and bibliographic and geographic entries. Electronic dictionaries on computers have expanded the capabilities of dictionaries. If you are unsure of a spelling, you can enter an approximation of the word and be given choices of possible entries. When looking for a word that fits a particular meaning, you can search the dictionary by entering one or more of the key words that might be found in its definition.

DIRECTIONS: *Read the entry for* gang *in Johnson's dictionary and list the different pieces of information he supplies about the word; then look up the word* gang *in a modern dictionary and note the similarities and differences in the kinds of information supplied. Fill in the Venn diagram to show the similarities and differences between Johnson's dictionary and a modern dictionary.*

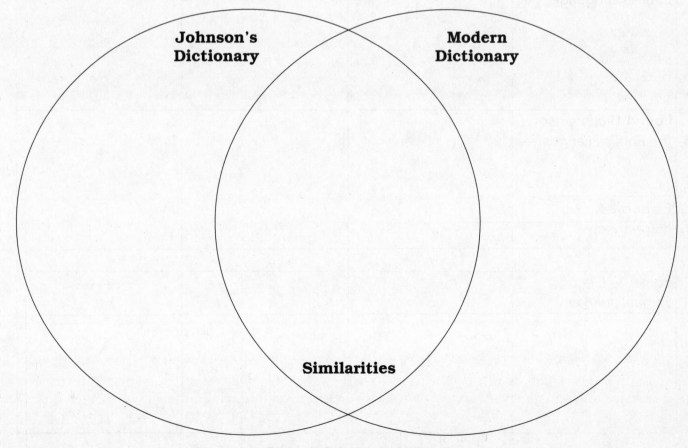

Johnson's Dictionary

Modern Dictionary

Similarities

© Pearson Education, Inc., publishing as Pearson Prentice Hall. All rights reserved.

from The Preface to A Dictionary of the English Language and *from* **A Dictionary of the English Language** by Samuel Johnson
from **The Life of Samuel Johnson** by James Boswell

Reading Strategy: Establish a Purpose

When you **establish a purpose** before reading, you are able to

- focus on the information you wish to find.
- add the knowledge you have gained to your framework of prior knowledge on the subject.
- increase your concentration and ability to retain what you have read.
- increase your pleasure in reading because you are taking an active rather than a passive part in the process.

DIRECTIONS: *Establish a specific purpose for reading the excerpts from* A Dictionary of the English Language *and* The Life of Samuel Johnson. *After you have set a purpose, use the following KWL chart to record what you* Know *about the subject, what you* Want *to find out, and what you* Learned *from your reading.*

Selection	What I Know	What I Want to Find Out (Purpose for Reading)	What I Learned
from The Preface to *A Dictionary of the English Language*			
from *A Dictionary of the English Language*			
from *The Life of Samuel Johnson*			

© Pearson Education, Inc., publishing as Pearson Prentice Hall. All rights reserved.

Name _____ Date _____

from The Preface to A Dictionary of the English Language and **from A Dictionary of the English Language** by Samuel Johnson
from The Life of Samuel Johnson by James Boswell
Vocabulary Builder

Using the Root -dict-

A. DIRECTIONS: *The words that follow each contain the word root -dict-, from the Latin for "to say." Information about the prefix or suffix of each word is contained in parentheses. On the line, write the word that best completes each sentence.*

dictate (-ate = "act on")
dictator (-or = "one that does something")
diction (-ion = "action or process")
predict (pre- = "before")

1. When the _____ seized power, he immediately censored the newspapers.

2. Because their scientific instruments were precise, the meteorologists were able to _____ accurately the arrival of the storm.

3. The executive began to _____ her speech into the tape recorder.

4. The actor's good _____ enhanced his reading of the short story.

Using the Word List

| recompense | caprices | adulterations | propagators | risible |
| abasement | credulity | malignity | pernicious | inculcated |

B. DIRECTIONS: *Match each word in the left column with its definition in the right column. Write the letter of the definition on the line next to the word it defines.*

___ 1. adulterations
___ 2. risible
___ 3. inculcated
___ 4. caprices
___ 5. abasement
___ 6. propagators
___ 7. malignity
___ 8. credulity
___ 9. pernicious
___10. recompense

A. condition of being put down or humbled
B. tendency to believe too readily
C. strong desire to harm others
D. causing serious injury; deadly
E. impressed upon the mind by repetition
F. prompting laughter
G. those who cause something to happen or to spread
H. reward, payment
I. whims
J. impurities

© Pearson Education, Inc., publishing as Pearson Prentice Hall. All rights reserved.

from **The Preface to A Dictionary of the English Language** and *from* **A Dictionary of the English Language** by Samuel Johnson

from **The Life of Samuel Johnson** by James Boswell

Grammar and Style: Parenthetical Expressions

Parenthetical expressions are words, phrases, or clauses which interrupt the main part of a sentence to comment on it or to give additional information. Listed below are several common parenthetical expressions.

I am sure	after all	incidentally	naturally	on the other
I believe	by the way	indeed	nevertheless	hand
I think	for example	in fact	of course	to tell the truth
I hope	however	in my opinion	on the contrary	

Wherever parenthetical expressions occur in a sentence—at the beginning, the middle, or the end—they need to be set off from the main part of the sentence by commas. The following examples are from *The Life of Samuel Johnson.*

> But however that might be, this speech was somewhat unlucky. . . .

> That, Sir, I find, is what a very great many of your countrymen cannot help.

A. PRACTICE: *For each of the following sentences, identify the parenthetical expression by underlining it. Then insert commas to set off the expression from the rest of the sentence.*

1. The character of Samuel Johnson has I trust been so developed in the course of this work. . . .

2. Man is in general made up of contradictory qualities. . . .

3. Ridicule has gone down before him, and I doubt Derrick is his enemy.

4. . . . so that the unavoidable consciousness of his superiority was in that respect a cause of disquiet.

5. . . . his poetical pieces in general have not much of that splendor. . . .

B. Writing Application: *Use each parenthetical expression below in a sentence.*

1. on the contrary

   _____

2. incidentally

   _____

3. to tell the truth

   _____

4. on the other hand

   _____

© Pearson Education, Inc., publishing as Pearson Prentice Hall. All rights reserved.

from The Preface to A Dictionary of the English Language and **from A Dictionary of the English Language** by Samuel Johnson
from The Life of Samuel Johnson by James Boswell

Support for Writing

Use the chart below to collect information that compares Johnson's *A Dictionary of the English Language* with a modern historical dictionary. Then, write a thesis statement that summarizes your findings.

	Johnson's *A Dicionary of the English Language*	A Modern Historical Dictionary
Pronunciation and Part of Speech		
Derivation		
Definition		
Historical Quotations		

Thesis:

On a separate page, write a draft that supports the points of your thesis. Note similarities and differences between Johnson's dictionary and modern historical dictionaries. Use passages from each dictionary to support your summary.

© Pearson Education, Inc., publishing as Pearson Prentice Hall. All rights reserved.

Name _____ Date _____

"Elegy Written in a Country Churchyard" by Thomas Gray
"A Nocturnal Reverie" by Anne Finch, Countess of Winchilsea
Literary Analysis: Pre-Romantic Poetry

The poems of Thomas Gray and Anne Finch celebrate the formal style of eighteenth-century poetry while at the same time ushering in the emotional expressiveness of the coming Romantic movement. Unlike many other poets of the time, Gray and Finch managed to create poems that stirred not only readers' minds but their emotions. In poems such as Gray's "Elegy Written in a Country Churchyard," for example, readers found themselves compelled and emotionally drawn to insights about the lives and deaths of common rural people, those whose existence supposedly held little meaning for the rest of the world. By concentrating on life's mysteries, the unanswerable questions that mark human experience, Gray and Finch were able to create poems of universal appeal and lasting literary significance.

DIRECTIONS: *Read the lines from "Elegy Written in a Country Churchyard" and "A Nocturnal Reverie" and answer the questions that follow.*

> Some village Hampden, that, with dauntless breast,
>   The little tyrant of his fields withstood,
> Some mute inglorious Milton here may rest,
>   Some Cromwell guiltless of his country's blood.

1. What is Gray saying about the lives of the common people laid to rest in the churchyard?

    _____

    _____

> Yet even these bones from insult to protect
>   Some frail memorial still erected nigh,
> With uncouth rhymes and shapeless sculpture decked,
>   Implores the passing tribute of a sigh.

> Their name, their years, spelt by the unlettered Muse,
>   The place of fame and elegy supply:
> And many a holy text around she strews,
>   That teach the rustic moralist to die.

2. What statement does Gray make about the importance of honoring the dead?

    _____

    _____

© Pearson Education, Inc., publishing as Pearson Prentice Hall. All rights reserved.

Name _____ Date _____

"Elegy Written in a Country Churchyard" by Thomas Gray
"A Nocturnal Reverie" by Anne Finch, Countess of Winchilsea
Reading Strategy: Paraphrase

Poetry presents readers with challenges different from those presented by prose. Poetry often uses dense language and imagery, which some readers find difficult to follow. **Paraphrasing** is a useful tool to help guide you through complex poetic passages. Look at the following example from Gray's "Elegy."

Original:

Full many a gem of purest ray serene
The dark unfathomed caves of ocean bear:
Full many a flower is born to blush unseen,
And waste its sweetness on the desert air.

Paraphrase:

Many precious gems are never seen by human eyes because they exist deep in the ocean. Many flowers bloom without ever being seen; their sweet smells dissipate in the desert.

DIRECTIONS: *Use the chart below to help you break down difficult passages in Thomas Gray's "Elegy Written in a Country Churchyard." When you encounter complex material, read it over twice; then try to paraphrase the meaning of the words. Continue reading to make sure that your paraphrase makes sense with regard to the rest of the poem. An example has been completed for you.*

Original	Paraphrase
1. "The boast of heraldry, the pomp of power,/ And all that beauty, all that wealth e'er gave,/ Awaits alike the inevitable hour./The paths of glory lead but to the grave." ("Elegy," lines 33–36)	Having a noble birthright, power, wealth, and beauty doesn't matter; in the end, everyone dies.
2.	
3.	
4.	
5.	

© Pearson Education, Inc., publishing as Pearson Prentice Hall. All rights reserved.

"Elegy Written in a Country Churchyard" by Thomas Gray
"A Nocturnal Reverie" by Anne Finch, Countess of Winchilsea
Vocabulary Builder

Using the Prefix *circum-*

A. DIRECTIONS: *Each of the following sentences includes an italicized word that contains the prefix* circum- *(or* circ-*), meaning "around." Fill in the blank with a word or phrase that completes the sentence and reveals the meaning of the italicized word.*

1. When a path is *circuitous*, it _____ .

2. When a person *circulates* at a party, he or she _____
   _____

3. A *circus* takes place in _____ .

4. If a patient is *circumambulating* the grounds, he or she is _____
   _____ .

Using the Word List

penury	circumscribed	ingenuous	ignoble
nocturnal	temperate	venerable	forage

B. DIRECTIONS: *Write a word or words from the Word List to complete each sentence.*

1. It is so cold here that I'm tempted to move someplace where the weather is
   _____ .

2. The pasture is full of rich _____ for the cattle to graze on.

3. Finch's poem describes _____ phenomena such as moonlight.

4. Gray describes the churchyard occupants as _____ regardless of their
   _____, or poverty.

5. The judge described the ex-senator as lowly and _____ for taking advantage
   of his _____, unsuspecting constituents.

6. The teacher _____ the topics for the final essay by requiring that they focus
   on plot.

© Pearson Education, Inc., publishing as Pearson Prentice Hall. All rights reserved.

"Elegy Written in a Country Churchyard" by Thomas Gray
"A Nocturnal Reverie" by Anne Finch, Countess of Winchilsea
Grammar and Style: Pronoun-Antecedent Agreement

You will find it easier to understand densely constructed poetry if you learn to recognize **pronoun-antecedent agreement.** Look, for example, at this excerpt from "A Nocturnal Reverie":

In such a night, when every louder wind
Is to *its* distant cavern safe confined;
And only gentle Zephyr fans *his* wings,
And lonely Philomel, still waking, sings;
Or from some tree, famed for the owl's delight,
She, hollowing clear, directs the wanderer right. . . .

Reading carefully, you will note that *its* in line 2 refers to line 1 and its antecedent *wind.* The pronoun *his* in line 3 refers to its antecedent, the proper noun *Zephyr.* The pronoun *She* in line 6 refers to its antecedent, the proper noun *Philomel* in line 4.

When using pronouns, make sure that the pronoun you choose agrees with its antecedent.

A. PRACTICE: *Circle the word in parentheses that correctly completes each sentence.*

1. The children patiently await (*his, their*) father's return.

2. Which one of the sons was (*his, their*) father's favorite?

3. The cows and the sheep are going to (*its, their*) pen for the night.

4. Gray's lonely musings reveal (*his, their*) serious frame of mind.

B. Writing Application: *For each of the antecedents below, write a sentence that uses a correct pronoun. Underline the pronoun in your completed sentence.*

1. The mothers and the children _____

_____ .

2. The cemetery _____

_____ .

3. Thomas Gray _____

_____ .

4. Anne Finch, Countress of Winchilsea, _____

_____ .

© Pearson Education, Inc., publishing as Pearson Prentice Hall. All rights reserved.

"Elegy Written in a Country Churchyard" by Thomas Gray
"A Nocturnal Reverie" by Anne Finch, Countess of Winchilsea
Support for Writing

Use the chart below to take notes for your reflective essay. Close your eyes and put yourself back at the place and time that inspired you. Write notes about your sensory experience of the place.

Time: _____

Place: _____

Sense	Details of the Setting
Sight	
Sound	
Touch	
Taste	
Smell	

Use a separate page to draft a reflective essay about a time and place that inspired you. In your draft, mention the details you have gathered, and clearly link the details to your thoughts and feelings.

© Pearson Education, Inc., publishing as Pearson Prentice Hall. All rights reserved.

"On Spring" by Samuel Johnson
from **"The Aims of the Spectator"** by Joseph Addison
Literary Analysis: Essay

An **essay** is a piece of short prose that explores a single topic. The word *essay* comes from a French word meaning an "attempt" or "a test." The word was first applied to the writing of Montaigne (1533–1592), a Frenchman whose essays dealt with the questions of life. Although Montaigne's essays were "attempts" to find answers to these enduring questions, they did not always end with definite answers. Montaigne wrote on a number of subjects, but he said that his aim was always to learn about himself.

In his essay "On Spring" Johnson "attempts" to relate the significance and meaning of springtime to our lives. In *The Aims of the Spectator* Addison is "trying" to express his goals for the periodical by describing its usefulness to different types of people. Both essays cause the reader to reflect on his or her own relationship to the given topic.

DIRECTIONS: *Read the following excerpts from the essays and answer the questions on another sheet of paper. Give quotations from the essay to support your interpretation.*

from "The Aims of the Spectator"

I shall be ambitious to have it said of me that I have brought philosophy out of closets and libraries, schools and colleges, to dwell in clubs and assemblies, at tea tables and in coffeehouses.

1. What is Addison's ultimate goal for *The Spectator*? Give evidence to support your ideas.

from "The Aims of the Spectator"

As they lie at the mercy of the first man they meet, and are grave or impertinent all the day long, according to the notions which they have imbibed in the morning, I would earnestly entreat them not to stir out of their chambers till they have read this paper, and do promise them that I will daily instill into them such sound and wholesome sentiments as shall have a good effect on their conversation for the ensuing twelve hours.

2. How would you describe the type of person Addison is writing about in this passage? How does Addison believe *The Spectator* will benefit this type of person?

from "On Spring"

A French author has advanced this seeming paradox, that very few men know how to take a walk; and, indeed, it is true, that few know how to take a walk with a prospect of any other pleasure than the same company would have afforded them at home.

3. How does the paradox that Johnson cites relate to the topic of the essay as a whole? What does the ability to "take a walk" have to do with Johnson's topic?

© Pearson Education, Inc., publishing as Pearson Prentice Hall. All rights reserved.

Name _____ Date _____

Reading Strategy: Draw Inferences

Both Samuel Johnson and Joseph Addison use subtle irony, complex attitudes, and shades of meaning in their essays. As you read their essays you need to **draw inferences** to reach logical conclusions about what the writers mean. For example, in the third paragraph of "The Aims of the Spectator" Addison writes

> . . . in the next place, I would recommend this paper to the daily perusal of those gentlemen whom I cannot but consider as my good brothers and allies, I mean the fraternity of spectators, who live in the world without having anything to do in it; and either by the affluence of their fortunes or laziness of their dispositions have no other business with the rest of mankind but to look upon them.

Addison is saying that there is a type of person who does not frequently engage or interact with people or the outside world. In the pages of *The Spectator* these people will find a means to engage the outside world and understand its workings. Although Addison counts himself among this "fraternity," you can infer from the use of the word "laziness" that he has some ambivalent feelings about these people.

DIRECTIONS: *Use this chart to draw inferences about ideas or attitudes that Johnson or Addison leave unstated. Write down passages that seem unclear, and make logical connections between what the writer says and what he might mean. An example has been done for you.*

Passage or Statement	Inference that Can Be Drawn
1. "I hope to increase the number of these by publishing this daily paper, which I shall always endeavor to make an innocent if not an improving entertainment, and by that means at least divert the minds of my female readers from greater trifles."	Addison is mocking the trivialities with which most women are forced to occupy their time.
2.	
3.	
4.	
5.	

© Pearson Education, Inc., publishing as Pearson Prentice Hall. All rights reserved.

Name _____ Date _____

"On Spring" by Samuel Johnson
from **"The Aims of the Spectator"** by Joseph Addison
Vocabulary Builder

Using the Root -*spec*-

A. DIRECTIONS: *Each of the following sentences includes an italicized word which contains the word root -spec- from a Latin word meaning "to look." Fill in the blank with a word or phrase that completes the sentence and reveals the meaning of the italicized word.*

1. When the detective *inspected* the room, he _____.

2. If she studied every *aspect* of the problem, she _____.

3. If you behold a *spectacle*, you _____.

Using the Word List

procured	divert	speculation	transient
affluence	contentious	trifles	embellishments

B. DIRECTIONS: *Write the word from the box that best completes each sentence.*

1. I don't know how he _____ the canoe, but it certainly made the trip more enjoyable.

2. I like her painting because she manages to describe a place or person without _____.

3. He was concerned that too much time was being spent on _____ during the meetings.

4. The houses in Great Neck were large and hinted at the _____ of the neighborhood.

5. Her brother seemed sad, so she tried to _____ him with a game of checkers.

6. Whether or not the candidate would run for office was merely a matter for _____.

7. After the season, the pitcher realized how fleeting and _____ were the joys of playing.

8. Because of their bickering, the partners' relationship could be described as _____.

© Pearson Education, Inc., publishing as Pearson Prentice Hall. All rights reserved.

Name _____ Date _____

Grammar and Style: Adjective Clauses

Adjective clauses are clauses that qualify or further describe the nouns or pronouns preceding them. These clauses begin with the relative pronouns *who, whom, which, that,* and *whose.* The following lines from "On Spring" and *The Aims of the Spectator* show examples of adjective clauses.

It may be laid down as a position *which will seldom deceive* . . .

There is another set of men that I must likewise lay a claim to, *whom I have lately called the blanks of society* . . .

It was said of Socrates *that he brought philosophy down from heaven, to inhabit among men* . . .

A. PRACTICE: *Underline the adjective clause in each of the following lines. In the blanks, write the relative pronoun with which the adjective clause begins.*

1. Samuel Johnson's *Dictionary of the English Language*, which was wildly popular in its day, greatly influenced the format of later dictionaries.

   _____

2. Irony and satire were popular tools of writers who hoped to make their mark in eighteenth-century literature.

   _____

3. The art of essay writing, which many writers hold to be among the most difficult, dates to the sixteenth century.

   _____

B. Writing Application: *Write an adjective clause that uses the relative pronoun shown in parentheses to qualify or further describe each noun below.*

1. the poet (*whose*)

   _____

2. a barking dog (*that*)

   _____

3. the president (*whom*)

   _____

4. ironic essays (*that*)

   _____

5. the dancer (*who*)

   _____

© Pearson Education, Inc., publishing as Pearson Prentice Hall. All rights reserved.

"On Spring" by Samuel Johnson
from **"The Aims of the Spectator"** by Joseph Addison
Support for Writing

Use the chart and lines below to take notes about human behavior. Note the type of behavior you will write about at the top. Then, take notes about your observations of this behavior. Finally, briefly compare and contrast the examples of human behavior.

Type of human behavior:	
Observed examples:	1.
	2.
	3.
	4.

How examples are alike: _____

_____

_____

How examples are different: _____

_____

_____

Use a separate page to write a draft for an essay about human behavior. Focus your essay on a few examples, and offer conclusions about what the behavior represents.

Name _____ Date _____

DIRECTIONS: *Use the space provided to answer the questions.*

1. **A.** According to Richard Rodriguez, what do the best journalists achieve?

   B. What noun would Rodriguez like to adopt from Joseph Addison as Rodriguez presents himself to the reader?

   _____

   _____

   _____

2. Briefly explain how Joseph Addison invented a "fictionalized persona."

   _____

   _____

   _____

3. What are some of the similarities Rodriguez sees between eighteenth-century London and modern-day Tijuana?

   _____

   _____

   _____

   _____

4. How does Rodriguez define his "journalistic obligation" to the reader?

   _____

   _____

5. How does the writer describe his "journalistic impulse"?

   _____

   _____

6. Why does Tijuana remind Rodriguez of himself?

   _____

   _____

   _____

   _____

© Pearson Education, Inc., publishing as Pearson Prentice Hall. All rights reserved.

Richard Rodriguez
Listening and Viewing

Segment 1: Meet Richard Rodriguez
- How did Richard Rodriguez's connection with language help him define who he is?
- Why do you think language is an important tool?

_____

_____

_____

Segment 2: Richard Rodriguez on Addison
- What are some characteristics of Joseph Addison's writing?
- How does Richard Rodriguez try to incorporate Addison's writing style in his own work?
- Why do you think that journalism is important to society?

_____

_____

_____

Segment 3: The Writing Process
- How does Richard Rodriguez prepare to begin writing a piece?
- What writing techniques of Richard Rodriguez's would you most likely use in your own writing? Why?

_____

_____

_____

Segment 4: The Rewards of Writing
- Why does Richard Rodriguez think it is important for students to read literature?
- What do you think you can learn by exploring literature?

_____

_____

_____

© Pearson Education, Inc., publishing as Pearson Prentice Hall. All rights reserved.

"A Modest Proposal" by Jonathan Swift
Literary Analysis: Satirical Essay

A **satirical essay** is a piece of prose writing that ridicules the faults and shortcomings of individuals, groups, institutions, or humanity in general. While a satirical essay is often written to be humorous, the main purpose is to encourage readers to bring about change. Writers of satire may use a variety of strategies.

- Exaggeration is a deliberate overstatement of some quality or characteristic. Swift uses exaggeration when he says, "A very worthy person, a true lover of his country, and whose virtues I highly esteem was lately pleased, in discoursing on this matter, to offer a refinement upon my scheme."
- Understatement is the opposite of exaggeration. Swift uses it in this statement: "I shall now therefore humbly propose my own thoughts, which I hope will not be liable to the least objection."
- Sarcasm can be bitter, rude, and sometimes personal. Swift attacks the wealthy landlords when he says that "landlords, who, as they have already devoured most of the parents, seem to have the best title to the children."

A. DIRECTIONS: *On the lines below, answer these questions about the use of satire in* "A Modest Proposal."

1. While the topic of "A Modest Proposal" is serious and the proposal shocking and terrible, the essay does have humorous elements. What makes it humorous?

_____

_____

_____

_____

2. The target of Swift's satire is the poverty in Ireland. What makes the satirical essay an effective method for drawing attention to this problem?

_____

_____

_____

_____

B. DIRECTIONS: *Today, as in Swift's time, the satirical essay can be a potent weapon in calling for social change. What present-day situation or event would make a good subject for a satirical essay? How could the subject be satirized?*

_____

_____

_____

_____

_____

© Pearson Education, Inc., publishing as Pearson Prentice Hall. All rights reserved.

Name _____ Date _____

Reading Strategy: Recognize Author's Purpose

An **author's purpose** is his or her reason for writing. Authors want their purpose to be understood, so they give many hints and may even state their purpose outright. Swift wants his purpose understood but does not state it directly. Instead, he disguises it in satire. What he really means is the opposite of what he says. He says in cold-hearted, practical terms that by killing and eating children, the poverty can be ended in Ireland. What he wants the reader to understand is that he does not want to eat the children, he wants to save them.

DIRECTIONS: *Read the following lines from "A Modest Proposal." Then, state Swift's true meaning.*

---

1. Some persons of a desponding spirit are in great concern about that vast number of poor people, who are aged, diseased, or maimed. . . . But I am not in the least pain upon that matter, because it is vey well known, that they are every day dying, and rotting, by cold, and famine, and filth, and vermin. . . ."

Author's Purpose:

---

2. I desire those politicians, who dislike my overture, . . . that they will first ask the parents of these mortals, whether they would not at this day think it a great happiness to have been sold for food at a year old, in the manner I prescribe, and thereby have avoided such a perpetual scene of misfortunes.

Author's Purpose:

© Pearson Education, Inc., publishing as Pearson Prentice Hall. All rights reserved.
153

Name _____ Date _____

"A Modest Proposal" by Jonathan Swift
Vocabulary Builder

Word Parts: Prefix en-

A. DIRECTIONS: *The following words all begin with the prefix* en-, *which means "in" or "into." Complete each sentence with the correct word from the list.*

encumbrance	endure
enrich	encourage

1. The narrator was able to _____ his readers to support his proposal.

2. Children are an _____ to parents who are too poor to feed them.

3. Old and sick people cannot _____ hunger as well as younger people.

4. The hard work of Ireland's poor served only to _____ the absentee English landlords.

Using the Word List

sustenance	commodity	collateral	deference
censure	encumbrance	contrive	incur

B. DIRECTIONS: *Write the word from the box that best describes the situation.*

1. Swift thinks up a clever way to draw people's attention to the poverty in Ireland.

   _____

2. Because he was a member of the clergy, people showed great respect for Swift.

   _____

3. The poor of Ireland suffer great hardships through no fault of their own.

   _____

4. In his essay, Swift says children are a great burden on their parents and on society.

   _____

5. Swift observes that it requires very little food or money to raise very young children.

   _____

6. Swift also describes infants as a valuable item of trade.

   _____

7. People are extremely poor, and a related problem is starvation.

   _____

8. Swift condemns the English government for doing so little to help the poor.

   _____

© Pearson Education, Inc., publishing as Pearson Prentice Hall. All rights reserved.

"A Modest Proposal" by Jonathan Swift

Grammar and Style: Vary Sentence Beginnings

When most of the sentences in a piece of writing begin with the same sentence structure, the writing becomes monotonous. Good writers **vary sentence beginnings** to make their writing more interesting. There are a variety of ways to start sentences.

- Subject: Jonathan Swift was born in Dublin, Ireland.
- Adverb: Actually, Swift published many satirical essays.
- Prepositional phrase: From the start, Swift attacked the short-comings of institutions through his biting essays.
- Participial phrase: Hoping to awaken people to the dangers of religious extremism, Pope wrote *A Tale of a Tub*.
- Subordinate clause: After Swift published his first poem in 1692, John Dryden told him "you will never be a poet."

DIRECTIONS: *Rewrite the following sentences to vary the sentence beginnings. Start each sentence with the beginning indicated.*

1. Swift arrived in England and stayed with his friend, Alexander Pope. (*participial phrase*)

   _____

   _____

2. Swift began writing *Gulliver's Travels* in 1720. (*prepositional phrase*)

   _____

   _____

3. Swift met "Stella," who became the love of his life, while working in England. (*subordinate clause*)

   _____

   _____

4. In the *Bickerstaff Papers,* Swift made satirical attacks on an astrologer. (*subject*)

   _____

   _____

5. Swift's inner ear disease got much worse as he got older. (*adverb*)

   _____

   _____

© Pearson Education, Inc., publishing as Pearson Prentice Hall. All rights reserved.

"A Modest Proposal" by Jonathan Swift

Support for Writing

Use the graphic organizer below to generate ideas for your **satirical essay.** First, write the behavior, trend, or attitude you want to ridicule in the center circle. Then, in the surrounding circles, list arguments that supporters of this behavior, trend, or attitude use to support their position.

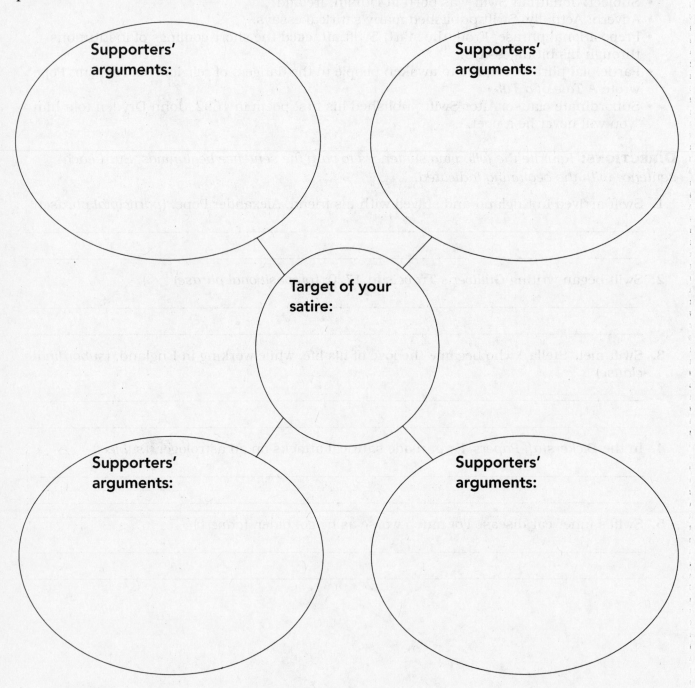

On a separate page, use your completed chart to help you write your satirical essay. As you write, exaggerate the arguments of supporters of your targeted subject to make the arguments look ridiculous.

© Pearson Education, Inc., publishing as Pearson Prentice Hall. All rights reserved.

"To a Mouse" and **"To a Louse"** by Robert Burns
"Woo'd and Married and A'" by Joanna Baillie
Literary Analysis: Dialect

Robert Burns was one of the first poets to write verse that incorporated the Scottish dialect of English. **Dialect** is the language, chiefly the speech habits and patterns, of a particular social class, region, or group. Usually dialect differs from the standard form of the language because it possesses its own unique grammar, pronunciation, and vocabulary.

In "To a Mouse," Burns's use of dialect adds to the poem's appeal and the reader's appreciation. If the poem had been written in standard English, it would lack the sense of immediacy and the color achieved in such lines as:

That wee bit heap o' leaves an' stibble, / Has cost thee mony a weary nibble!

By using Scottish dialect, Burns succeeded in capturing his people's tenderness for and intimacy with nature and their shared acceptance of the prospect of "nought but grief an' pain" in the wake of "promised joy."

DIRECTIONS: *The following lines are from "To a Mouse." Rewrite each line in standard English and explain the effect that the use of Scottish dialect alone can achieve.*

1. "Wee, sleekit, cow'rin', tim'rous beastie,"

   _____

   _____

   _____

2. "A daimen icker in a thrave / 'S a sma' request:"

   _____

   _____

   _____

3. "An' naething, now, to big a new ane,"

   _____

   _____

   _____

4. "To thole the winter's sleety dribble, / An' cranreuch cauld!"

   _____

   _____

   _____

© Pearson Education, Inc., publishing as Pearson Prentice Hall. All rights reserved.

Name _____ Date _____

Reading Strategy: Translate Dialect

A **dialect** is the language and speech habits of the members of a particular group, class, or region. Each dialect has its own unique grammar, pronunciation, and vocabulary. Robert Burns and Joanna Baillie wrote their poems in the Scottish dialect of English. Their use of dialect made their poems more accessible and familiar to their contemporaries in Scotland. Modern readers can use a number of different strategies to **translate dialect:**

- Read footnotes to get definitions.
- Use context to guess meaning.
- Speak words aloud and listen for similarities to standard English words.
- Look for similarities between printed dialect words and English words.
- Note apostrophes, which often signal that a letter has been omitted.

DIRECTIONS: *After reading the following lines from "To a Mouse," translate each word in italics, identifying the strategy you used to determine each word's meaning.*

1. "I wad be laith to *rin* an' chase thee / Wi' murd'ring pattle."

_____

_____

_____

2. "I doubt na, *whyles*,[8] but thou may thieve;"

_____

_____

_____

3. "Thy wee bit *housie*, too, in ruin!"

_____

_____

_____

4. "An' *lea'e* us nought but grief an' pain,"

_____

_____

_____

[8]whyles: At times.

Name _____ Date _____

"To a Mouse" and **"To a Louse"** by Robert Burns
"Woo'd and Married and A'" by Joanna Baillie
Vocabulary Builder

Using the Suffix *-some*

A. DIRECTIONS: *The following words all contain the suffix—some, meaning "having specific qualities." Using the word's context along with what you know about this suffix, write a definition of each italicized word in the blank.*

1. At first the jokes were funny, but they became *tiresome.*

   _____

2. When Jerome went to the zoo, he thought the snakes were *loathsome,* but Janelle enjoyed them.

   _____

3. Bees abuzzing around your head at a picini are so *bothersome,* aren't they?

   _____

Using the Word List

dominion	impudence	winsome
discretion	inconstantly	

B. DIRECTIONS: *Write a word from the Word List to answer each question.*

1. Which word means most nearly the opposite of *imprudence?* _____

2. If you observe someone acting rudely toward a stranger, what word might you use to describe such behavior? _____

3. Which word is closest in meaning to *changeably?* _____

4. Which word describes a monarch's authority over his or her subjects?

   _____

5. What word might you use to describe a person who has a charming manner and appearance? _____

© Pearson Education, Inc., publishing as Pearson Prentice Hall. All rights reserved.

Name _____ Date _____

"To a Mouse" and **"To a Louse"** by Robert Burns
"Woo'd and Married and A'" by Joanna Baillie

Grammar and Style: Interjections

An **interjection** is a word or phrase that can stand by itself and that is used to express emotion. Consider these examples from "To a Louse."

> *My sooth!* right bauld ye set your nose out. . . .
>
> *O,* Jenny, dinna toss your head. . . .

Notice that an exclamation mark often follows an interjection to show the strong emotion being expressed.

A. PRACTICE: *Underline the interjection in each sentence.*

1. My gosh! There's a bug in that woman's hair.

2. Hey! It's only a louse.

3. Good grief! You say that as if a louse were nothing at all to have in your hair.

4. Aha! It's not a louse—it's a bee!

5. Yikes! I remember when a bee flew into my mother's hair while she was driving.

6. I didn't think she would stop the car in time! Whew! It was close.

B. Writing Application: *For each of the following interjections, write a sentence that incorporates it. Punctuate each interjection by using an exclamation mark.*

1. well

_____

2. hurrah

_____

3. hey

_____

4. alas

_____

5. whoa

_____

6. oh

_____

7. my goodness

_____

© Pearson Education, Inc., publishing as Pearson Prentice Hall. All rights reserved.

Name _____   Date _____

"To a Mouse" and **"To a Louse"** by Robert Burns
"Woo'd and Married and A'" by Joanna Baillie

Support for Writing

Use the Venn diagram below to take notes comparing the vain churchgoer and the moping young bride. Write how they are alike where the circles overlap. Write how they are different where the circles are separate.

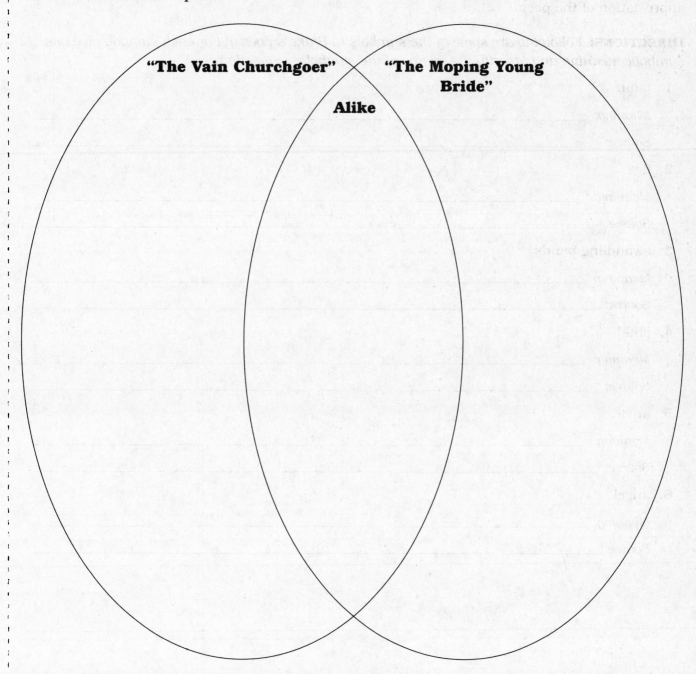

"The Vain Churchgoer"   **"The Moping Young Bride"**

Alike

On a separate page, use the details about the churchgoer and the bride to write an essay comparing the two.

© Pearson Education, Inc., publishing as Pearson Prentice Hall. All rights reserved.

Name _____ Date _____

"The Lamb," "The Tyger," "The Chimney Sweeper," and **"Infant Sorrow"** by William Blake
Literary Analysis: Symbols

Poets sometimes create their own **symbols,** but frequently they draw on symbols that should be familiar to everyone. Such symbols come from religious texts such as the Bible, as well as from stories that are common throughout a culture, such as a fairy tale or a beloved book. The more associations the reader can make with a given symbol in a poem, the richer the appreciation of the poem.

DIRECTIONS: *Following are some of the symbols in Blake's poetry. For each symbol, give one symbolic meaning and identify the source of the symbolic connection.*

1. lamb

   Meaning: _____

   Source: _____

2. fire

   Meaning: _____

   Source: _____

3. swaddling bands

   Meaning: _____

   Source: _____

4. child

   Meaning: _____

   Source: _____

5. anvil

   Meaning: _____

   Source: _____

6. angel

   Meaning: _____

   Source: _____

© Pearson Education, Inc., publishing as Pearson Prentice Hall. All rights reserved.

"The Lamb," "The Tyger," "The Chimney Sweeper," and **"Infant Sorrow"** by William Blake

Reading Strategy: Use Visuals as a Key to Meaning

When you read any form of literature that has accompanying illustrations, you can **use the visuals as a key to meaning** by studying the details of the illustrations and thinking about how they relate to the information provided by the author's words. Look at visuals and consider how they support or add to information about characters or events. Blake's vivid illustrations accompany both "The Lamb" and "The Tyger." A late-nineteenth-century engraving, accompanies the poems "The Chimney Sweeper" and "Infant Sorrow" in your textbook. By looking closely at the details of these illustrations you can gather clues about Blake's meaning and about the characters, ideas, or situations described in the poems.

DIRECTIONS: *Use the graphic organizer below to help you use the visuals as a key to Blake's meaning. Study the illustrations as you read each poem. Gather and chart clues that support or add to information in the poems. The first one has been done for you.*

Poem	What the Illustrations Add to the Meaning
"The Lamb"	**1.** One of the lambs in the illustration is eating from the boy's hand, supporting the description of the lamb as meek and docile.
"The Tyger"	**2.**
"The Chimney Sweeper"	**3.**
"Infant Sorrow"	**4.**

© Pearson Education, Inc., publishing as Pearson Prentice Hall. All rights reserved.

"The Lamb," "The Tyger," "The Chimney Sweeper," and **"Infant Sorrow"** by William Blake
Vocabulary Builder

Using the Root *-spir-*

A. DIRECTIONS: *Each of the following sentences includes an italicized word that contains the word root* -spir-, *which means "breath" or "life." Fill in each blank with a word or phrase to complete the sentence and reveal the meaning of the italicized word.*

1. If the young woman is *spirited*, she _____.

2. If he was *dispirited* by the bad news, he _____.

3. If we waited to see what would *transpire*, we _____.

4. If the council member's term *expired*, it _____.

5. If the poem *inspires* the reader, it _____.

Using the Word List

vales	symmetry	aspire

B. DIRECTIONS: *Match each word in the left column with its definition in the right column. Write the letter of the definition on the line next to the word it defines.*

___ 1. vales   **A.** balance of forms

___ 2. symmetry   **B.** hollows

___ 3. aspire   **C.** seek after

C. DIRECTIONS: *Complete each sentence by filling in the blank with one of the words from the word bank.*

1. The rolling hills and grassy _____ were the landscape of his earliest memories.

2. Early on he learned to appreciate the veins of leaves, the wings of butterflies—in short, all of nature's _____.

3. With all of these influences it was only natural that he would _____ to become a nature photographer.

© Pearson Education, Inc., publishing as Pearson Prentice Hall. All rights reserved.

"The Lamb," "The Tyger," "The Chimney Sweeper," and **"Infant Sorrow"** by William Blake
Grammar and Style: Commonly Confused Words: *Rise* and *Raise*

The forms of the irregular verb *rise*, which means "to get up," are often confused with those of the regular verb *raise*, which means "to lift or elevate." The forms of the verb *rise* are *rise*, *rose*, *had risen*. The forms of the verb *raise* are *raise*, *raised*, *had raised*. Note the following examples:

Rise
Present: We *rise* early in the morning.
Past: I *rose* before the sun came up.
Past Participle: We *had risen* early in order to catch the first train.

Raise
Present: He *raises* the canoe onto the truck's roof.
Past: I *raised* the bookshelf up a few inches.
Past Participle: She *had raised* both of the ladders onto the platform.

A. PRACTICE: *Underline the forms of the verb* rise *or* raise *in each of the following lines. In the blank, identify whether the verb is a form of* rise *or* raise *and identify the form in which it appears. The first one is done for you.*

1. The King <u>rose</u> one morning and decided he wanted to conquer the world.
   rise: past tense

2. One night the King had a dream that the sun had risen in the west.
   _____

3. He called his ministers into council and raised the issue of conquest.
   _____

4. He took this dream as a bad omen and doubts rose in his mind.
   _____

B. Writing Application: *Rewrite each sentence using the verb tense of* rise *or* raise *indicated in parentheses.*

1. The sun had risen over the far horizon. (present)
   _____

2. We rise and gather up our camp equipment. (past)
   _____

3. Abigail and John raised the kayak onto the roof of the car. (past participle)
   _____

4. I watch as morning mist rises from the nearby river. (past)
   _____

© Pearson Education, Inc., publishing as Pearson Prentice Hall. All rights reserved.

Name _____ Date _____

"The Lamb," "The Tyger," "The Chimney Sweeper," and **"Infant Sorrow"** by William Blake
Support for Writing

Use the chart below to take notes for your literary analysis. First, write your thesis statement in the center circle. Then, find details in the two poems to support your comparison and the poems' connection to Blake's life.

Details from "The Tyger"   **Details from "The Lamb"**

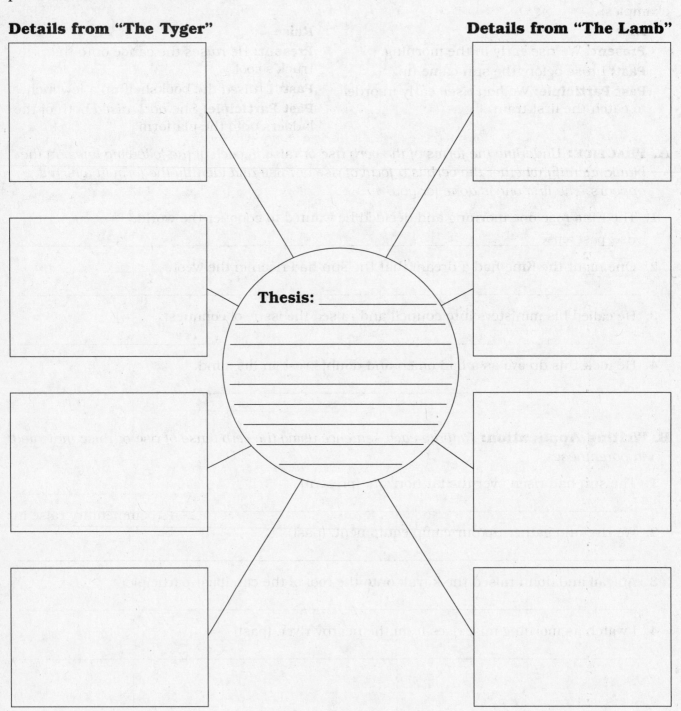

Thesis: _____

On a separate page, use the information in your chart to write your comparative literary analysis.

© Pearson Education, Inc., publishing as Pearson Prentice Hall. All rights reserved.

Name _____ Date _____

Elizabeth McCracken Introduces "Introduction" to *Frankenstein* by Mary Shelley

DIRECTIONS: *Use the space provided to answer the questions.*

1. What was McCracken's recurring nightmare when she was a child?

_____

_____

_____

_____

2. A. What does McCracken mean by "the thrill of the terrifying"?

_____

_____

   B. Do you agree with McCracken that horror has a strange but widespread appeal to both children and adults? How would you explain this appeal?

_____

_____

_____

_____

3. According to McCracken, why did her dream about a Frankenstein monster impress her?

_____

_____

4. Why did McCracken become a fiction writer?

_____

_____

5. What questions about Mary Shelley's *Frankenstein* does McCracken's commentary raise in your mind at this point?

_____

_____

_____

_____

_____

_____

_____

© Pearson Education, Inc., publishing as Pearson Prentice Hall. All rights reserved.

Elizabeth McCracken
Listening and Viewing

Segment 1: Meet Elizabeth McCracken
- How does Elizabeth McCracken draw on her personal experiences to create characters for her stories?
- Why might real-life experiences be a good starting point for a story?

_____

_____

_____

_____

Segment 2: On Frankenstein
- Why is *Frankenstein* considered a "gothic novel"?
- Although *Frankenstein* was first published in 1818, people are still intrigued by this story today. What do you find timeless about the motivations of Dr. Frankenstein as described by McCracken?

_____

_____

_____

_____

Segment 3: The Writing Process
- How does Elizabeth McCracken "find" her plot?
- Why do you think it is important to be flexible when you develop plot?

_____

_____

_____

_____

Segment 4: The Rewards of Writing
- What advice does Elizabeth McCracken have for young writers?
- Do you agree or disagree with her advice?

_____

_____

_____

_____

© Pearson Education, Inc., publishing as Pearson Prentice Hall. All rights reserved.

Introduction to Frankenstein by Mary Wollstonecraft Shelley

Literary Analysis: The Gothic Tradition

To the Romantics of the early nineteenth century, the **Gothic** elements of mystery, variety, richness, and primitive wildness suggested the natural, free, authentic aspects of life that they valued. The Gothic novel was characterized by mystery, chivalry, and horror. The Gothic tradition emphasized setting and plot more than character; often, an atmosphere of brooding and terror pervaded Gothic novels.

DIRECTIONS: *Answer the following questions about how Mary Shelley's Introduction to* Frankenstein *reflects the Gothic tradition.*

1. How might the Swiss setting in which Mary Wollstonecraft Shelley found herself in the summer of 1816 have inspired her to write a Gothic novel?

_____

_____

_____

_____

_____

_____

2. How did the stories that the writers read to amuse themselves help produce a frame of mind conducive to Gothic writing?

_____

_____

_____

_____

_____

3. How is the waking dream that Mary Wollstonecraft Shelley describes characteristic of the Gothic tradition?

_____

_____

_____

_____

_____

_____

© Pearson Education, Inc., publishing as Pearson Prentice Hall. All rights reserved.

Introduction to Frankenstein by Mary Wollstonecraft Shelley
Reading Strategy: Predict

Making **predictions** about what will happen in a literary work keeps you involved in your reading. Use clues that the writer provides, along with what you learn about the characters and the pattern in which the work is organized. As you read, check your predictions and revise them as necessary.

DIRECTIONS: *In the lines following each excerpt, record what predictions you might make about Mary Shelly's novel Frankenstein.*

1. "'How I, then a young girl, came to think of, and to dilate upon, so very hideous an idea?'"

   _____

   _____

   _____

   _____

2. "I busied myself to think of a story—a story to rival those which had excited us to this task. One which would speak to the mysterious fears of our nature . . ."

   _____

   _____

   _____

   _____

3. ". . . various philosophical doctrines were discussed, and among others the nature of the principle of life and whether there was any probability of its ever being discovered and communicated."

   _____

   _____

   _____

   _____

4. "When I placed my head on my pillow, I did not sleep, nor could I be said to think. My imagination, unbidden, possessed and guided me, gifting the successive images that arose in my mind with a vividness far beyond the usual bounds of reverie."

   _____

   _____

   _____

   _____

© Pearson Education, Inc., publishing as Pearson Prentice Hall. All rights reserved.

Name _____ Date _____

Introduction to Frankenstein by Mary Wollstonecraft Shelley
Vocabulary Builder

Using Related Words: *Phantasm* and *Fantasy*

A. DIRECTIONS: *The word* phantasm *means "supernatural form or shape." It is related to the word* fantasy, *which means "a product of the imagination." Each italicized word in the following sentences is related to* phantasm *or* fantasy. *Replace each one with a synonymous word or phrase. Write the new word or phrase on the line following the sentence.*

1. To Dexter, the shadows looked like a parade of *fantastic* creatures. _____

2. When Sono opened her eyes, the *phantasm* was still there. _____

3. Angela liked to *fantasize* about quitting her job and moving to Alaska. _____

4. Scowling, Greg pronounced, "If you think you're entitled to another week of vacation, you're living in a *fantasy* land!" _____

5. The special effects in that movie were *phantasmagorical*! _____

Using the Word List

| appendage | ungenial | acceded |
| platitude | phantasm | incitement |

B. DIRECTIONS: *Fill in each blank with a word from the Word List to complete the sentence.*

1. Alex _____ to Lori's request not to reveal the plans for the surprise party.

2. Without much imagination, the speaker often used a _____ like "All's well that ends well."

3. The shimmering mist in Margo's office turned out to be steam from her teacup, not a _____.

4. The stock market always seems to crash during the _____ weather of October.

5. Tasha's encouragement was all the _____ Li needed to convince her to apply for the job.

6. Dan's pencil looked like an extra _____ growing above his ear.

© Pearson Education, Inc., publishing as Pearson Prentice Hall. All rights reserved.

Introduction to Frankenstein by Mary Wollstonecraft Shelley
Grammar and Style: Past Participial Phrases

A **past participle** is the form of a verb that is used along with a form of the verb "to have." In the following sentences, the past participle is italicized.

Juan wasn't hungry because he had already *eaten*.

I have *had* enough of your teasing!

A **past participial phrase** is a phrase that includes a past participle and acts as an adjective. The past participle and all the other words in the phrase work together to modify a noun or pronoun. In the following sentence, the past participial phrase is italicized.

Percy Bysshe Shelley wrote a ghost story *based on his childhood experiences*.

The past participial phrase "based on his childhood experiences" acts as an adjective for the noun "story."

A. PRACTICE: *Underline the past participial phrase in each sentence below, and circle the word it modifies.*

1. The illustrious poets also, annoyed by the platitude of prose, speedily relinquished their uncongenial task.

2. . . . he advanced to the couch of the blooming youths, cradled in healthy sleep.

3. Eternal sorrow sat upon his face as he bent down and kissed the foreheads of the boys, who from that hour withered like flowers snapped from the stalk.

4. He would hope that, left to itself, the slight spark of life which he had communicated would fade. . . .

B. Writing Application: *Rewrite each of these sentences, adding a past participial phrase that acts as an adjective to modify the italicized word.*

1. On Friday, all her best *students* were late to class.

_____

2. The *plants* on Sara's windowsill withered and died.

_____

3. The *house* was more dilapidated than haunted.

_____

4. Several of the *stuffed animals* were in danger of falling to the floor.

_____

5. *Samuel* did not listen to the train conductor's announcements and consequently missed his stop.

_____

_____

© Pearson Education, Inc., publishing as Pearson Prentice Hall. All rights reserved.

Name _____ Date _____

Introduction to Frankenstein by Mary Wollstonecraft Shelley
Support for Writing

Use the two charts below to take notes about your impressions of Dr. Frankenstein and his monster before reading the Introduction and after reading it.

Impressions: Dr. Frankenstein	
Before Reading	**After Reading**

Impressions: The Monster	
Before Reading	**After Reading**

On a separate page, use your charts to write an essay comparing your impressions of *Frankenstein* before you read the Introduction to your impressions after reading it.

© Pearson Education, Inc., publishing as Pearson Prentice Hall. All rights reserved.

Name _____ Date _____

Poetry of William Wordsworth
Literary Analysis: Romanticism

During the European Enlightenment, a period that preceded Romanticism, writers and poets believed that intellect and reason were the most important aspects of humanity. They also felt that life was a universal experience for all people, no matter their background or living situation. Romanticism argued against those beliefs. Romantic poets felt that emotions were at least as important as reason, if not more so. They felt that each individual was unique, and that each person's individual life and experiences were important. They also believed that turning away from intellect and toward emotions would lead one away from society and technology and closer to nature.

DIRECTIONS: *Read the lines from the poems, and answer the questions that follow.*

Though changed, no doubt, from what I was when first
I came among these hills; when like a roe
I bounded o'er the mountains, by the sides
Of the deep rivers, and the lonely streams. . . .
("Tintern Abbey")

1. How does the narrator describe his younger self? What is he implying with these descriptions?

   _____

   _____

Little we see in Nature that is ours;
We have given our hearts away, a sordid boon! . . .
. . . —Great God! I'd rather be
A Pagan suckled in a creed outworn;
So might I, standing on this pleasant lea,
Have glimpses that would make me less forlorn;
Have sight of Proteus rising from the sea;
Or hear old Triton blow his wreathed horn.
("The World Is Too Much with Us")

2. Do you think that Wordsworth really wished he could believe in ancient Greek gods? If you do, explain why. If you don't, explain what he meant instead.

   _____

   _____

Milton! thou should'st be living at this hour:
England hath need of thee. . .
. . . Thy soul was like a Star, and dwelt apart:
Thou hadst a voice whose sound was like the sea:
Pure as the naked heavens, majestic, free. . . .
("London, 1802")

© Pearson Education, Inc., publishing as Pearson Prentice Hall. All rights reserved.

Poetry of William Wordsworth
Reading Strategy: Use Literary Context

Romantic poets and writers, like Romantic musicians and artists, were revolutionary in their time. They were revolting against an earlier literary movement called the European Enlightenment. The Enlightenment stressed intellect and reason. It said that all people were essentially the same, no matter who they were or where they lived. The Romantics stressed the importance of emotions over reason, and believed in the importance of each individual's expression, based on his or her own feelings and life experiences.

DIRECTIONS: *Use this graphic organizer to help you record Romantic elements from Wordsworth's poems. When you find a passage that exemplifies Romantic ideals, think about it. Decide why it exemplifies the Romantic period rather than the European Enlightenment. One passage has already been chosen and analyzed for you.*

Passage	Why Passage Characterizes Romantic Period, Not Enlightenment
1. "But oft . . . / . . . I have owed to them / . . . sensations sweet, / Felt in the blood, and felt along the heart; / . . . feelings too / Of unremembered pleasure . . ." ("Tintern Abbey," 25–30)	It describes the emotional response that memories of the landscape provoked in the narrator rather than describing the landscape rationally and realistically.
2.	
3.	
4.	
5.	

Poetry of William Wordsworth
Vocabulary Builder

Using Related Words: *Anatomize*

A. DIRECTIONS: *Answer the following questions about* anatomize *and words related to it.*

1. What does *anatomize* mean? _____

2. What type of tool might an anatomist use? _____

3. If someone were making an anatomic study of mole rats, would she be more interested in the rats' feeding habits or in their internal organs? _____

4. In 1958, Robert Travers wrote a book called *Anatomy of a Murder.* How do you think the book treats the crime in question? _____

Using the Word List

recompense	roused	presumption	antomize
confounded	sordid	stagnant	

B. DIRECTIONS: *Each item below consists of a related pair of words in CAPITAL LETTERS followed by four lettered pairs of words. Choose the pair that best expresses a relationship similar to that expressed in the pair in capital letters. Circle the letter of your choice.*

1. EGOTIST : PRESUMPTION ::
   A. traitor : treachery
   B. doctor : stethoscope
   C. coward : bravery
   D. lawyer : summation

2. CONFOUNDED : CLEAR-HEADED ::
   A. enraged : even-tempered
   B. amused : laughing
   C. saddened : regretful
   D. wondrous : awesome

3. RECOMPENSE : SALARY ::
   A. fairness : injustice
   B. indebtedness : mortgage
   C. heat : perspiration
   D. interest : payment

4. ROUSED : EXCITED ::
   A. sympathetic : saddened
   B. curious : uninterested
   C. offended : insulted
   D. sleeping : awakened

5. SORDID : FILTHY ::
   A. frigid : lukewarm
   B. amusing : ridiculous
   C. untimely : early
   D. angry : irate

6. SWAMP : STAGNANT ::
   A. ocean : salty
   B. river : flowing
   C. pond : tidal
   D. lake : frozen

7. ANATOMIZE : DISSECT ::
   A. infantilize : mature
   B. categorize : difference
   C. prioritize : equate
   D. analyze : study

© Pearson Education, Inc., publishing as Pearson Prentice Hall. All rights reserved.

Name _____ Date _____

Poetry of William Wordsworth
Grammar and Style: Present Participial Phrases

A participle is a verb that is used as an adjective: The *folded* blanket is warmer. A present participle uses the present tense: A *rolling* stone gathers no moss. A **present participial phrase** consists of a present participle plus one or more words that modify it. The entire phrase is used as an adjective.

Example: *Walking down the street,* I ran into my friend Ken.

A. PRACTICE: *Read each of the following lines from "Lines Composed a Few Miles Above Tintern Abbey." If the underlined words are a present participial phrase, write "yes." If not, write "no" and explain why not.*

1. "And <u>passing even into my purer mind</u> / . . . feelings too/Of unremembered pleasure . . ."

_____

2. "we are laid asleep/In body, and become a <u>living</u> soul. . . ."

_____

3. "Have hung upon the <u>beatings of my heart</u> . . ."

_____

4. "more like a man/<u>Flying from something</u> that he dreads . . ."

_____

5. "The <u>sounding</u> cataract/Haunted me like a passion . . ."

_____

B. Writing Application: *Rewrite each of the following sentences, adding a present participial phrase that modifies the subject.*

1. I lost my key.

_____

2. That dog looks like my dog.

_____

3. The car is out of control.

_____

4. The man seems familiar.

_____

5. The movie is great!

_____

© Pearson Education, Inc., publishing as Pearson Prentice Hall. All rights reserved.

Poetry of William Wordsworth
Support for Writing

Use the organizer below to take notes for a response to criticism. Review the poems, and then write notes and cite lines that support or argue against Thomas Wolfe's statement.

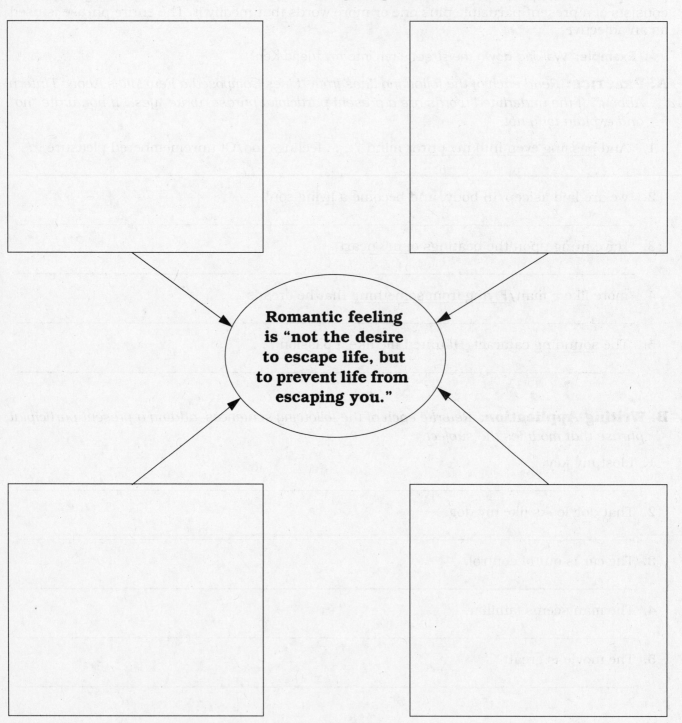

Romantic feeling is "not the desire to escape life, but to prevent life from escaping you."

On a separate page, write a response to criticism. Clearly state whether or not you agree with Wolfe. Then, use evidence from the organizer to support your position.

"The Rime of the Ancient Mariner" and **"Kubla Khan"** by Samuel Taylor Coleridge
Literary Analysis: Poetic Sound Devices

Alliteration is the repetition of a consonant sound at the beginnings of words. **Consonance** is the repetition of consonant sounds in stressed syllables with dissimilar vowel sounds. **Assonance** is repetition of vowel sounds in stressed syllables with dissimilar consonant sounds. **Internal rhyme** is the use of rhyming words within a line.

DIRECTIONS: *In each of the following passages from "The Rime of the Ancient Mariner" and "Kubla Kahn," certain letters are italicized. For each passage, write on the line the* **sound device** *that is used.*

1. "As who pursued with ye*ll* and b*l*ow" _____
2. "The ice did spl*it* with a thunder-f*it*" _____
3. "*H*e *h*olds *h*im with *h*is skinny *h*and" _____
4. "The ship was ch*eered*, the harbor cl*eared*" _____
5. "And we did spea*k* only to brea*k*" _____
6. "*R*ed as a *r*ose is she" _____
7. "All in a h*o*t and c*o*pper sky" _____
8. "The Wedding G*uest* he beat his br*east*" _____
9. "The death f*i*res danced at n*ight*" _____
10. "The *f*air breeze blew, the white *f*oam *f*lew" _____
11. "His *f*lashing eyes, his *f*loating hair!" _____
12. "A *d*amsel with a *d*ulcimer" _____
13. "For *h*e on *h*oneydew *h*ath fed," _____
14. "And *cl*ose your eyes with h*ol*y dread" _____
15. "And from this chasm, with *c*easeless turmoil s*ee*thing" _____

© Pearson Education, Inc., publishing as Pearson Prentice Hall. All rights reserved.

"The Rime of the Ancient Mariner" and **"Kubla Khan"** by Samuel Taylor Coleridge

Reading Strategy: Analyze Poetic Effects

One of the primary characteristics that sets verse apart from prose is the range of poetic and sound devices commonly used in poetry. These devices enhance the musical qualities of the language by pleasing the ear, but they also serve to emphasize meaning and create mood. By paying attention to these devices you can become more sensitive to the nuances and effects of poetic language. The following are several different types of sound devices:

alliteration:	repetition of consonant sounds at the beginnings of words
consonance:	repetition of consonant sounds at the ends of words
assonance:	repetition of vowel sounds in nearby words or syllables
internal rhyme:	rhymes occurring within a poetic line
ordinary repetition:	repetition of entire words

DIRECTIONS: *Use this chart to keep track of poetic effects as you read "The Rime of the Ancient Mariner" and "Kubla Khan." Each time you encounter a poetic sound device, write the example in the left column. Then, in the right column, explain the effect of the device, or how it enhances the text. The first passage has been done for you.*

Line or Phrase	Device	Effect
1. "Water, water, everywhere,/ Nor any drop to drink." ("Rime," lines 121–122)	repetition and alliteration	Repetition of the word *water* and of the *w* sound emphasizes the amount of water. Repetition of the *dr-* sound in *drop* and *drink* also emphasizes the lack of drinking water. The differing alliteration in each line contrats the amount of water with the lack of drinking water.
2.		
3.		
4.		
5.		

© Pearson Education, Inc., publishing as Pearson Prentice Hall. All rights reserved.

Name _____   Date _____

"The Rime of the Ancient Mariner" and "Kubla Khan" by Samuel Taylor Coleridge
Vocabulary Builder

Using the Root -journ-

A. DIRECTIONS: *Each of the following words contains the Latin root -journ-, which comes from the French and Latin words for "day." For each of the following sentences, choose one of the five words or phrases to replace the italicized word or phrase.*

adjourn	du jour	journal
journalism	journey	

1. The long day's *trip* had wiped me out completely. _____
2. I'm not so interested in writing fiction; I prefer *reporting*. _____
3. Kevin wrote all of his secret sorrows in his *diary*. _____
4. At midnight, the council finally decided that it was time for the meeting *to end for the day*. _____
5. Maggie ordered the radish salad and the soup *of the day*. _____

Using the Word List

averred	sojourn	expiated
reverence	sinuous	tumult

B. DIRECTIONS: *Choose the letter of the description that best fits each word below. Write the letters on the lines provided.*

___ 1. tumult
   A. commotion
   B. height
   C. depth
   D. gathering

___ 2. sinuous
   A. weak
   B. strong
   C. straight
   D. curving

___ 3. averred
   A. expressed ignorance
   B. stated to be true
   C. stated to be false
   D. defended weakly

___ 4. expiated
   A. breathed
   B. blamed
   C. explained
   D. atoned

___ 5. sojourn
   A. stay for a while
   B. visit briefly
   C. travel widely
   D. carry to

___ 6. reverence
   A. sadness
   B. veneration
   C. revisitation
   D. abhorrence

© Pearson Education, Inc., publishing as Pearson Prentice Hall. All rights reserved.

Name _____ Date _____

"The Rime of the Ancient Mariner" and **"Kubla Khan"** by Samuel Taylor Coleridge
Grammar and Style: Inverted Word Order

In standard English word order, the subject precedes the verb, the verb precedes the direct object, and a prepositional phrase follows the word it modifies. Sometimes a writer uses **inverted word order** to achieve a certain effect. The following lines from "Kubla Khan" provide an example.

Inverted word order: In Xanadu did Kubla Khan/A stately pleasure dome decree. . . .

Normal word order: Kubla Khan did decree a stately pleasure dome in Xanadu. . . .

A. PRACTICE: *For each of the following phrases, identify the sentence parts that have been inverted. Then rewrite the phrase or sentence, using normal word order.*

from "The Rime of the Ancient Mariner":

1. "At length did cross an Albatross. . . ."

_____

_____

2. "Instead of the cross, the Albatross/About my neck was hung."

_____

_____

from "Kubla Khan":

3. "Where was heard the mingled measure/From the fountain and the caves."

_____

_____

4. "A damsel with a dulcimer/In a vision once I saw. . . ."

_____

_____

B. Writing Application: *Rewrite each of these sentences using inverted word order.*

1. I saw a sprite in that light.

_____

2. His fingers wrapped around the pole; I knew that it would snap.

_____

3. The man and his dog ran up the walk to fetch the injured bird.

_____

4. Soft music slipped into my ears and sent me right to sleep.

_____

© Pearson Education, Inc., publishing as Pearson Prentice Hall. All rights reserved.

Name _____   Date _____

"The Rime of the Ancient Mariner" and **"Kubla Khan"** by Samuel Taylor Coleridge
Support for Writing

Use the cluster diagram to gather details from "The Rime of the Ancient Mariner" about the albatross and about its effects on the Mariner.

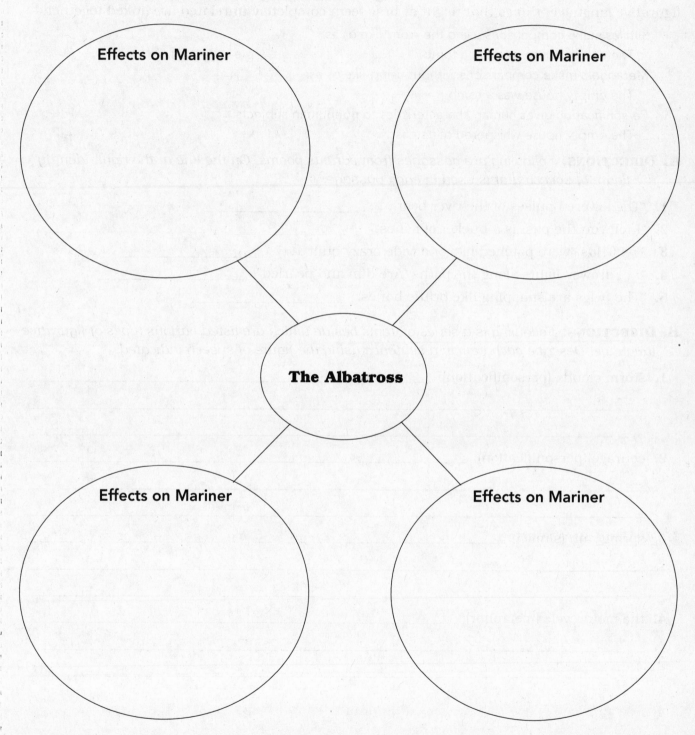

On a separate page, use the information you have gathered in your cluster diagram as you write your essay analyzing the meanings of the Albatross as a symbol.

© Pearson Education, Inc., publishing as Pearson Prentice Hall. All rights reserved.

"She Walks in Beauty," *from* **Childe Harold's Pilgrimage,**
and *from* **Don Juan** by George Gordon, Lord Byron
Literary Analysis: Figurative Language

To build powerful images, writers use **figurative language,** or figures of speech. Through figurative language, things that might at first seem completely unrelated are linked together.

   Similes make comparisons using the word *like* or *as:*

     The empty house was like a tomb.

   Metaphors make comparisons without using *like* or *as:*

     The empty house was a tomb.

   Personification gives human characteristics to nonhuman subjects:

     The empty house whispered of its past.

A. DIRECTIONS: *Following are passages from various poems. On the line at the right, identify the figure of speech that is used in each passage.*

1. "The lowered pulses of the river beat . . ." _____

2. "I tell you the past is a bucket of ashes." _____

3. The fields "were patched like one wide crazy quilt . . ." _____

4. ". . . drowsy lights along the paths/Are dim and pearled" _____

5. "The twigs are snapping like brittle bones." _____

B. DIRECTIONS: *Following is a series of items beside which are listed various types of figurative language. Describe each item in a sentence using the figure of speech indicated.*

1. storm clouds (personification) _____

   _____

2. courage (personification) _____

   _____

3. spring rain (simile) _____

   _____

4. the motorcycle (metaphor) _____

   _____

© Pearson Education, Inc., publishing as Pearson Prentice Hall. All rights reserved.

Name _____   Date _____

"She Walks in Beauty," *from* Childe Harold's Pilgrimage, and *from* Don Juan by George Gordon, Lord Byron
Reading Strategy: Question

Poetry is meant to be read several times. You might read a poem once to get a general sense of its themes. On another reading, you might focus on the language and rhythm of the poem. Next you might pay special attention to its images. At least one of your readings should be devoted to achieving a basic understanding of what the poet is trying to communicate. You can do this by reading actively—asking questions about the poem and answering them. Ask questions that use the words *who, what, where, when,* and *why.* For example, consider the excerpt in your textbook from *Childe Harold's Pilgrimage:*

- **Question:** *What* does the speaker hope to communicate? **Answer:** He expresses admiration for the ocean.
- **Question:** *Why* does the speaker admire the ocean? **Answer:** Humans and human activities are insignificant in comparison to the ocean; the ocean is unchanging; it rules its domain and cannot be tamed by humans.

DIRECTIONS: *Read the excerpt in your textbook from* Don Juan. *Write questions about the poem using the words listed below. Then answer your questions.*

1. Who _____

   _____?

   _____

   _____

2. What _____

   _____?

   _____

   _____

3. What _____

   _____?

   _____

   _____

4. Why _____

   _____?

   _____

   _____

5. Why _____

   _____?

   _____

   _____

© Pearson Education, Inc., publishing as Pearson Prentice Hall. All rights reserved.

"She Walks in Beauty," *from* Childe Harold's Pilgrimage, and *from* Don Juan by George Gordon, Lord Byron
Vocabulary Builder

Using the Suffix *-ous*

A. DIRECTIONS: *The following words all contain the suffix -ous, meaning "full of." In the blanks, complete each sentence with the appropriate word or words from the list.*

famous	delicious	miraculous	rebellious
ominous	adventurous	humorous	

1. The mushrooms tasted _____, but they were poisonous.

2. The _____ hero walked forward boldly into the storm, undeterred by the _____ lightning flashing all around him.

3. The politician was _____ for always beginning his speeches with a _____ anecdote.

4. Maude made a _____ recovery following cardiac surgery.

5. Feeling _____, Theo refused to celebrate the holidays.

Using the Word List

arbiter	credulous	retort	torrid	avarice
fathomless	tempests	copious	insensible	

B. DIRECTIONS: *Match each word in the left column with its definition in the right column. Write the letter of the definition on the line next to the word it defines.*

___ 1. retort   **A.** willing to believe

___ 2. credulous   **B.** numb

___ 3. copious   **C.** plentiful

___ 4. avarice   **D.** greed

___ 5. insensible   **E.** storms

___ 6. fathomless   **F.** reply with a wisecrack

___ 7. arbiter   **G.** too deep to measure

___ 8. tempests   **H.** very hot

___ 9. torrid   **I.** judge

© Pearson Education, Inc., publishing as Pearson Prentice Hall. All rights reserved.

Name _____ Date _____

"She Walks in Beauty," *from* Childe Harold's Pilgrimage, and *from* Don Juan by George Gordon, Lord Byron
Grammar and Style: Subject and Verb Agreement

Every **verb** form that you write should agree in number with the noun that is its **subject**. A singular subject must have a singular verb, and a plural subject must have a plural verb.

Singular subject and verb:	*Time writes* no wrinkle on thine azure brow. . . .
	Where a *thought* serenely sweet *expresses*/How pure, how dear its dwelling place.
Plural subject and verb:	*Time and adversity write* no wrinkle on thine azure brow. . . . Where *thoughts* serenely sweet *express*/How pure, how dear their dwelling place.

A. PRACTICE: *Check each of the following sentences to see if its subject and verb agree in number. If they agree, write* agree *in the blank next to the sentence. If they do not agree, write the correct form of the verb in the blank next to the sentence. If there are two verbs, be sure to write the correct form of each in the blank.*

1. She *walks* in beauty, like the night. . . . _____

2. The smiles that win, the tints that glow, but *tells* of days in goodness spent . . .

   _____

3. There *are* a pleasure in the pathless woods. . . . _____

4. These *is* thy toys, and, as the snowy flake, / They *melts* into thy yeast of waves. . . .

   _____

5. their decay/*Have dried* up realms to deserts. . . . _____

6. *Roll* on, thou deep and dark blue ocean—*roll!* _____

B. Writing Application: *Write a sentence using each word or phrase below as the subject. Make sure that the verb agrees with the subject in each case.*

1. raindrop

   _____

2. dancer

   _____

3. coffee and tea

   _____

4. olives

   _____

5. strangers

   _____

© Pearson Education, Inc., publishing as Pearson Prentice Hall. All rights reserved.

"She Walks in Beauty," *from* Childe Harold's Pilgrimage, and *from* Don Juan by George Gordon, Lord Byron
Support for Writing

Use the chart below to gather and record ideas for your monologue.

Byronic Opinions that Fit Today's World	Byron's Circumstances and Attitude	Words and Phrases That Convey his Attitude

On a separate page, use the information you have gathered as you write your monologue.

© Pearson Education, Inc., publishing as Pearson Prentice Hall. All rights reserved.

"Ozymandias," "Ode to the West Wind," and **"To a Skylark"**
by Percy Bysshe Shelley
Literary Analysis: Imagery

Poets use vivid **imagery** for many reasons. Appealing to a reader's senses of sight, hearing, taste, smell, and touch can make the poem seem more real to the reader. Certain images may also inspire a reader to respond with feelings of awe, disgust, fear, desire, amusement, or joy, to name just a few. But poets do not use images purely to keep the reader's interest—often, the images in a poem help to develop the poem's theme. For example, in "To a Skylark," Shelley uses imagery to reinforce the theme of creativity. He compares the bird to the moon, a poet, a highborn maiden, a glowworm, and a rose. The subject of each image emits or creates a beautiful thing: The moon and glowworm both emit light, the poet creates poetry, the maiden sings, and the rose emits a pleasant odor.

DIRECTIONS: *Answer the following questions on the lines provided.*

> . . . Two vast and trunkless legs of stone
> Stand in the desert. Near them, on the sand,
> Half sunk, a shattered visage lies, whose frown,
> And wrinkled lip, and sneer of cold command . . .
> ("Ozymandias," lines 2–5)

1. To what senses does this image appeal?

   _____

2. What emotions might this image provoke in a reader?

   _____

3. To what senses does this image appeal?

   _____

4. What emotions might this image provoke in a reader?

   _____

5. How is this image related to the theme of the poem?

   _____

© Pearson Education, Inc., publishing as Pearson Prentice Hall. All rights reserved.

Name _____ Date _____

"Ozymandias," "Ode to the West Wind," and "To a Skylark"
by Percy Bysshe Shelley
Reading Strategy: Respond to Imagery

Poets use descriptive language, or **imagery,** to make their writing seem more real and vivid to the reader. They do this by appealing to a reader's physical senses with visual details, sounds, smells, tastes, and textures. In order to **respond to a poem's imagery,** you must use your imagination and draw on your life experience. For example, you might respond to Shelley's mention of rain by imagining what rain feels like against your skin.

DIRECTIONS: *As you read these poems, copy several passages that contain vivid images in the first column of the graphic organizer below. In the second column, describe the image in your own words. Include details that Shelley implies but may not specifically mention. Remember to include sounds, smells, tastes, and textures, as well as sights, if appropriate. In the third column list the senses (sight, hearing, touch, smell, or taste) through which the image can be experienced.*

Passage	Description of Image	Senses
1. "Round the decay / Of that colossal wreck, boundless and bare, / The lone and level sands stretch far away." ("Ozymandias," lines 12–14)	The statue is surrounded by a vast empty desert where it is dry and hot and there is no sound but the wind.	sight, touch, sound
2.		
3.		
4.		
5.		

"Ozymandias," "Ode to the West Wind," and "To a Skylark"
by Percy Bysshe Shelley
Vocabulary Builder

Using the Root -puls-

A. DIRECTIONS: *The word root -puls- means "push" or "drive." Using your knowledge of the word root -puls- and the information in parentheses, replace each italicized word or phrase with a word that includes the word root -puls-. Write the new word on the line that follows the sentence.*

compulsive (*com-* = with)	repulse (*re-* = against)
pulsar (*-ar* = of or relating to)	impulsiveness (*im-* = toward)

1. Astronomers began to pick up waves of electromagnetic radiation that were being emitted from a previously unknown *neutron star.* _____

2. Because he is *a/an obsessive* shopper, Isaiah can't save money. _____

3. Maddie regretted her *spontaneity* after she threw her book out the window. _____

4. The army used tanks to *drive back* the attacking forces. _____

Using the Word List

visage	verge	sepulcher	impulse
blithe	profuse	vernal	satiety

B. DIRECTIONS: *Fill in each blank with a word from the Word List.*

1. Mary visited the graveyard to put flowers by her ancestor's _____.

2. It was difficult to stop the flooding because the flow of water was so _____

3. The _____ equinox signals the first day of spring.

4. Don't ever show your sorry _____ around here again!

5. After the pie-eating contest, Harold was beyond _____; he was on the _____ of being sick.

6. José loved his grandmother, but her _____ response to even the most depressing events irritated him.

7. When the rescue ship sailed into the harbor and unloaded the survivors, Sarah obeyed her sudden _____ to kneel and kiss the solid ground.

© Pearson Education, Inc., publishing as Pearson Prentice Hall. All rights reserved.

Name _____ Date _____

"Ozymandias," "Ode to the West Wind," and "To a Skylark"
by Percy Bysshe Shelley
Grammar and Style: Subjunctive Mood

The **subjunctive mood** is used to refer to possible rather than actual actions. For example, writers use the subjunctive mood to suggest that something might happen, express doubt that something will happen, voice a desire for something to happen, or note that if one action occurs another is likely to follow. The subjunctive can be formed with the plural past tense of the verb *to be (were)* or with helping verbs like *could, would,* or *should.*

Subjunctive:

The skylark could fly away.

The skylark should fly away.

I insist that the skylark fly away.

The skylark would fall out of the sky,

    were it not to spread its wings and fly.

Not subjunctive:

The skylark will fly away.

The skylark is flying away.

The skylark flew away.

The skylark has flown away,

A. PRACTICE: *Underline the subjunctive verbs in the following verses from "Ode to the West Wind."*

If I were a dead leaf thou mightest bear;

If I were a swift cloud to fly with thee;

A wave to pant beneath thy power, and share

The impulse of thy strength, only less free

Than thou, O uncontrollable! If even

I were as in my boyhood, and could be

The comrade of thy wanderings over Heaven,

As then, when to outstrip thy skyey speed

Scarce seemed a vision; I would ne'er have striven

As thus with thee in prayer in my sore need.

B. Writing Application: *Rewrite each of the following sentences, changing the verb form to the subjunctive. Be sure to change the rest of the sentence too, if necessary.*

1. That apple cannot fall far from the tree.

    _____

2. Samantha will hurt herself when she loses her balance on those slippery steps.

    _____

3. I am sorry you are not happy about this decision.

    _____

4. Marty refused to resign from the company.

    _____

5. Bruno is not able to talk, even though he may want to—he's only a dog.

    _____

© Pearson Education, Inc., publishing as Pearson Prentice Hall. All rights reserved.

"Ozymandias," "Ode to the West Wind," and **"To a Skylark"**
by Percy Bysshe Shelley
Support for Writing

Use the lines below to record questions and to organize your research into the scientific and historical background of one of Shelley's poems.

1. Specific question: _____

   _____

   A. General question: _____

   _____

   B. General question: _____

   _____

2. Specific question: _____

   _____

   A. General question: _____

   _____

   B. General question: _____

   _____

3. Specific question: _____

   _____

   A. General question: _____

   _____

   B. General question: _____

   _____

Use your questions to guide your research into the background of your poem. On a separate page, use the information you gather to support your introduction.

© Pearson Education, Inc., publishing as Pearson Prentice Hall. All rights reserved.

Name _____ Date _____

Poetry of John Keats
Literary Analysis: Ode

The **ode** is a long lyric poem with a serious subject. Written in an elevated style, the ode usually honors its subject and addresses it directly. There are three types of odes in English. The **Pindaric ode** is written in sets of three stanzas and is modeled after the odes of the Greek poet Pindar. Pindar's odes were chanted by a chorus onstage, in the Greek dramatic tradition. With the first stanza, or strophe, the chorus moved to the right; with the second, or antistrophe, it moved to the left. For the third and final stanza, or epode, the chorus stood still. In the English Pindaric ode, the strophes and antistrophes have one stanza pattern and the epode has another. The **Horatian ode** is modeled after the odes of the Roman poet Horace. It is homostrophic, or contains only one type of stanza, and tends to be more restrained and meditative in tone. Finally, the **irregular ode** contains no set strophic pattern.

DIRECTIONS: *Fill in the following table to determine which type of odes Keats has written. When analyzing the stanzas, be sure to count out the number of lines, rhyme scheme, and meter for each stanza.*

	"Ode to a Nightingale"	**"Ode on a Grecian Urn"**
Number of stanzas		
Number of lines per stanza		
Rhyme scheme(s)		
Meter(s)		
Type of ode		

© Pearson Education, Inc., publishing as Pearson Prentice Hall. All rights reserved.

Poetry of John Keats
Reading Strategy: Paraphrase

Keats's nineteenth-century language and complex figures of speech can be difficult to understand. If you come to the end of a stanza and have no idea what you have just read, go back and read each phrase or sentence one at a time. Once you've identified the spots that are giving you trouble, you can **paraphrase** them, or restate them in your own words. Read the following example from Keats's "On First Looking into Chapman's Homer":

Oft of one wide expanse had I been told

That deep-browed Homer ruled as his demesne:

Yet did I never breathe its pure serene

Till I heard Chapman speak out loud and bold. . . .

Paraphrase:

I had often been told of a great place, ruled by the thoughtful Homer. However, I never breathed its pure air until I heard Chapman speak of it loudly and boldly.

The paraphrased version uses simple words and phrases in the place of more difficult ones and rearranges the order of the sentence parts. Once you have paraphrased the passage you can more easily see that the "wide expanse," or "great place," refers to Homer's poetry and that Chapman's speaking of this place refers to his translation of Homer's work.

DIRECTIONS: *Paraphrase the following difficult passages from Keats's poems. Use the footnotes and a dictionary, if necessary, to define difficult words.*

from "When I Have Fears That I May Cease to Be":

1. "When I have fears that I may cease to be
   Before my pen has gleaned my teeming brain . . ."

   _____

   _____

from "Ode to a Nightingale":

2. "Fade far away, dissolve, and quite forget
   What thou among the leaves hast never known,
   The weariness, the fever, and the fret. . . ."

   _____

   _____

   _____

Name _____ Date _____

Poetry of John Keats
Vocabulary Builder

Using the Suffix -age

A. DIRECTIONS: *Each of the following sentences contains an italicized word ending with the suffix -age, one meaning of which is "state, condition, or quality." Using the word's context along with what you know about this suffix, write a definition of each italicized word in the blank.*

1. The backyard always floods because of poor *drainage.*

   _____

2. Alfred and Olivia wanted nothing more than to be joined in *marriage.*

   _____

3. The terrorists kept their prisoners in *bondage* for thirty days.

   _____

4. The war led to a great *shortage* of many goods.

   _____

5. The garage and its contents lay in *wreckage* around me.

   _____

Using the Word List

ken	surmise	gleaned
teeming	vintage	requiem

B. DIRECTIONS: *Fill in the blank in each sentence with the correct word from the Word List.*

1. I _____ that the trouble began long before we got here.
2. He _____ as much information as he could from the newspaper article.
3. The cathedral choir sang a _____ at his funeral.
4. Jack just bought a Model T to add to his collection of _____ cars.
5. The bag of rotten apples was _____ with ants.
6. The secrets of the universe are far beyond my _____.

© Pearson Education, Inc., publishing as Pearson Prentice Hall. All rights reserved.

Name _____ Date _____

Poetry of John Keats
Grammar and Style: Direct Address

Direct address is the calling of a person or thing by name. Terms of direct address are generally set off by commas. This device can create a tone of intimacy and provide information about the person or thing being addressed as well as the writer's thoughts or feelings about the subject being addressed. The following lines from "When I Have Fears That I May Cease to Be" show the use of direct address:

> And when I feel, *fair creature of an hour,*
> That I shall never look upon thee more . . .

A. PRACTICE: *The following passages from "Ode on a Grecian Urn" contain examples of direct address. Underline the words of direct address within each passage.*

1. Thou still unravished bride of quietness
   Thou foster child of silence and slow time,
   Sylvan historian, who canst thus express
   A flowery tale more sweetly than our rhyme . . .

2. Fair youth, beneath the trees, thou canst not leave
   Thy song, nor ever can those trees be bare. . . .

3. Ah, happy, happy boughs! that cannot shed
   Your leaves, nor ever bid the Spring adieu . . .

4. O Attic shape! Fair attitude! with brede
   Of marble men and maidens overwrought . . .

B. Writing Application: *Rewrite the following sentences using one form of direct address in each sentence.*

1. I wish I could forget you and your wicked birds.

   _____

2. Some day you will all see that I'm no child, that I knew the truth.

   _____

3. If only you would look my way, you'd know my mind.

   _____

4. I wonder what secrets hide behind those bricks of yours.

   _____

5. Did you know that the sight of you knocks me speechless?

   _____

© Pearson Education, Inc., publishing as Pearson Prentice Hall. All rights reserved.

Name _____ Date _____

Poetry of John Keats
Support for Writing

Complete the chart below by writing quotations about extreme feelings or ideas from two of Keats's poems. Then, think about the quotations and draw a conclusion.

Quotations Expressing Feelings and Ideas

	Poem title: _____	**Poem title:** _____
Expresses extreme feelings	Quotation:	Quotation:
	Quotation:	Quotation:
Expresses balanced feelings	Quotation:	Quotation:
	Quotation:	Quotation:

Conclusion: _____

_____

_____

_____

On a separate page, draw on information from the chart to support your response to literature.

© Pearson Education, Inc., publishing as Pearson Prentice Hall. All rights reserved.

Name _____ Date _____

"Speech to Parliament: In Defense of the Lower Classes" by George Gordon, Lord Byron
"A Song: 'Men of England'" by Percy Bysshe Shelley
"On the Passing of the Reform Bill" by Thomas Babington Macaulay

Literary Analysis: Political Commentary

Political commentary, or opinions on political and social issues, can be delivered in a variety of literary forms, including speeches, essays, poems, letters, and even novels. Effective political commentators identify the ideas they wish to express, choose an appropriate literary form, and tailor their message to a particular audience. For instance, the subject of Lord Byron's commentary is a defense of the actions of workers who destroyed factory equipment to protest losing their jobs. Knowing that his audience would be members of Parliament, Byron wrote his commentary as a speech and addressed his remarks (in respectful but confrontational language) directly to his listeners. Being a member of the House of Lords as well as a poet, Byron understood that oration was the most productive form for communicating ideas to a large group of statesmen. He also believed that his fellow legislators must be challenged openly about their responsibilities toward the unemployed workers.

DIRECTIONS: *Choose one of the three literary works in this section. After reading the selection, answer the following questions.*

1. How would you describe the author's message in a sentence or two? Identify two or three sentences in which the author addresses this central idea.

   _____

   _____

   _____

2. What goal do you think the author hopes to achieve with this commentary?

   _____

   _____

   _____

3. Why do you think the author chose to write in this literary form?

   _____

   _____

   _____

4. How would you describe the audience for this political commentary?

   _____

   _____

   _____

5. List several examples of language or ideas that reflect the author's awareness of his audience.

   _____

   _____

   _____

Name _____ Date _____

"Speech to Parliament: In Defense of the Lower Classes" by George Gordon, Lord Byron
"A Song: 'Men of England'" by Percy Bysshe Shelley
"On the Passing of the Reform Bill" by Thomas Babington Macaulay
Reading Strategy: Set a Purpose for Reading

If you **set a purpose for reading,** you can focus your attention on particular aspects of a literary work and enrich your reading experience. For instance, if you decide to read "A Song: 'Men of England'" for pleasure, you might take special note of Shelley's use of language, his sound devices, and his passionate tone. On the other hand, you could choose to read the poem to identify its Romantic characteristics; in this case, you might pay close attention to the poet's use of nature imagery and to his challenging attitude about employers' poor treatment of workers.

DIRECTIONS: *This graphic organizer can help you set a purpose for reading, note specific passages in the literature, and reflect on these passages in light of your purpose. Before reading, state your purpose in the center box. Then, as you read, write down at least four passages from the work that relate to or answer your purpose. Beneath each quoted passage, explain how it deepens your understanding and helps fulfill your purpose.*

Purpose

_____
_____
_____
_____
_____
_____
_____
_____

Passages

_____	_____	_____	_____
_____	_____	_____	_____
_____	_____	_____	_____
_____	_____	_____	_____
_____	_____	_____	_____
_____	_____	_____	_____

© Pearson Education, Inc., publishing as Pearson Prentice Hall. All rights reserved.

Name _____ Date _____

"Speech to Parliament: In Defense of the Lower Classes" by George Gordon, Lord Byron
"A Song: 'Men of England'" by Percy Bysshe Shelley
"On the Passing of the Reform Bill" by Thomas Babington Macaulay
Vocabulary Builder

Using the Roots -dec-

A. DIRECTIONS: *Each of the words in the left column contains the roots -deci- or -deca-, meaning "ten." Match each word with its definition in the right column. Write the letter of the definition on the line next to the word it defines.*

___ 1. decade
___ 2. decimal
___ 3. decahedron
___ 4. decibel
___ 5. decathlon

A. an athletic contest consisting of ten events
B. a solid figure with ten plane surfaces
C. a period of ten years
D. a fraction expressed in base 10
E. a numerical expression of the relative loudness of sounds

Using the Word List

| impediments | decimation | efficacious |
| emancipate | balm | inauspicious |

B. DIRECTIONS: *Choose the letter of the word or phrase that is most nearly the same as each numbered word. Write the letters on the lines provided.*

___ 1. inauspicious
   A. unlikeable
   B. unmentionable
   C. unfavorable
   D. uneasy

___ 2. emancipate
   A. trap
   B. free
   C. enliven
   D. elevate

___ 3. balm
   A. something disturbing
   B. something healing
   C. something flat
   D. something powdery

___ 4. efficacious
   A. affluent
   B. effusive
   C. efficient
   D. effective

___ 5. impediments
   A. obstructions
   B. detours
   C. pedestals
   D. openings

___ 6. decimation
   A. harm
   B. destruction
   C. support
   D. addition

© Pearson Education, Inc., publishing as Pearson Prentice Hall. All rights reserved.

"Speech to Parliament: In Defense of the Lower Classes" by George Gordon, Lord Byron
"A Song: 'Men of England'" by Percy Bysshe Shelley
"On the Passing of the Reform Bill" by Thomas Babington Macaulay

Grammar and Style: Correlative Conjunctions

Correlative conjunctions work in pairs to link two words or groups of words of equal importance. Writers use correlative conjunctions such as *just as . . . so (too)* and *whether . . . or,* to present their ideas in a balanced manner. The following lines from "Speech to Parliament: In Defense of the Lower Classes" show how a pair of correlative conjunctions works in a sentence.

> When we were told that these men are leagued together, *not only* for the destruction of their own comfort, *but* of their very means of subsistence, can we forget that it is the bitter policy . . . unto the third and fourth generation!

A. PRACTICE: *Underline the correlative conjunctions in each of the following sentences.*

1. It is widely believed that both Shelley and Byron are among the most important English poets of the early nineteenth century.

2. Do you know whether Lord Byron is considered a Romantic or a Victorian writer?

3. Neither Byron nor Shelley possessed Thomas Babington Macaulay's qualifications as a statesman.

4. Just as repetition can underscore a poem's musicality, so too can it intensify the persuasiveness of a piece of oration.

5. The anthology contains not only examples of Shelley's verses but also a selection of his personal letters.

B. Writing Application: *Rewrite each pair of sentences below as a single sentence. In your sentence, use the pair of correlative conjunctions that appears in brackets.*

1. You may write your research report on the life and literary works of Percy Bysshe Shelley. You may write your report on the life and literary works of Mary Shelley. [*either . . . or*]

   _____

2. Poets must consider carefully the connotations of the words they choose to express their ideas. Poets must consider with great care the sound of the words they use. [*not only . . . but also*]

   _____

3. If you are writing a speech, you must pay close attention to your audience. If you are writing a persuasive essay, you must pay close attention to your audience. [*whether . . . or*]

   _____

© Pearson Education, Inc., publishing as Pearson Prentice Hall. All rights reserved.

Name _____   Date _____

"Speech to Parliament: In Defense of the Lower Classes" by George Gordon, Lord Byron
"A Song: 'Men of England'" by Percy Bysshe Shelley
"On the Passing of the Reform Bill" by Thomas Babington Macaulay

Support for Writing

Use the chart below to take notes for your editorial. First, write down the issue you want to argue in the first line. Then, gather and jot down the facts about the issue. After you have had a chance to gather and think about the facts, state your opinion.

Political issue:	
Who?	
What?	
When?	
Where?	
Why?	
How	
My opinion: _____ _____ _____ _____	

On a separate page, use information from the chart to help you write your editorial. You will probably want to revise how you stated your opinion in the chart as you work it into your editorial. Use details from the chart to support your position.

© Pearson Education, Inc., publishing as Pearson Prentice Hall. All rights reserved.

"On Making an Agreeable Marriage" by Jane Austen
from **A Vindication of the Rights of Woman** by Mary Wollstonecraft

Literary Analysis: Social Commentary

Mary Wollstonecraft and Jane Austen were writers who were enormously gifted in the art of **social commentary.** These women looked closely at the world around them, thought deeply about what they saw, and put their views down on paper for the betterment and enjoyment of others. For example, Austen begins her letter to her niece by gently prodding Fanny to remember all her gentleman friend's wonderful qualities. But Austen's letter slowly transforms into an appeal to consider carefully before accepting a marriage proposal, and thereby avoid a marriage of convenience or a marriage for the sake of money. Her point, in the end, is that there is nothing worse than marriage without mutual affection and respect. Austen, who remained unmarried throughout her brief life, was nonetheless able to view the institution of marriage with great perception and evenhandedness.

DIRECTIONS: *Read the excerpts from the selections and answer the questions that follow.*

And from the time of our being in London together, I thought you really very much in love.—But you certainly are not at all—there is no concealing it.—What strange creatures we are!—It seems as if your being made secure of him (as you say yourself) had made you Indifferent.

(from "On Making an Agreeable Marriage")

1. What point does Austen make about the fickle nature of some human relationships?

_____

_____

_____

_____

It is acknowledged that they spend many of the first years of their lives in acquiring a smattering of accomplishments; meanwhile strength of body and mind are sacrificed to libertine notions of beauty, to the desire of establishing themselves—the only way women can rise in the world—by marriage. And this desire making mere animals of them, when they marry they act as such children may be expected to act—they dress, they paint, and nickname God's creatures. Can they be expected to govern a family with judgment, or take care of the poor babes whom they bring into the world?

(from A Vindication of the Rights of Women)

2. What point is Wollstonecraft making about women's place in society?

_____

_____

_____

_____

_____

"On Making an Agreeable Marriage" by Jane Austen
from **A Vindication of the Rights of Woman** by Mary Wollstonecraft
Reading Strategy: Determine the Writer's Purpose

It is particularly important to **determine the writer's purpose** when you're reading essays, speeches, or works of social commentary. Authors of these works can have a variety of purposes. Some seek to explain an issue or a process; others attempt to persuade a certain group or society in general to think in a particular way. Still others write to incite their audience to take action.

DIRECTIONS: *Use this graphic organizer to help you record and analyze Mary Wollstonecraft's purpose for writing "A Vindication of the Rights of Women." For each paragraph write down clues that reflect the author's tone and attitude. Decide what you think the author's purpose was. Then think about how the paragraph affected your own opinion on the topic. The first paragraph has been analyzed for you.*

Author's Tone/Attitude	Author's Purpose	Personal Reaction
Paragraph 1: The author takes a tone that reveals her to be saddened and frustrated by the way women of her generation are being educated. She feels strongly that women are sacrificing their intellects in order to gain the attentions of men. Wollstonecraft keeps her tone low-key, but it is clear that the situation she is writing about also makes her angry.	The author is attempting to persuade readers that women have been unfairly treated.	Some of the points about society that Wollstonecraft makes are still relevant today. Many women act nice or pretend they're not overly intelligent so that men won't feel threatened.
Paragraph 2:		
Paragraph 3:		
Paragraph 4:		
Paragraph 5:		

© Pearson Education, Inc., publishing as Pearson Prentice Hall. All rights reserved.
205

Name _____ Date _____

"On Making an Agreeable Marriage" by Jane Austen
from **A Vindication of the Rights of Woman** by Mary Wollstonecraft
Vocabulary Builder

Using the Root *-fort-*

A. DIRECTIONS: *Each of the following sentences includes an italicized word that contains the word root -fort-, meaning "strong." Fill in the blank with a word or phrase that completes the sentence and reveals the meaning of the italicized word.*

1. A musical analogy Mary Wollstonecraft might have used is that while women were expected to play the piano softly and prettily, men could be counted on to play *fortissimo*, _____.

2. The *fortress* stood upon a hill and was _____.

3. Jane Austen wrote to her friend Fanny to provide *fortification* for Fanny to make up her own mind about marriage. Austen wanted to _____ Fanny's resolve.

4. Mary Wollstonecraft put a lot of *effort* into her essay on woman's rights. It was a _____ to put her deepest feelings into words.

Using the Word List

scruple	amiable	vindication	fortitude	gravity
solicitude	fastidious	specious	preponderates	

B. DIRECTIONS: *In the following paragraph, fill in the blanks using words from the Word List.*

Jane Austen wrote to Fanny out of (1) _____ with regard to her friend's future marriage. Austen's argument was certainly not (2) _____, or deceptively attractive. To Austen, choosing the right husband was a matter of great (3) _____. In Austen's mind, there was no need to provide (4) _____ for *not* marrying someone; one either loved the other person or one didn't. She had no regard for women who behaved in a false manner by only pretending to care for someone. Nor did Austen advocate being so (5) _____ as to be pleased by no man. She recommended a clear head, an open heart, and (6) _____ of spirit. Austen's philosophy seemed to be that if one of those things (7) _____ over the others, all is lost. Although she had no (8) _____ about speaking her mind, Austen's tone remained (9) _____ throughout her letter to Fanny.

Name _____ Date _____

"On Making an Agreeable Marriage" by Jane Austen
from **A Vindication of the Rights of Woman** by Mary Wollstonecraft
Grammar and Style: Commas in a Series

It is important to be consistent when using a grammatical device such as **commas in a series.** Although it is usual to use commas in a series to ensure clear writing, modern rules of grammar also allow for omitting the final comma before a conjunction. Look at these examples.

Final comma: Jane Austen recommends that young women be amiable, discerning, and scrupulous when it comes to choosing a mate.

No final comma: She warns against loveless marriage, a fastidious nature and specious behavior.

Each of the sentences above is correct in terms of proper usage. However, if the two example sentences were to appear within the same piece of writing, they would create a consistency problem. Remember that whichever comma style you decide to employ, you must use it consistently throughout a single piece of writing.

A. PRACTICE: *Decide whether each of the sentences uses series commas appropriately. If a sentence does not use series commas correctly, rewrite the corrected sentence on the blank line. If the sentence is correct as written, write* correct *on the blank line.*

1. Fanny, and her friends, and family addressed the problem of her impending marriage.

   _____

2. You might say that honesty, happiness, and respect are the three main requirements for a happy marriage.

   _____

3. Mary Wollstonecraft felt that young women were taught to behave in a deceptive, conniving, and, ridiculous way.

   _____

B. Writing Application: *Follow the directions to create sentences that correctly use commas in a series.*

1. Write a sentence that uses three adjectives about women's societal roles according to Mary Wollstonecraft.

   _____

   _____

2. Write a sentence about the possible importance of a large family in Mary Wollstonecraft's day.

   _____

   _____

3. Write a sentence about love and marriage in Jane Austen's day.

   _____

   _____

© Pearson Education, Inc., publishing as Pearson Prentice Hall. All rights reserved.

Name _____   Date _____

"On Making an Agreeable Marriage" by Jane Austen
from **A Vindication of the Rights of Woman** by Mary Wollstonecraft
Support for Writing

Use the chart below to take notes for your letter to an author. Review the selection and jot down notes about the author's opinion in the first column. Then, jot down notes about your response in the second column. Include reasons and facts to support your opinion.

Author:

Author's Opinion	My Reaction

On a separate page, use the information in the chart to write your letter to an author.

© Pearson Education, Inc., publishing as Pearson Prentice Hall. All rights reserved.

from In Memoriam, A.H.H., "The Lady of Shalott," "Ulysses," and from The Princess: "Tears, Idle Tears" by Alfred, Lord Tennyson

Literary Analysis: The Speaker in Poetry

We can truly understand a poem only when we understand who is speaking and what motivated him or her to do so. In Tennyson's "Ulysses," the hero is an adventurer who not only reveals his longing to roam "with a hungry heart," but also attempts to persuade his aging followers and subjects that he and his band should leave the kingdom and "sail beyond the sunset."

DIRECTIONS: *On the lines, describe what Ulysses reveals in each quotation about his own thoughts and feelings or how he hopes to persuade his listeners with his words. Remember that both ordinary subjects and Ulysses's fellow adventurers are listening to him speak.*

1. How dull it is to pause, to make an end, / To rust unburnished, not to shine in use!

   _____
   _____
   _____
   _____

2. This is my son, mine own Telemachus, / To whom I leave the scepter and the isle / Well-loved of me, discerning to fulfill / This labor, . . .

   _____
   _____
   _____
   _____

3. . . . My mariners, / Souls that have toiled and wrought, and thought with me— / That ever with a frolic welcome took / The thunder and the sunshine, . . .

   _____
   _____
   _____
   _____

4. 'Tis not too late to seek a newer world. / Push off, and sitting well in order smite / The sounding furrows; . . .

   _____
   _____
   _____
   _____

© Pearson Education, Inc., publishing as Pearson Prentice Hall. All rights reserved.
209

Name _____ Date _____

from **In Memoriam, A.H.H.**, **"The Lady of Shalott," "Ulysses,"** and *from* **The Princess:**
"Tears, Idle Tears" by Alfred, Lord Tennyson

Reading Strategy: Judge a Poet's Message

Beneath the surface of most poetry are powerful messages about some of life's big issues—love, death, and war, for example. You can apply your critical judgement and experiences to the work to determine whether you think the poet's views are accurate. As you look at a poem, notice clues about the poet's message. What is the message? Do the ideas follow logically? Is the evidence appropriate and relevant? Are Characters and situations true to life? How does it relate to your own experiences or observations of life? Once you have answered these questions, you can make your own judgment about the validity of the poet's message.

DIRECTIONS: *In the following chart, record your own experiences and then make a judgment about each excerpt.*

Poet's Message	+ My Experiences/ Observations of Life	= My Judgment of Poet's Message
Far off thou art, but ever nigh/I have thee still, and I rejoice:/I prosper, circled with thy voice;/I shall not lose thee though I die. ("In Memoriam, A.H.H.")		
I am a part of all that I have met;/Yet all experience is an arch wherethrough/Gleams that untraveled world, whose margin fades/Forever and forever when I move. ("Ulysses")		
Tear, idle tears, I know not what they mean,/Tears from the depth of some divine despair/Rise in the heart and gather to the eyes,/In looking on the happy autumn fields,/And thinking of the days that are no more. ("Tears, Idle Tears" from The Princess)		

© Pearson Education, Inc., publishing as Pearson Prentice Hall. All rights reserved.

from In Memoriam, A.H.H., "The Lady of Shalott," "Ulysses," and from The Princess:
"Tears, Idle Tears" by Alfred, Lord Tennyson

Vocabulary Builder

Using Medieval Words

The Word List word *churls* is an Old English word meaning "farmers or peasants." In his poems, Tennyson uses a number of medieval words to add atmosphere and help create the setting.

A. DIRECTIONS: *Using the context of the sentence, write a definition of each underlined Old English or other medieval word.*

1. Roland earned 100 gold crowns as the village blacksmith, and so was obligated to <u>tithe</u> 10 crowns to the parish.

   _____

2. The knight, smiling, raised only his <u>buckler</u> to fend off the wooden swords of the children who had gathered around him.

   _____

3. Only the old woman's eyes were visible from within the folds of the <u>wimple</u> wrapped around her head.

   _____

Using the Word List

> diffusive   churls   waning   furrows

B. DIRECTIONS: *Choose the letter of the word or phrase most nearly similar in meaning to each numbered word. Write the letter of your choice in the blank.*

___ 1. diffusive
    A. polluted
    B. fervent
    C. dispersed
    D. alternate

___ 2. churls
    A. attitudes
    B. coarse persons
    C. emblems
    D. assigned duties

___ 3. waning
    A. bathing
    B. waxing
    C. expanding
    D. declining

___ 4. furrows
    A. grooves
    B. ponders
    C. plants
    D. lairs

© Pearson Education, Inc., publishing as Pearson Prentice Hall. All rights reserved.

Name _____ Date _____

from **In Memoriam, A.H.H.**, **"The Lady of Shalott," "Ulysses,"** and *from* **The Princess:**
"Tears, Idle Tears" by Alfred, Lord Tennyson

Grammar and Style: Parallel Structure

Sometimes for effect, writers repeat words and phrases, or place them in grammatically similar clauses or structures. **Parallel structure** adds rhetorical and emotional power through rhythm, repetition, and emphasis. Writers may use single words, infinitive phrases, prepositional phrases, or clauses in parallel structure.

A. PRACTICE: *Underline each parallel structure in the following passages and identify its grammatical element.*

1. There she sees the highway near
   Winding down to Camelot:
   There the river eddy whirls,
   And there the surly village churls,
   And the red cloaks of market girls,
   Pass onward from Shallot.

2. Let Love clasp Grief lest both be drowned,
   Let darkness keep her raven gloss.
   Ah, sweeter to be drunk with loss,
   To dance with death, to beat the ground. . .

B. Writing Application: *Create sentences with parallel structure for each of the following items, using the prompts provided.*

1. (Repeat article *the*) Damsels, abbot, shepherd, page, and knight may see Camelot, but not the Lady of Shallot.

   _____

   _____

2. (Make one sentence with compound verbs) In order to bear the fate of the curse, the Lady should not look at Camelot. She should not wonder about it. She should not dream of the town. She must not go to it.

   _____

   _____

3. (Make infinitive phrases of gerunds) Sharing, striving, questioning, and discovering is living, whatever one's age, says Tennyson in "Ulysses."

   _____

   _____

4. (Repeat brief rhetorical questions) What are faith, friendship, memory, and life itself? "In Memoriam, A.H.H." asks these essential questions about relationships in the face of death.

   _____

   _____

© Pearson Education, Inc., publishing as Pearson Prentice Hall. All rights reserved.

***from* In Memoriam, A.H.H., "The Lady of Shalott," "Ulysses," and *from* The Princess: "Tears, Idle Tears"** by Alfred, Lord Tennyson

Support for Writing

Use the chart below to record information about Tennyson's life and poetry. Write an event from Tennyson's life in each box in the left column. Write his literary achievements in the boxes on the right. Then, circle the arrow that shows whether each literary achievement was an effect or a cause of the corresponding event in his life.

Tennyson's Life   **Tennyson's Poetry**

Cause and Effect

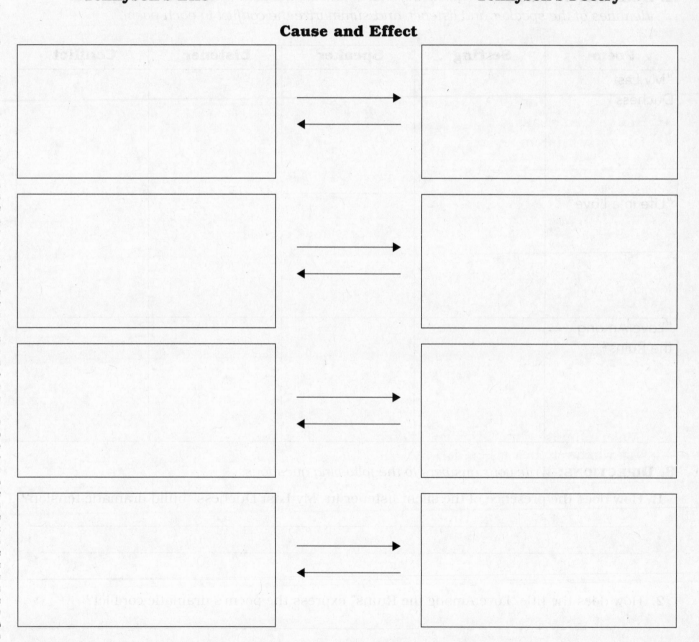

On a separate page, use the information you have recorded in the chart as you write a draft of your biographical essay on Tennyson. Discuss the cause-and-effect relationship between his life and his work.

© Pearson Education, Inc., publishing as Pearson Prentice Hall. All rights reserved.

Name _____ Date _____

Literary Analysis: Dramatic Monologue

A **dramatic monologue** is a speech, sometimes to a silent listener, in which a character indicates a setting and a dramatic conflict. In the monologue, this character reveals his or her inmost feelings, sometimes without knowing it.

A. DIRECTIONS: *Complete the following chart. Indicate the setting and names or general identities of the speaker and listener, and summarize the conflict in each poem.*

Poem	Setting	Speaker	Listener	Conflict
"My Last Duchess"				
"Life in a Love"				
"Love Among the Ruins"				

B. DIRECTIONS: *Write your answers to the following questions.*

1. How does the presence of the silent listener in "My Last Duchess" build dramatic tension?

_____

_____

_____

2. How does the title "Love Among the Ruins" express the poem's dramatic conflict?

_____

_____

_____

© Pearson Education, Inc., publishing as Pearson Prentice Hall. All rights reserved.

Name _____ Date _____

"My Last Duchess," "Life in a Love," and **"Love Among the Ruins"**
by Robert Browning
Sonnet 43 by Elizabeth Barrett Browning
Reading Strategy: Make Inferences About the Speaker

When you read a poem, look for meaning behind the speaker's words and actions. Make inferences about the speaker's thoughts, feelings, and motivations. Be aware, too, that the speaker's words sometimes reveal more than he or she realizes.

DIRECTIONS: *Read the following lines from "My Last Duchess" and "Love Among the Ruins." Answer the questions related to each set of lines.*

from **"My Last Duchess"** (lines 24–28)
. . . she liked whate'er
She looked on, and her looks went everywhere.
Sir, 'twas all one! My favor at her breast,
The dropping of the daylight in the West,
The bough of cherries some officious fool
Broke in the orchard for her . . .

1. What can you infer about the Duke's attitude toward his wife?

    _____

    _____

2. What can you infer about the Duke's personality from lines 27–28?

    _____

    _____

from **"Love Among the Ruins"** (lines 67–72)
When I do come, she will speak not, she will stand,
Either hand
On my shoulder, give her eyes the first embrace
Of my face,
Ere we rush, ere we extinguish sight and speech
Each on each.

3. What can you infer about the speaker's feelings for the woman?

    _____

    _____

4. What can you infer about the speaker's attitude toward love?

    _____

    _____

© Pearson Education, Inc., publishing as Pearson Prentice Hall. All rights reserved.

"My Last Duchess," "Life in a Love," and "Love Among the Ruins"
by Robert Browning
Sonnet 43 by Elizabeth Barrett Browning
Vocabulary Builder

Using the Suffix -ence

A. DIRECTIONS: *Answer each of the following questions, changing the underlined word to a word with the suffix -ence.*

1. Why was Alan <u>absent</u> from the meeting?

   _____

   _____

2. How did the class behave when there was an observer <u>present</u>?

   _____

   _____

3. Why did the teacher praise the <u>diligent</u> students?

   _____

   _____

4. How did the suspect prove he was <u>innocent</u> of the charge?

   _____

   _____

Using the Word List

countenance	officious	munificence	dowry
eludes	vestige	sublime	minions

B. DIRECTIONS: *Match each word in the left column with its definition in the right column. Write the letter of the definition on the line next to the word it defines.*

___ 1. countenance   **A.** overly eager to please

___ 2. officious   **B.** state of being generous; lavish

___ 3. munificence   **C.** avoids or escapes

___ 4. dowry   **D.** inspiring admiration through greatness or beauty

___ 5. vestige   **E.** face

___ 6. sublime   **F.** natural talent, gift, or endowment

___ 7. minions   **G.** attendants or agents

___ 8. eludes   **H.** trace; bit

© Pearson Education, Inc., publishing as Pearson Prentice Hall. All rights reserved.

"My Last Duchess," "Life in a Love," and **"Love Among the Ruins"**
by Robert Browning
Sonnet 43 by Elizabeth Barrett Browning

Grammar and Style: The Use of *Like* and *As*

Like, meaning "similar to," is used to compare nouns or pronouns. It introduces a prepositional phrase, which consists of a preposition and a noun or pronoun. *As* is a subordinating conjunction and is used to compare actions. It introduces a clause with a noun and a verb. Look at the following examples from poems by Robert Browning and Elizabeth Barrett Browning:

Strangers *like* you . . .
I love thee purely, *as* they turn from Praise.

A. PRACTICE: *Correctly complete each of the following sentences by writing either* like *or* as *on the line.*

1. Robert Browning wrote many dramatic monologues, _____ "My Last Duchess."

2. A dramatic monologue reads _____ lines from a play.

3. The Duke in "My Last Duchess" doesn't act _____ I'd expect an aristocrat to act.

4. Elizabeth Barrett Browning's "Sonnet 43" has fourteen lines _____ all sonnets do.

5. Many of her sonnets, _____ "Sonnet 43," are well-known love poems.

B. Writing Application: *Write a paragraph in which you describe another famous love story* like *the one between Robert Browning and Elizabeth Barrett. Use* like *and* as *at least once each.*

_____

_____

_____

_____

_____

_____

_____

_____

_____

_____

© Pearson Education, Inc., publishing as Pearson Prentice Hall. All rights reserved.

"My Last Duchess," "Life in a Love," and **"Love Among the Ruins"**
by Robert Browning
Sonnet 43 by Elizabeth Barrett Browning
Support for Writing

Use the cluster diagram to gather details from "My Last Duchess" about the duke's character and first marriage.

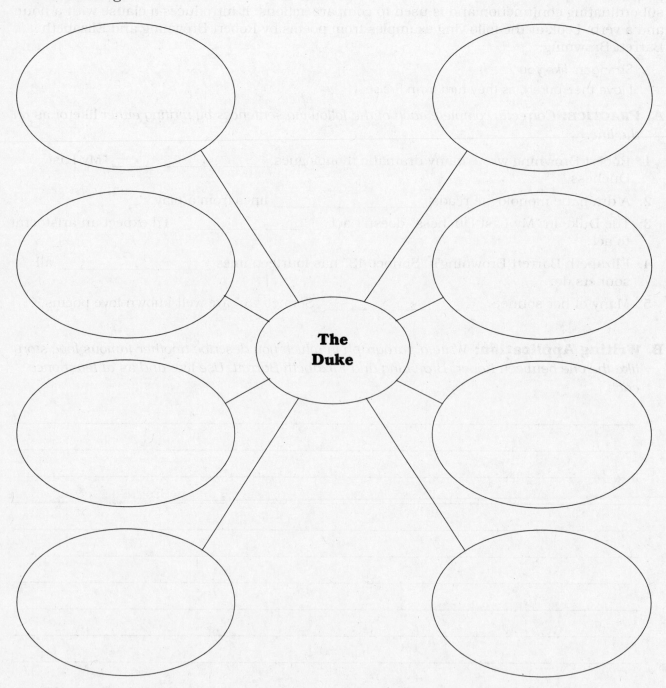

On a separate page, use the information you have gathered in your cluster diagram to help you draft a recommendation to the girl's father about the duke's proposal. Start by presenting your position. Then, explain the reasons behind your position.

© Pearson Education, Inc., publishing as Pearson Prentice Hall. All rights reserved.

from **Hard Times** by Charles Dickens
from **Jane Eyre** by Charlotte Brontë

Literary Analysis: The Novel and Social Criticism

A **novel** is a long work of fiction, usually featuring a complex plot, major and minor characters, a significant theme, and several settings. Like many novelists in nineteenth-century England, Charles Dickens and Charlotte Brontë created the fictional worlds in their novels to reflect real people and social institutions. Through their novels, they could comment on what they saw as problems and injustices in their society. This type of commentary through fiction is known as **social criticism.**

DIRECTIONS: *Examine the social criticism in* Hard Times *and* Jane Eyre *by answering the following questions.*

Hard Times

1. Of Thomas Gradgrind, Dickens writes: ". . . he seemed a kind of cannon loaded to the muzzle with facts, and prepared to blow [the students] clean out of the regions of childhood at one discharge." What is Dickens's attitude toward Thomas Gradgrind's teaching style? Why is this passage an example of social criticism?

   _____

   _____

2. When Mr. Gradgrind addresses student Sissy Jupe, he refers to her only as "girl number twenty." Why does he refer to her in this way? What viewpoint is Dickens criticizing by drawing attention to this? What aspect of the school is he criticizing?

   _____

   _____

Jane Eyre

3. Helen explains why she was punished by saying "'I seldom put, and never keep, things in order; I am careless; I forget rules; I read when I should learn my lessons; I have no method; and sometimes I say, like you, I *cannot bear* to be subjected to systematic arrangements. This is all very provoking to Miss Scatcherd, who is naturally neat, punctual, and particular.'" Are Helen's "faults" truly bad? In this passage, what is Brontë criticizing about the world in which the two girls live?

   _____

   _____

4. While Jane feels anger when she is treated unfairly, Helen, who is older, says only: "'degradation never too deeply disgusts me, injustice never crushes me too low: I live in calm, looking to the end.'" How much value does Helen place on her life? In what ways are Helen's statements a criticism of what she has been taught at Lowood?

   _____

   _____

© Pearson Education, Inc., publishing as Pearson Prentice Hall. All rights reserved.

from **Hard Times** by Charles Dickens
from **Jane Eyre** by Charlotte Brontë
Reading Strategy: Recognize the Writer's Purpose

A **writer's purpose** is his or her reason for writing a literary work. An author might write a novel for one or more of the following reasons: to address a social problem, to satirize a particular institution, or to entertain readers with humor or adventure. To understand a writer's purpose, pay close attention to the details he or she uses to describe characters, events and ideas. These details reveal the writer's attitude, or feelings, toward what he or she is describing. The writer's attitude, in turn, suggests his or her purpose.

DIRECTIONS: *As you read the selections, try to determine the writer's purpose by answering the following questions.*

Hard Times

1. In Chapter 1 of *Hard Times,* what details does Dickens use to describe the schoolroom? What details does he use to describe the physical appearance of "the speaker" in the schoolroom? What might these details say about the author's attitude and purpose?

   _____

   _____

   _____

2. What details does Dickens use to create a contrast between Sissy Jupe and Bitzer? Why does Sissy clash with her teachers? What might the incident surrounding Sissy indicate about the author's attitude and purpose?

   _____

   _____

   _____

Jane Eyre

3. What details does Brontë give about Miss Scatcherd and her treatment of Helen Burns? What might these details reveal about the author's attitude and purpose?

   _____

   _____

   _____

4. What two contrasting outlooks are presented in the discussion between Helen and Jane? What does the conversation reveal about their character and their school? Why might this discussion be important to the author's purpose?

   _____

   _____

   _____

Name _____ Date _____

from **Hard Times** by Charles Dickens
from **Jane Eyre** by Charlotte Brontë
Vocabulary Builder

Using the Prefix *mono-*

The Greek word prefix *mono-* means "single" or "alone." This meaning appears in *monotonous*, meaning "having a single 'tone'" or "dull and unwavering."

A. DIRECTIONS: *Complete each sentence with a word from the box.*

monolithic	monophony	monosyllabic	monogram

1. The old library was a _____ stone structure.
2. His initials formed a _____ on his writing paper.
3. The song was a simple _____, without harmonizing parts.
4. The teacher repeated the _____ word *facts*.

Using the Word List

monotonous	obstinate	adversary	indignant
approbation	obscure	comprised	sundry

B. DIRECTIONS: *For each numbered word, choose the word that is most similar in meaning.*

___ 1. monotonous
   A. alone
   B. quiet
   C. exciting
   D. dull

___ 2. obstinate
   A. approving
   B. displeased
   C. stubborn
   D. slow

___ 3. adversary
   A. opponent
   B. partner
   C. student
   D. teacher

___ 4. indignant
   A. thoughtful
   B. displeased
   C. agreeable
   D. strict

___ 5. approbation
   A. punishment
   B. lesson
   C. approval
   D. plan

___ 6. obscure
   A. vague
   B. correct
   C. clear
   D. lonely

___ 7. comprised
   A. organized
   B. taught
   C. argued
   D. contained

___ 8. sundry
   A. few
   B. angry
   C. ridiculous
   D. various

© Pearson Education, Inc., publishing as Pearson Prentice Hall. All rights reserved.

from **Hard Times** by Charles Dickens; *from* **Jane Eyre** by Charlotte Brontë
Grammar and Style: Punctuation of Dialogue

For the **proper punctuation of dialogue,** observe the following rules:

- Place commas and periods within closing quotation marks. Place a comma introducing a quotation before opening quotation marks.

   "Yes," the young girl explained, "my name is Sissy."

- Place question marks and exclamation marks within closing quotation marks when they end quotations, and outside closing quotation marks when they belong to a sentence that includes a quotation.

   Miss Scatcherd cried out, "You disagreeable girl!"

   "Why doesn't she wish to leave Lowood?" Jane wondered.

   Was it Gradgrind who said, "Stick to Facts, sir!"**?**

A. Practice: *Read the following lines of dialogue from* Hard Times *and* Jane Eyre. *Where they are needed, place quotation marks correctly in relation to commas, periods, exclamation points, and question marks.*

1. After a pause, one half of the children cried in chorus, Yes, Sir!

2. You must paper it, said Thomas Gradgrind, whether you like it or not.

3. Fact, fact, fact! said the gentleman.

4. Why, thought I, does she not explain that she could neither clean her nails nor wash her face, as the water was frozen?

B. Writing Application: *Rewrite the following, placing commas and quotation marks where they are needed.*

I thought I heard Mr. Gradgrind shout Just give me facts! Did he really say Facts alone are needed in life?

In response to his statements, the fearful children in the room said Yes, sir!

I don't understand Sissy Jupe said.

_____

_____

_____

_____

_____

_____

_____

© Pearson Education, Inc., publishing as Pearson Prentice Hall. All rights reserved.

from Hard Times by Charles Dickens; *from* Jane Eyre by Charlotte Brontë
Support for Writing

Use the chart below to record information about each source.

Bibliographic information for print sources should include the title, author's name, place of publication, publisher, and date of publication. Internet sources should have as much of the print information as you can find plus the Internet address and the date the site was researched.

Primary or Secondary	Bibliographic Information	Content and Comments

On a separate page, use the information in your chart to prepare your annotated bibliography. Include annotations that explain why each source is useful.

© Pearson Education, Inc., publishing as Pearson Prentice Hall. All rights reserved.

"Dover Beach" by Matthew Arnold

"Recessional" and **"The Widow at Windsor"** by Rudyard Kipling

Literary Analysis: Mood as a Key to Theme

The feelings that a poem creates in the reader make up the **mood** of the poem. How you feel after you read a poem can give you a hint as to the poem's central idea, or **theme.**

If you go away from a poem feeling happy, the poem likely expressed an optimistic outlook or a pleasing image. If, however, a poem's theme has to do with the evils of imperialism, for example, it probably will not contain optimism or pleasing images. A reader might come away from such a poem feeling threatened, sober, or scared. Those feelings can be a clue that the poem's central idea is to be taken seriously.

To create mood, poets use vivid images and words that have emotional appeal. Notice how Matthew Arnold creates a rhythm that imitates the sound of the ocean. Notice, too, the vivid verbs and adjectives he uses, which have more emotional appeal than less colorful language.

> Listen! you hear the grating roar
> Of pebbles which the waves draw back, and fling,
> At their return, up the high strand,
> Begin, and cease, and then again begin,
> With tremulous cadence slow, and bring
> The eternal note of sadness in.

DIRECTIONS: *Following each passage, describe the mood of the passage—the feelings the passage creates in you—and indicate the words or phrases that create that mood. Then interpret those feelings in connection with the theme of that poem.*

1. lines 9-14 from "Dover Beach" (see above)

   _____

   _____

2. lines 13-18 from "Recessional":

   > Far-called, our navies melt away—
   > On dune and headland sinks the fire—
   > Lo, all our pomp of yesterday
   > Is one with Nineveh and Tyre!
   > Judge of the Nations, spare us yet,
   > Lest we forget—lest we forget!

   _____

   _____

© Pearson Education, Inc., publishing as Pearson Prentice Hall. All rights reserved.

Name _____ Date _____

"Dover Beach" by Matthew Arnold
"Recessional" and "The Widow at Windsor" by Rudyard Kipling
Reading Strategy: Draw Conclusions

As we read, sometimes we piece together information in order to **draw conclusions** based on that information. Readers who do this can enhance their understanding of a poem or story. At the beginning of "Dover Beach," for example, readers may think that the poem is simply about a person admiring a view of the ocean. Then, at the end of the second stanza, the cadence of the waves brings the "eternal note of sadness in." This should raise a question in readers' minds. Why is there sadness? As readers continue, they should be able to draw a conclusion as to why the speaker of the poem feels sadness.

DIRECTIONS: *As you read each poem, record two sets of details from which you draw conclusions about the speaker's attitude toward events in the poem or toward the larger subject of the poem. An example has been provided for you.*

"Dover Beach"

Details	Conclusions
"eternal note of sadness"; Sophocles heard it; "human misery"; "Sea of Faith" once full but now retreating	The speaker feels the world is a lesser place—a sadder place—because people don't have the faith in God they once did.

"Recessional"

Details	Conclusions

"The Widow at Windsor"

Details	Conclusions

© Pearson Education, Inc., publishing as Pearson Prentice Hall. All rights reserved.

"Dover Beach" by Matthew Arnold
"Recessional" and **"The Widow at Windsor"** by Rudyard Kipling
Vocabulary Builder

Using the Root *-domi-*

A. DIRECTIONS: *From the Latin* dominus, *English acquires several words whose meanings relate to the word's meaning of "lord" or "master." Keep this in mind as you answer questions about some words that include the -domi- root. Use a dictionary if you wish.*

1. How is someone who *dominates* different from someone who *domineers*?

   _____

2. Portuguese and Brazilian royalty are allowed to add the word *Dom* to their names, as a sign of their status. What, in your opinion, does this signify?

   _____

3. What is an *indomitable* enemy?

   _____

Using the Word List

tranquil	cadence	turbid	dominion	contrite

B. DIRECTIONS: *Match each word in the left column with its definition in the right column. Write the letter of the definition on the line next to the word it defines.*

___ 1. cadence   A. repenting for sin
___ 2. contrite   B. murky
___ 3. dominion   C. free from disturbance
___ 4. tranquil   D. rhythmic sequence
___ 5. turbid   E. power

© Pearson Education, Inc., publishing as Pearson Prentice Hall. All rights reserved.

"Dover Beach" by Matthew Arnold
"Recessional" and **"The Widow at Windsor"** by Rudyard Kipling
Grammar and Style: Present Tense

The **present tense** of a verb expresses an action or a state of being that is occurring now. A present tense verb may also express a general truth. Following are several examples of sentences from "Dover Beach" that contain present tense verbs.

The sea *is* calm tonight.
The tide *is* full, the moon *lies* fair
Upon the straits:

Arnold, in particular, uses many present tense verbs in his poem. This helps readers feel close to the ideas the poet is expressing.

A. PRACTICE: *Place a check mark next to each sentence whose main verb is in the present tense.*

_____ 1. Arnold's and Kipling's lives overlap by twenty-three years.

_____ 2. Both poets lived during Queen Victoria's reign.

_____ 3. Kipling receives the Nobel Prize for Literature in 1907.

_____ 4. A Nobel Prize carries with it great distinction.

_____ 5. Matthew Arnold was never honored with such an award.

_____ 6. His ideas, however, are admirable.

_____ 7. In a volume on social criticism, Arnold urges people to base their lives on the "best that has been thought and said in the world."

_____ 8. Kipling, on the other hand, is known as an imperialist, though perhaps a cautious one.

_____ 9. After a long absence, he returned to India at the age of seventeen.

_____ 10. Many of Kipling's writings display his affection for Indian life.

B. Writing Application: *Write two original sentences according to the following instructions.*

Write one sentence in the present tense about a captivating view you have seen, whether of the ocean, a mountain, or a cityscape.

1. _____

_____

Write one sentence in the present tense about a parade you have watched or in which you have participated.

2. _____

_____

"Dover Beach" by Matthew Arnold
"Recessional" and "The Widow at Windsor" by Rudyard Kipling
Support for Writing

Use the charts below to gather details for your response to critic Walter E. Houghton's statement that the Victorian Age was characterized by "widespread doubt about the nature of man, society, and the universe." Then, use your information to write a thesis statement for your essay.

"Recessional"

	Images	Moods	Themes
Doubt			
Self-Confidence			

"The Widow of Windsor"

	Images	Moods	Themes
Doubt			
Self-Confidence			

Thesis Statement (agree or disagree with Houghton's statement):

_____

_____

_____

On a separate page, use the thesis statement to help you write your response. Support your thesis with the details you have gathered from the poems.

© Pearson Education, Inc., publishing as Pearson Prentice Hall. All rights reserved.

From the Author's Desk
James Berry Introduces "From Lucy: Englan' Lady," "Time Removed," and "Freedom"

DIRECTIONS: *Use the space provided to answer the questions.*

1. Briefly describe the author's roots, mentioned by James Berry in the first paragraph of his essay.

   _____

   _____

2. Why is Rudyard Kipling's poem "Recessional" significant for Berry?

   _____

   _____

3. According to Berry, what is Lucy's attitude toward the Queen of England? What does Lucy's outlook represent?

   _____

   _____

   _____

   _____

4. When James Berry returned to Jamaica after a long absence, how did he feel when he saw his homeland again?

   _____

   _____

5. According to Berry, how did England contrast with Jamaica?

   _____

   _____

   _____

6. What explanation does Berry offer for the title of his poem "Time Removed"?

   _____

   _____

7. What seems to be Berry's attitude toward the pain and suffering of the past? How do you evaluate this attitude? Briefly explain your answer.

   _____

   _____

   _____

   _____

   _____

© Pearson Education, Inc., publishing as Pearson Prentice Hall. All rights reserved.

James Berry
Listening and Viewing

Segment 1: Meet James Berry
- As a young boy, how did James Berry use his interests as the basis of his writing?
- What interests have you pursued as writing topics and why?

_____

_____

_____

Segment 2: James Berry Introduces "Lucy: Englan' Lady"
- What inspired James Berry to write the poem "Lucy: Englan' Lady"?
- How does James Berry's reading of this poem change the way you might understand it if you read the poem yourself?

_____

_____

_____

Segment 3: The Writing Process
- What process does James Berry follow when he develops a character?
- As a writer, do you think you would rather create characters from your own imagination or base them on real people? Explain your answer.

_____

_____

_____

_____

Segment 4: The Rewards of Writing
- James Berry believes that literature helps "widen the human vision of experience." What do you think he means by this?
- What do you think you can learn about yourself by reading and writing?

_____

_____

_____

_____

"Condition of Ireland," *The Illustrated London News*
"Progress in Personal Comfort" by Sydney Smith
Literary Analysis: Journalistic Essay

Journalistic essays are short prose pieces that describe current events or trends. Unlike personal essays, which focus on a writer's inner reflections and personal reactions to experiences, journalistic essays examine news, facts, and events and try to make them directly relevant to a wider audience. The writer of a journalistic essay gathers facts and weaves them into a unified story.

DIRECTIONS: *Answer the following questions.*

1. What purely factual information does the journalistic essay "Condition of Ireland" present about the Famine and Britain's Poor-Laws?

   _____

   _____

   _____

2. What voice is used in *The Illustrated London News* article? What perspective does this voice provide on the facts surrounding the famine? Name specific examples from the selection that demonstrate the writer's perspective.

   _____

   _____

   _____

   _____

   _____

3. According to "Progress in Personal Comfort," what inventions and services came about during Sydney Smith's life?

   _____

   _____

4. How might you describe the voice of Sydney Smith in "Progress in Personal Comfort"? What unique story about progress and a changing world does he tell? Give specific examples of Smith's perspective on these events.

   _____

   _____

   _____

   _____

   _____

© Pearson Education, Inc., publishing as Pearson Prentice Hall. All rights reserved.

"Condition of Ireland," *The Illustrated London News*
"Progress in Personal Comfort" by Sydney Smith

Reading Strategy: Distinguish Emotive and Informative Language

Emotive language includes words, phrases, and examples that appeal to a reader's feelings. **Informative language** conveys facts. Often emotive language is woven into the informative language of an essay to capture the interest and emotions of readers and to reveal the attitude of a writer toward his or her subject.

DIRECTIONS: *As you read the selections, identify examples of emotive and informative language. In each of the following passages from the selections, underline emotive language and circle informative language. Then analyze the emotive words in the passages to determine the writer's attitude toward a particular subject or idea.*

"Condition of Ireland"

1. The Poor-Law, said to be for the relief of the people and the means of their salvation, was the instrument of their destruction. In their terrible distress, from that temporary calamity with which they were visited, they were to have no relief unless they gave up their holdings.

   Attitude: _____

2. Calmly and quietly, but very ignorantly—though we cheerfully exonerate the parties from any malevolence; they only committed a great mistake, a terrible blunder, which in legislation is worse than a crime—but calmly and quietly from Westminster itself . . . did the decree go forth . . .

   Attitude: _____

"Progress in Personal Comfort"

3. It took me nine hours to go from Taunton to Bath, before the invention of the railroads, and I now go in six hours from Taunton to London! In going from Taunton to Bath, I suffered between 10,000 and 12,000 severe contusions, before stone-breaking Macadam was born.

   Attitude: _____

4. There were no banks to receive the savings of the poor. The Poor Laws were gradually sapping the vitals of the country; and whatever miseries I suffered, I had no post to whisk my complaints for a single penny to the remotest corners of the empire . . .

   Attitude: _____

© Pearson Education, Inc., publishing as Pearson Prentice Hall. All rights reserved.

Name _____ Date _____

"Condition of Ireland," *The Illustrated London News*
"Progress in Personal Comfort" by Sydney Smith
Vocabulary Builder

Using "Humor" Words

The Illustrated London News article describes problems faced by the Irish as melancholy, or sad. The word *melancholy* originally meant "black bile," which is one of the four principal humors, or liquids, that people believed controlled health and personality. The other humors were yellow bile, blood, and phlegm. Modern English contains words originating from the theory of humors.

A. DIRECTIONS: *Answer the following questions, based on clues given about the humors.*

1. Phlegm is a thick, slow-moving fluid, so a *phlegmatic* person probably feels
   _____.

2. A person controlled by the warm, life-giving flow of blood can be described as *sanguine*, or
   _____.

Using the Word List

requisites	sanction	exonerate
melancholy	indolence	depredation

B. DIRECTIONS: *For each sentence, choose the Word List word that best completes its meaning. Write the word on the line.*

1. Some landowners were lazy, and everyone suffered from this _____.

2. The writer will _____ people who meant no harm.

3. More food, more cultivation, and more employment were the _____ for maintaining the Irish in existence.

4. When walking at night without streetlights, the writer felt exposed to danger and
   _____.

5. The law gave landowners the _____ and encouragement to evict people.

6. They could not get over the _____ sight of people needing to work for food.

© Pearson Education, Inc., publishing as Pearson Prentice Hall. All rights reserved.

"Condition of Ireland," *The Illustrated London News*
"Progress in Personal Comfort" by Sydney Smith

Grammar and Style: Coordinating Conjunctions

A **coordinating conjunction** links two sentence parts of the same grammatical kind. The seven coordinating conjunctions are *and, but, or, nor, yet, so,* and *for.* Notice the use of coordinating conjunctions in the following passages.

from "Condition of Ireland"

The present condition of the Irish . . . has been mainly brought on by ignorant *and* vicious legislation. . . .

We shall fully consider that question before we quit the subject, *but* we shall now only say . . .

from "Progress in Personal Comfort"

. . . I now glide without noise *or* fracture, on wooden pavements.

A. PRACTICE: *Read the following passages from "Progress in Personal Comfort" and "Condition of Ireland." Underline any coordinating conjunctions that you find.*

1. I can walk, by the assistance of the police, from one end of London to the other, without molestation; or, if tired, get into a cheap and active cab . . .

2. Calmly and quietly, but very ignorantly . . . did the decree go forth which has made the temporary but terrible visitation of a potato rot the means of exterminating, through the slow process of disease and houseless starvation, nearly the half of the Irish.

B. Writing Application: *Rewrite each of the following pairs of sentences, connecting them with a coordinating conjunction.*

1. Most people believe progress is always good. "Condition of Ireland" reveals something different.

_____

_____

2. In the name of economic progress, many people suffered. Many people died.

_____

_____

3. The Poor-Laws were supposed to provide relief for the people in Ireland. The laws instead caused the people's destruction.

_____

_____

4. People lost their land. They lost their livelihoods.

_____

_____

© Pearson Education, Inc., publishing as Pearson Prentice Hall. All rights reserved.

"Condition of Ireland," *The Illustrated London News*
"Progress in Personal Comfort" by Sydney Smith
Support for Writing

Use the chart below to take notes for your comparison-and-contrast essay. List the viewpoints expressed in each essay along with details that support the viewpoint. Finally, draw a conclusion about the similarities and differences between the viewpoints.

	"Condition of Ireland"	**"Progress in Personal Comfort"**
View:		
View:		
View:		

Conclusion

On a separate page, use the information from your conclusion to draft a thesis statement for your essay. Then, use details from the chart of viewpoints as you write.

© Pearson Education, Inc., publishing as Pearson Prentice Hall. All rights reserved.

Name _____ Date _____

"Remembrance" by Emily Brontë
"The Darkling Thrush" and "Ah, Are You Digging on My Grave?"
by Thomas Hardy

Literary Analysis: Stanza Structure and Irony

A **stanza** usually contains a certain number of lines arranged to show a recurring pattern, rhythmic structure, and rhyme scheme. **Irony** is a deliberate contradiction between expectation and reality. Poets can establish certain expectations in their readers through a regular stanza structure. When poets then inject surprising events or ideas within the stanza structure, they create irony. The contrast between expectation and reality can make a poem more memorable.

DIRECTIONS: *Write your answers to the following questions on the chart.*

Questions for Analysis	"Remembrance"	"The Darkling Thrush"	"Ah, Are You Digging on My Grave?"
1. How many stanzas are in the poem?			
2. What is the stanza type (number of lines, meter, rhyme scheme)?			
3. What expectation is established by the stanza structure?			
4. What change or surprise occurs in the poem?			
5. What is the irony in the poem?			

© Pearson Education, Inc., publishing as Pearson Prentice Hall. All rights reserved.

"Remembrance" by Emily Brontë
"The Darkling Thrush" and **"Ah, Are You Digging on My Grave?"**
by Thomas Hardy
Reading Strategy: Reading Stanzas as Units of Meaning

Like paragraphs in prose, stanzas in poetry are usually a unit of meaning—they convey a main idea. Sometimes, a stanza will create a unified mood. Taken together, the stanzas of a poem express a larger theme or idea. As you read, analyze the stanzas in a poem for a progression of thoughts, a sequence of events, or a building of an argument or mood within the poem.

A. DIRECTIONS: *On the lines, write your answers to the following questions.*

1. In "Remembrance," what progression of thoughts or sequence of events does the speaker describe in stanzas one through five?

   _____

2. What change in the speaker's attitude occurs in stanzas six through eight?

   _____

3. What pattern is established in the first four stanzas of "Ah, Are You Digging on My Grave"?

   _____

B. DIRECTIONS: *On the flow chart, write a summary of each stanza in "The Darkling Thrush."*
Then write a sentence stating how the stanzas work together to create meaning.

Stanza 1:

⬇

Stanza 2:

⬇

Stanza 3:

⬇

Stanza 4:

⬇

Overall Meaning:

© Pearson Education, Inc., publishing as Pearson Prentice Hall. All rights reserved.

"Remembrance" by Emily Brontë
"The Darkling Thrush" and **"Ah, Are You Digging on My Grave?"**
by Thomas Hardy
Vocabulary Builder

Using the Root -*terr(a)*-

A. DIRECTIONS: *Match each word in the left column with its definition in the right column. Write the letter of the definition on the line next to the word it defines.*

___ 1. territorial
___ 2. terrace
___ 3. subterranean
___ 4. terra-cotta
___ 5. terrarium

A. beneath the earth
B. fired clay used as building material
C. a glass container containing a garden of small plants and perhaps some small land animals
D. relating to a geographical area
E. a flat roof or paved outdoor space

Using the Word List

languish	rapturous	gaunt	terrestrial

B. DIRECTIONS: *On the line, write the Word List word that best completes the meaning of the sentence as a whole.*

1. The thrush in Hardy's poem sings a _____ song.
2. While in mourning, the woman refused to eat and became _____ and pale.
3. The turn of the century causes the speaker to _____ rather than celebrate.
4. Unable to fly, the ostrich is a more _____ creature than other birds.

C. DIRECTIONS: *Match each word in the left column with its definition in the right column. Write the letter of the definition on the line next to the word it defines.*

___ 1. languish
___ 2. rapturous
___ 3. gaunt
___ 4. terrestrial

A. of the earth
B. weaken
C. thin
D. ecstatic

© Pearson Education, Inc., publishing as Pearson Prentice Hall. All rights reserved.

Name _____ Date _____

"Remembrance" by Emily Brontë
"The Darkling Thrush" and **"Ah, Are You Digging on My Grave?"**
by Thomas Hardy

Grammar and Style: Pronoun Case Following *Than* or *As*

An incomplete construction is a clause in which key words are not stated, even while their meaning is understood. Sentences are often abbreviated in real speech, as well as in dialogue in poetry and prose, especially after the words *than* or *as*. A common mistake is using an incorrect pronoun to follow these words. To make sure you choose the pronoun after *than* or *as* correctly, mentally complete the sentence.

In the following example, an incomplete construction contains the pronoun *I* following the word *as*. The word in brackets is the unspoken word that is understood and that completes the clause.

And every spirit upon earth / Seemed fervorless *as I* [was].

A. PRACTICE: *Circle the pronoun that correctly completes each construction.*

1. Few siblings were closer to one another than (*they, them*).
2. Everyone at the New Year's party seemed to have a better time than (he, him).
3. No one was as disappointed by the party as (*I, me*).
4. I enjoy poetry more than (*she, her*).
5. No group was more prepared for the presentation than (*we, us*).
6. My partner was as nervous as (*I, me*).

B. Writing Application: *Complete each construction with an appropriate pronoun.*

1. No one enjoyed the play more than _____.
2. The lead actor was more impressive than _____.
3. Few actors are as talented as _____.
4. Everyone was as pleased with the performance as _____.

© Pearson Education, Inc., publishing as Pearson Prentice Hall. All rights reserved.

"Remembrance" by Emily Brontë
"The Darkling Thrush" and **"Ah, Are You Digging on My Grave?"**
by Thomas Hardy
Support for Writing

Use the chart below to gather information for your comparison of literary sources. Use a variety of sources, such as an encyclopedia, an online review, or an article written by a scholar.

Title of work analyzed: _____

Source	Contents	Analysis

Choose two of the sources to draft your analysis. On a separate page, use details from the chart as you compare them to one another and analyze their literary value.

© Pearson Education, Inc., publishing as Pearson Prentice Hall. All rights reserved.

"God's Grandeur" and **"Spring and Fall: To a Young Child"**
by Gerard Manley Hopkins
"To an Athlete Dying Young" and **"When I Was One-and-Twenty"**
by A. E. Housman

Literary Analysis: Rhythm and Meter

Rhythm is the alternation of strong and weak—or stressed and unstressed—syllables, which creates a flow or movement. **Meter** describes or "measures" rhythm when it follows a regular pattern. When poets or readers examine the meter of a poem, they "scan" the poem, marking stressed syllables with a ´ mark and unstressed syllables with a ˘ mark.

The meter of a poem is measured in feet. A foot is a combination of two or more syllables, at least one of which is typically stressed. There are specific kinds of feet. Here are two examples.

Metrical Foot	Pattern of Syllables	Example
iamb	one unstressed, one stressed (˘´)	The time you won your town the race
trochee	one stressed, one unstressed (´˘)	It will come to such sights colder

Another way to measure and label meter is to count how many feet there are in a line. In the iambic example in the chart, the line contains four iambic feet. Thus the line is said to be in iambic *tetrameter*. The words *trimeter* and *pentameter* refer to lines of poetry with three feet and five feet, respectively.

Hopkins is known for experimenting with rhythm. He uses counterpoint rhythm, which consists of two opposing rhythms in one line of poetry. He also uses what he called "sprung rhythm," which he felt closely imitates the flow of natural speech. In sprung rhythm, each foot begins with a stressed syllable, which may then be followed by any number of unstressed syllables. Scanning a poem written in sprung rhythm reveals its lack of conventional meter.

DIRECTIONS: *Follow the instructions given to examine the meter of Hopkins's and Housman's poems. (Scansion is not an exact science, but you should be able to find general patterns.)*

1. Scan the second stanza of "To an Athlete Dying Young." Then identify the meter of each line.

   Today, the road all runners come,
   Shoulder-high we bring you home,
   And set you at your threshold down,
   Townsman of a stiller town.

2. Scan these two lines from "God's Grandeur."

   And for all this, nature is never spent:
     There lives the dearest freshness deep down things; . . .

   What effect does the meter have on the meaning of these lines?

   _____

© Pearson Education, Inc., publishing as Pearson Prentice Hall. All rights reserved.

"God's Grandeur" and **"Spring and Fall: To a Young Child"**
by Gerard Manley Hopkins
"To an Athlete Dying Young" and **"When I Was One-and-Twenty"**
by A. E. Housman

Reading Strategy: Apply Biography

Knowing something about a poet can help readers understand that person's poetry more fully. Even simple details, such as knowing whether a poet is a man or a woman, can make a poem's meaning more clear. Whenever you read an author's **biography** in a textbook or anthology, be sure to apply what you learn to that person's writings.

Perhaps the most significant and startling fact about Gerard Manley Hopkins, for example, is that he was a Jesuit priest for all of his adult life. As you read his poems, look for signs of his religious beliefs. You may also see signs of the conflict he felt between his vocation and his other interests.

DIRECTIONS: *Use the charts on this page to record what you learn about each poet from the biographies on page 856. Then look for evidence of each man's character or personality in his poems. Quote lines or phrases from the poems that reveal the poets' backgrounds. An example entry has been provided.*

Characteristic of Hopkins	Where Characteristic Is Seen in Poems
strong religious beliefs	"The world is charged with the grandeur of God." ("God's Grandeur," line 1)

Characteristic of Housman	Where Characteristic Is Seen in Poems

© Pearson Education, Inc., publishing as Pearson Prentice Hall. All rights reserved.

"God's Grandeur" and **"Spring and Fall: To a Young Child"**
by Gerard Manley Hopkins
"To an Athlete Dying Young" and **"When I Was One-and-Twenty"**
by A. E. Housman
Vocabulary Builder

Using Coined Words

A. DIRECTIONS: *In "Spring and Fall," Hopkins uses* unleaving *to describe the falling of the leaves from the branches. This coined word concisely and descriptively expresses the poet's idea. For each of the following phrases, either coin a noun that names the idea or image in a descriptive way, or coin an adjective that would suit the subject.*

1. a puddle _____
2. the first leaf buds of spring _____
3. puppies _____
4. a playground full of children _____

Using the Word List

grandeur   blight   rue

B. DIRECTIONS: *Choose the letter of the word or phrase most nearly* similar *in meaning to each numbered word below. Write the letters on the lines provided.*

____ 1. blight
    A. disease
    B. rotten
    C. dim
    D. understandable

____ 2. grandeur
    A. more grand
    B. larger
    C. magnificence
    D. haughtiness

____ 3. rue
    A. mourn
    B. rejoice
    C. blush
    D. regret

C. DIRECTIONS: *On the line, write the Word List word that best completes the sentence.*

1. The great cathedral had a _____ that took one's breath away.
2. The tumble-down shack in the middle of the block was a _____ on the neighborhood.
3. My decision to leave before the end of the performance later caused me much _____.

© Pearson Education, Inc., publishing as Pearson Prentice Hall. All rights reserved.

Name _____ Date _____

"God's Grandeur" and **"Spring and Fall: To a Young Child"**
by Gerard Manley Hopkins
"To an Athlete Dying Young" and **"When I Was One-and-Twenty"**
by A. E. Housman

Grammar and Style: Capitalization of Compass Points

When a compass point—a direction word—is used to refer to a region, the word is capitalized.

I find the **S**outhwest a fascinating place to read about.

I decorated my bedroom in **S**outhwestern style.

I have lived in the **E**ast all my life.

When a compass point is used to indicate direction, the word is not capitalized.

We drove **s**outh about twenty miles to the riding stables.

Once there, we wandered **e**astward along a stream.

Later, we saw the city lights glowing to the **n**orth of us.

A. PRACTICE: *Write a D in front of each sentence in which the italicized word indicates direction. Write an R in front of each sentence in which the italicized word refers to a region, and capitalize the first letter of the word.*

_____ 1. Driving *westward* at sunset, we almost wished for a cloud to block the bright sun.

_____ 2. Our morning schedule took us *north* to view a historic site.

_____ 3. The *west* was our destination, and once we reached the Black Hills, we felt as if we had made it.

_____ 4. The next day, our progress was slowed by road construction on the *westbound* lanes of the highway.

_____ 5. Two days later I saw Mt. Rainier looming in the distance and knew that we had reached the *northwest*.

_____ 6. Our homeward journey, though pleasant, had little of the excitement of our *western* travels.

B. Writing Application: *Follow the instructions to write sentences that contain compass points, or direction words. Remember to capitalize a word that refers to a region.*

1. Make a statement about the states of Georgia and South Carolina. Refer to the region in which those states lie.

_____

2. Write a sentence about traveling from Texas to Montana.

_____

3. In what direction would you have to travel to get to Maine? In your answer, name the region in which Maine lies.

_____

© Pearson Education, Inc., publishing as Pearson Prentice Hall. All rights reserved.

Name _____ Date _____

"God's Grandeur" and "Spring and Fall: To a Young Child"
by Gerard Manley Hopkins
"To an Athlete Dying Young" and "When I Was One-and-Twenty"
by A. E. Housman
Support for Writing

Choose a poem and write a thesis for your analytical essay in the space provided below. Then, use the organizer to take notes from the poem that supports your thesis.

Poem: _____

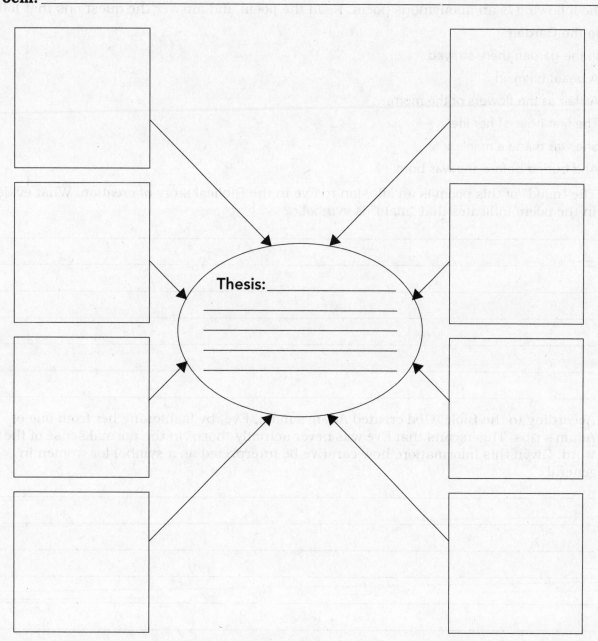

Thesis:_____

On a separate page, use details from the graphic organizer as your draft your analytical essay. Write a thesis. Then, develop it into paragraphs that use details from the poem to support your thesis.

© Pearson Education, Inc., publishing as Pearson Prentice Hall. All rights reserved.
245

Poetry of William Butler Yeats
Literary Analysis: Symbolism

A **symbol** is a word, character, object, or action that stands for something beyond itself. To determine whether a word has symbolic meaning, consider it within the context of the poem. For example, the city of Byzantium, which symbolically represents the poetic imagination, is central to the meaning of "Sailing to Byzantium." It is in Byzantium that the speaker finds "the singing masters of (his) soul." That Byzantium is part of the title is another clue to its significance.

The following is an anonymous poem. Read the poem and answer the questions that follow.

In the Garden

In the garden there strayed

A beautiful maid

As fair as the flowers of the morn;

The first hour of her life

She was made a man's wife,

And buried before she was born.

1. The "maid" of this poem is an allusion to Eve in the Biblical story of creation. What evidence in the poem indicates that "maid" is symbolic?

   _____

   _____

   _____

   _____

   _____

   _____

2. According to the Bible, God created Adam's mate, Eve, by fashioning her from one of Adam's ribs. This means that Eve was never actually "born" in the normal sense of the word. Given this information, how can Eve be interpreted as a symbol for women in general?

   _____

   _____

   _____

   _____

   _____

   _____

   _____

© Pearson Education, Inc., publishing as Pearson Prentice Hall. All rights reserved.

Name _____ Date _____

Poetry of William Butler Yeats
Reading Strategy: Apply Literary Background

Many readers focus closely on the words of a poem for understanding. After understanding the writer's work as it exists on the page, though, readers may find it helpful and interesting to consider a work in the larger context of the artist's life. What might have led a writer to a specific subject? What was he or she doing when this work was composed? What was the social or historical climate of the period?

It is not necessarily safe or correct, however, to assume that what is in a writer's work gives the exact story of his or her life. Events in writers' lives may not adequately explain their work. For example, one need not know or understand the full details of Yeats's involvement with Irish politics to appreciate his poetry. In some of his poems, however, having knowledge of the issues helps explain references and attitudes.

DIRECTIONS: *For each poem, use the third column to write the impact the information in the second column might have had on the poem's composition. Cite specific lines or sections when you can.*

Poem	Background Information	Impact on the Poem
1. "When You Are Old"	Actress Maud Gonne, a founder of Sinn Fein, met Yeats three years before the poem was written. She starred in his first play. He proposed, but she married another Irish revolutionary.	
2. "The Wild Swans at Coole"	Yeats summered for years at Coole Park, elegant home of Lady Gregory, founder of the Irish National Theater.	
3. "The Second Coming"	The poem was written in 1920. After the Russian revolution in 1917, counterrevolution, chaos, and famine persisted in the new state into the 1920's.	
4. "Sailing to Byzantium"	In a prose work, *The Vision*, Yeats wrote "I think that if I were given a month of antiquity . . . I would spend it in Byzantium [circa 535 AD] . . ."	

Unit 6 Resources: A Time of Rapid Change
© Pearson Education, Inc., publishing as Pearson Prentice Hall. All rights reserved.
247

Poetry of William Butler Yeats
Vocabulary Builder

Using the Root -ques-

The root -ques- derives from the Latin verb *quaerere*, which means "to ask."

A. DIRECTIONS: *The words in the list use the -ques- root. Choose the word that best completes each sentence and write in on the line.*

request   quest

1. The explorer's _____ for adventure caused him to undertake a voyage around the world.

2. The employee had to _____ another copy of the company's pension plan.

Using the Word List

clamorous	conquest	anarchy
conviction	paltry	artifice

B. DIRECTIONS: *Each item consists of a word from the Word List followed by four lettered words or phrases. Choose the word or phrase most nearly* opposite *in meaning to the Word List word. Circle the letter of your choice.*

1. clamorous
   A. miserable
   B. joyful
   C. quiet
   D. timid

2. conquest
   A. defeat
   B. plunder
   C. strategy
   D. battle

3. anarchy
   A. faith
   B. order
   C. power
   D. hope

4. conviction
   A. freedom
   B. certainty
   C. weakness
   D. doubt

5. paltry
   A. simple
   B. valuable
   C. clear
   D. kind

6. artifice
   A. destruction
   B. ingenuity
   C. dumbness
   D. incivility

© Pearson Education, Inc., publishing as Pearson Prentice Hall. All rights reserved.

Poetry of William Butler Yeats
Grammar and Style: Noun Clauses

Subordinate clauses of every type can function as single parts of speech. One type of clause, a **noun clause**, can serve any function that a noun can serve in a sentence. Here are examples of noun clauses:

Subject:	*What Yeats believed about history* shows in his poems.
Direct Object:	Yeats thought *that history runs in cycles.*
Indirect Object:	Yeats gives *what he believes* free rein in some poems, but not all.
Object of Preposition:	His general theory of *what determines history* produces sometimes complicated imagery.
Predicate Noun or Subject Complement:	The important thing to remember is *that one need not understand all Yeats's theories to enjoy the poetry.*
Appositive:	The essential thing, *what one should go by,* is whether a poem speaks to you.

A. PRACTICE: *Underline the noun clauses in the following sentences. Above each, indicate how the noun clause functions.*

1. In "When You Are Old," the speaker expresses an idea of what the thoughts of a woman he once loved might one day be.

2. Who you are may determine whether you believe "The Lake Isle of Innisfree" refers to a type of place or a kind of work.

3. Knowledge that the world will go on without you, that stark recognition, glides also across the water in "The Wild Swans at Coole."

B. Writing Application: *Write a sentence that uses the noun clause in the way indicated in parentheses.*

1. That Yeats is the best Irish poet (subject)

_____

_____

2. How Yeats creates memorable images (complement)

_____

_____

3. What Yeats says about aging (direct object)

_____

_____

© Pearson Education, Inc., publishing as Pearson Prentice Hall. All rights reserved.

Poetry of William Butler Yeats
Support for Writing

Review Yeats's poetry to find examples of "dreamlike symbols" and "symbols expressing conflict." Write examples in the chart. Think about whether your examples support Brower's statement that Yeats succeeded by letting these symbols express conflict he could not deal with outside of his poetry. Write your opinion below.

"dreamlike symbols"	"symbols expressing conflict"

My opinion:

_____

_____

_____

_____

On a separate page, use the statement of your opinion to write a thesis statement for your response to criticism. Then, use details from the chart to support your thesis statement as you write.

© Pearson Education, Inc., publishing as Pearson Prentice Hall. All rights reserved.

Name _____   Date _____

"Preludes," "Journey of the Magi," and "The Hollow Men" by T. S. Eliot
Literary Analysis: Modernism

Modernism was a literary movement of the early-to-mid twentieth century in which writers attempted to break away from traditional forms and styles of the past. Modernist literature was highly influenced by industrialization and by World War I, which many writers felt left the world chaotic, fragmented, and sad. In poetry, the Modernist movement brought forth a technique known as imagism. Imagist poets, including T. S. Eliot, stood back from their subjects, not commenting outright on feeling or meaning. They used suggestive, musical language and clear images to evoke emotions in readers. Their images are like snapshots, which capture important moments of perception.

DIRECTIONS: *Connect the elements of Modernism with the following excerpts from the Modernist poems you have read.*

1. The morning comes to consciousness . . . From the sawdust-trampled street / With all its muddy feet that press / To early coffee-stands. / With the other masquerades / That time resumes, / One thinks of all the hands / That are raising dingy shades / In a thousand furnished rooms.
   In what way is the style and theme of this excerpt from "Preludes" uniquely Modernist?

   _____

   _____

   _____

2. And the night-fires going out, and the lack of shelters, / And the cities hostile and the towns unfriendly / And the villages dirty and charging high prices: / A hard time we had of it. / At the end we preferred to travel all night. / Sleeping in snatches, / With the voices singing in our ears, saying / That this was all folly.
   In what way is the style of this excerpt reflective of the Modernist movement? In what way does the subject matter of "The Journey of the Magi," and the faithful dedication of the Magi revealed in this excerpt, set it apart from the strictly Modernist viewpoints expressed in the other two poems?

   _____

   _____

   _____

3. The eyes are not here / There are no eyes here / In this valley of dying stars / In this hollow valley / This broken jaw of our lost kingdoms / In this last of meeting places / We grope together / And avoid speech / Gathered on this beach of the tumid river
   What attitude toward people and the modern world is expressed in this excerpt from "The Hollow Men"? In what way is its style and theme similar to that of "Preludes"?

   _____

   _____

   _____

© Pearson Education, Inc., publishing as Pearson Prentice Hall. All rights reserved.

"Preludes," "Journey of the Magi," and "The Hollow Men" by T. S. Eliot
Reading Strategy: Interpret

In order to understand the themes in T. S. Eliot's poetry, you must **interpret**, or find meaning, in repeated images, words, and phrases. By linking these elements, you can find the meanings they suggest. For example, notice the images Eliot presents of urban life in "Preludes." If you put these images together, what do you learn about Eliot's view of the modern world?

DIRECTIONS: *As you read the poems, use the following questions as a guide to search for meaning in the images and patterns of Eliot's poems.*

1. What images does Eliot use to describe the city in "Preludes"? What feeling is created by these images? What do these images say about his perception of modern, urban life?

   _____

   _____

   _____

2. What images in "Preludes" relate directly to the actions of humans in the urban setting? What does the pattern of these images suggest about the lives of the people?

   _____

   _____

   _____

3. In "Journey of the Magi," what images does Eliot give of the journey? What do these images suggest about the journey?

   _____

   _____

   _____

4. What images and repeated words in "Journey of the Magi" describe the feelings of the Magi after their journey? What do these elements suggest about the importance of the journey?

   _____

   _____

   _____

5. What images in "The Hollow Men" describe specific limitations of the hollow men? What do these details reveal about the men's situation in life?

   _____

   _____

   _____

© Pearson Education, Inc., publishing as Pearson Prentice Hall. All rights reserved.

"Preludes," "Journey of the Magi," and "The Hollow Men" by T. S. Eliot
Vocabulary Builder

Using the Root *-fract-*

In "Journey of the Magi," T. S. Eliot describes camels as "sore-footed and *refractory.*" The word *refractory* means "stubborn" or "hard to manage." It contains the root *-fract-*, meaning "to break." A *refractory* camel is one that breaks away from the path which you want to take.

A. DIRECTIONS: *Complete each sentence with a word from the following list.*

refract   fractional   fractious

1. He ate only a _____ portion of his meal.

2. Guards were trying to control the loud and _____ crowd.

3. A prism hanging in a window will _____ sunlight into different colors.

Using the Word List

galled	refractory	dispensation
supplication	tumid	

B. DIRECTIONS: *Choose a lettered pair that best expresses a relationship* similar *to that expressed in the numbered pair. Circle the letter of your choice.*

1. GALLED : FRICTION ::
   A. worked : accomplishment
   B. consume : food
   C. rested : sleep
   D. injury : sore

2. REFRACTORY : STUBBORN ::
   A. generous : unselfish
   B. organize : arrange
   C. ancient : contemporary
   D. quietly : whisper

3. DISPENSATION : BELIEF ::
   A. creation : invent
   B. theory : philosophy
   C. operation : machine
   D. thought : concentrate

4. SUPPLICATION : PRAYER ::
   A. organization : society
   B. belief : knowledge
   C. education : lesson
   D. instruction : learn

5. TUMID : SHRIVELED ::
   A. pester : annoy
   B. heat : scorching
   C. massive : miniature
   D. simple : plain

© Pearson Education, Inc., publishing as Pearson Prentice Hall. All rights reserved.

"Preludes," "Journey of the Magi," and **"The Hollow Men"** by T. S. Eliot

Grammar and Style: Adjectival Modifiers

An **adjectival modifier** is any word or word group that functions as an adjective. The poems of T. S. Eliot contain many examples of prepositional phrases, participial phrases, and adjective clauses used as adjectival modifiers. For example:

Prepositional phrase: "In this valley of dying stars"

The prepositional phrase of *dying stars* modifies *valley*.

Participial phrase: ". . . And the silken girls bringing sherbet."

The participial phrase *bringing sherbet* modifies *girls*.

Adjective clause: "I am moved by fancies/that are curled around these images . . ."

The adjective clause *that are curled around these images* modifies *fancies*.

A. PRACTICE: *For each of the following excerpts from "Preludes," "Journey of the Magi," and "The Hollow Men," underline the adjectival modifier and circle the word it modifies. Then, on the line following the excerpt, identify the modifier as a prepositional phrase, a participial phrase, or an adjective clause.*

1. And now a gusty shower wraps / The grimy scraps / Of withered leaves . . . _____

2. The worlds revolve like ancient women / Gathering fuel . . . _____

3. Those who have crossed / With direct eyes . . . _____

4. And newspapers from vacant lots . . . _____

5. With all its muddy feet that press . . . _____

6. Then the camel men cursing and grumbling . . . _____

B. Writing Application: *Write a description of the scene in "Preludes," using a variety of adjectival modifiers. Experiment with prepositional phrases, participial phrases, and adjective clauses. Underline each modifier in your paragraph.*

_____

_____

_____

_____

_____

_____

_____

_____

© Pearson Education, Inc., publishing as Pearson Prentice Hall. All rights reserved.

"Preludes," "Journey of the Magi," and **"The Hollow Men"** by T. S. Eliot
Support for Writing

Review "Preludes" and "Journey of the Magi" and think about the quotation that suggests that "humanity is trapped in a dreary, meaningless cycle of time." As you read, gather details about time and the human sense of not belonging. Record your details in the organizers.

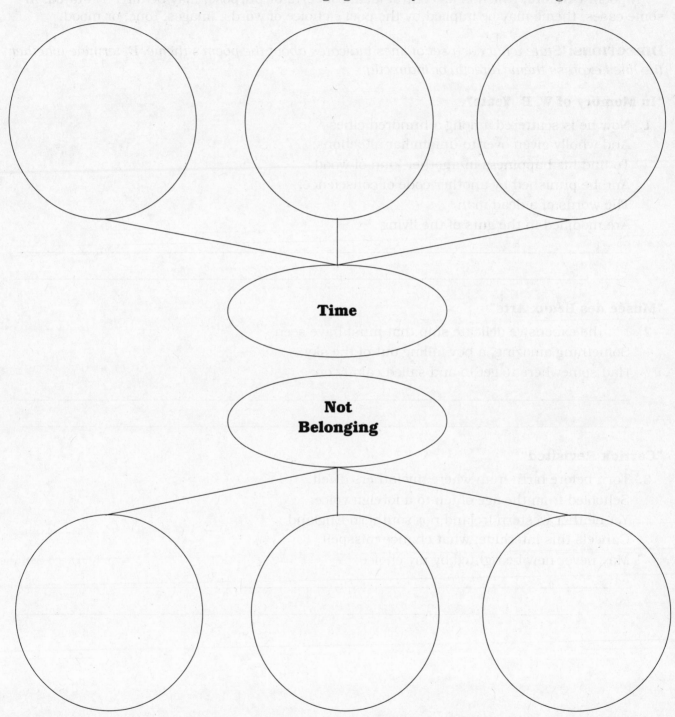

Look at the details you have collected and draw conclusions about Eliot's attitude toward these themes. Then, on a separate page, write your response to criticism.

© Pearson Education, Inc., publishing as Pearson Prentice Hall. All rights reserved.
255

Name _____ Date _____

"In Memory of W. B. Yeats" and **"Musée des Beaux Arts"** by W. H. Auden
"Carrick Revisited" by Louis MacNeice
"Not Palaces" by Stephen Spender
Literary Analysis: Theme

A poem's **theme,** which is its central idea, concern, or purpose, may be directly stated. In some cases, theme may be implied by the poet's choice of words, images, tone, or mood.

DIRECTIONS: *State what each set of lines indicates about the poem's theme. Determine whether the lines express theme directly or indirectly.*

"In Memory of W. B. Yeats"

1. Now he is scattered among a hundred cities
   And wholly given over to unfamiliar affections;
   To find his happiness in another kind of wood
   And be punished by another code of conscience.
   The words of a dead man
   Are modified in the guts of the living.

   _____

   _____

"Musée des Beaux Arts"

2. . . . the expensive delicate ship that must have seen
   Something amazing, a boy falling out of the sky,
   Had somewhere to get to and sailed calmly on.

   _____

   _____

"Carrick Revisited"

3. Torn before birth from where my fathers dwelt,
   Schooled from the age of ten to a foreign voice,
   Yet neither western Ireland nor southern England
   Cancels this interlude; what chance misspelt
   May never now be righted by my choice.

   _____

   _____

© Pearson Education, Inc., publishing as Pearson Prentice Hall. All rights reserved.

Name _____ Date _____

"In Memory of W. B. Yeats" and **"Musée des Beaux Arts"** by W. H. Auden
"Carrick Revisited" by Louis MacNeice
"Not Palaces" by Stephen Spender
Reading Strategy: Paraphrase

When you **paraphrase** a poet's words, or restate them in your own words, you can check your understanding of the poem's basic idea. Then you can interpret the poet's original work and appreciate how its language, imagery, and tone add depth to its meaning.

A. DIRECTIONS: *Write a paraphrase for each set of lines.*

"Musée des Beaux Arts"

1. . . . even the dreadful martyrdom must run its course
   Anyhow in a corner, some untidy spot
   Where the dogs go on with their doggy life . . .

   _____

   _____

"Carrick Revisited"

2. Time and place—our bridgeheads into reality
   But also its concealment! Out of the sea
   We land on the Particular and lose
   All other possible bird's-eye views, the Truth
   That is of Itself for Itself—but not for me.

   _____

   _____

"Not Palaces"

3. It is too late for rare accumulation,
   For family pride, for beauty's filtered dusts;
   I say, stamping the words with emphasis,
   Drink from here energy and only energy
   To will this time's change.

   _____

   _____

B. DIRECTIONS: *Write an explanation of how each paraphrase in Part A helps you understand the poet's original words.*

1. _____

2. _____

3. _____

© Pearson Education, Inc., publishing as Pearson Prentice Hall. All rights reserved.

"In Memory of W. B. Yeats" and **"Musée des Beaux Arts"** by W. H. Auden
"Carrick Revisited" by Louis MacNeice
"Not Palaces" by Stephen Spender
Vocabulary Builder

Using the Root *-top-*

A. DIRECTIONS: *Knowing that the word root -top- means "place" and drawing upon your knowledge of other word roots, circle the letter of the best answer for each question.*

1. What does a *topographer* do?
   A. designs buildings
   B. plans cities
   C. records geographical features
   D. studies the use of electricity

2. Where would you find a *utopia*?
   A. in someone's imagination
   B. in the ocean
   C. on a plain
   D. in a distant galaxy

Using the Word List

sequestered	topographical	affinities
prenatal	intrigues	

B. DIRECTIONS: *Choose the phrase that is the most appropriate description for each numbered word. Circle the letter of your choice.*

1. sequestered
   A. a small fish in a big pond
   B. a knight on a mission
   C. a dancer on a stage
   D. a patient in quarantine

2. topographical
   A. a political map of Britain
   B. a spinning carnival ride
   C. a relief chart of a park
   D. a featureless, grassy plain

3. affinities
   A. a group of total strangers
   B. a network of interpersonal relationships
   C. an endless universe
   D. a structure made of building blocks

4. prenatal
   A. a ship being repaired
   B. a poet's first book
   C. a check-up for a mother-to-be
   D. a cat lapping up a large saucer of cream

5. intrigues
   A. conspirators' plots
   B. pilots' instruments
   C. students' textbooks
   D. priests' vestments

"In Memory of W. B. Yeats" and **"Musée des Beaux Arts"** by W. H. Auden
"Carrick Revisited" by Louis MacNeice
"Not Palaces" by Stephen Spender

Grammar and Style: Parallel Structure

Parallel structure is the repeated use of the same grammatical form or pattern. Poets may use parallel structure to create a natural rhythm or flow in their writing or to emphasize an idea. In the following lines from "Not Palaces," the parallel prepositional phrases are underlined:

> It is too late for rare accumulation,
> For family pride, for beauty's filtered dusts.

A. PRACTICE: *Rewrite the italicized words to make the sentence structures parallel.*

1. W. H. Auden wrote poetry and *was a teacher* in numerous universities.

   _____

2. Auden speaks of Yeats as a poet and *he was* a man.

   _____

3. Returning to his childhood home makes MacNeice recall his youth and *he considers* his identity.

   _____

4. For Spender, poetry has a way of changing attitudes and *it can promote* social equality.

   _____

B. Writing Application: *Rewrite each of the following sentences, incorporating parallel sentence structure.*

1. Yeats died on a day that was dark, and it was cold.

   _____

   _____

2. The "Old Masters" refers to artists from Belgium and Holland and others from Italy.

   _____

   _____

3. Bruegel enjoyed painting scenes of laborers, including harvesters and hunting scenes.

   _____

   _____

4. The speaker in "Carrick Revisited" admires the landscape and is remembering his childhood.

   _____

   _____

© Pearson Education, Inc., publishing as Pearson Prentice Hall. All rights reserved.

"In Memory of W. B. Yeats" and **"Musée des Beaux Arts"** by W. H. Auden
"Carrick Revisited" by Louis MacNeice
"Not Palaces" by Stephen Spender

Support for Writing

Write the details and images about the artwork you chose in the chart below. Then, list words and phrases to describe these details. Try to think of vivid and precise words and phrases that will help the reader "see" the details in the painting.

Images and Details	Vivid Words and Phrases

On a separate page, use the ideas you have gathered to draft your poem about the artwork. Try to get across one main impression in your work.

© Pearson Education, Inc., publishing as Pearson Prentice Hall. All rights reserved.

"Shooting an Elephant" by George Orwell
Literary Analysis: Irony

Irony is a literary device that brings out contradictions between appearance and reality, or between expectation and reality, or between words and reality. In **verbal irony,** the intended meaning of words clashes with their usual meaning, as when Orwell describes the dangerous elephant as "grandmotherly." In **irony of situation,** events contradict what you expect to happen, as when the young Buddhist priests are revealed to be the most insulting toward the British.

DIRECTIONS: *Explain what is ironic about the following facts, events, or descriptions.*

1. Orwell's attitude toward Buddhist priests

_____

_____

2. Burmese population's lack of weapons

_____

_____

3. "Grinning" mouth of man trampled by elephant

_____

_____

4. Crowd gathering to watch shooting of elephant

_____

_____

5. Value of a living elephant compared to a dead one

_____

_____

6. Orwell's assessment that it was "perfectly clear" what he should do about killing the elephant

_____

_____

7. Comparison of rifle to something "beautiful"

_____

_____

8. Orwell's gladness that the coolie had been killed by the elephant

_____

_____

© Pearson Education, Inc., publishing as Pearson Prentice Hall. All rights reserved.

Name _____ Date _____

"Shooting an Elephant" by George Orwell
Reading Strategy: Recognize the Writer's Attitudes

Orwell reveals in his essay that his attitudes toward British rule in Burma are not always clear cut. At times, he expresses conflicting attitudes. When you recognize the writer's attitudes, you uncover clues to the meaning in a literary work.

DIRECTIONS: *Complete each cluster diagram by writing words and phrases, including quotations from the essay, that reflect Orwell's conflicting attitudes. Add branches to the diagram as needed. On the lines following each diagram, write your conclusion about Orwell's attitudes.*

1.

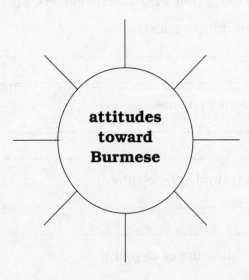

_____

_____

2.

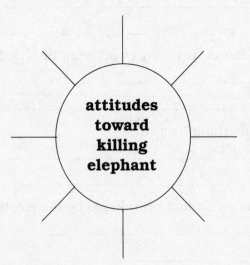

_____

_____

Name _____ Date _____

"Shooting an Elephant" by George Orwell
Vocabulary Builder

Using Words About Politics

A. DIRECTIONS: *In a few sentences, describe Orwell's experiences as a British police officer in Burma. Use the following words:* imperialism, despotic, dominion.

_____

_____

_____

_____

_____

_____

_____

_____

_____

_____

Using the Word List

prostate	imperialism	despotic
squalid	dominion	senility

B. DIRECTIONS: *Match each word in the left column with its definition in the right column. Write the letter of the definition on the line next to the word it defines.*

___ 1. prostrate

___ 2. imperialism

___ 3. despotic

___ 4. squalid

___ 5. dominion

___ 6. senility

A. miserably poor; wretched

B. defenseless; in a prone or lying position

C. mental or physical decay due to old age

D. rule or power to rule; a governed territory

E. tyrannical

F. policy and practice of forming and maintaining an empire in order to control raw materials and world markets by the conquest of other countries and the establishment of colonies

© Pearson Education, Inc., publishing as Pearson Prentice Hall. All rights reserved.

Name _____   Date _____

"**Shooting an Elephant**" by George Orwell
Grammar and Style: Restrictive and Nonrestrictive Participial Phrases

Participial phrases, or groups of words with a participle, modify nouns and pronouns. A **restrictive participial phrase** is essential to the meaning of the word it modifies and is not separated by commas. A **nonrestrictive participial phrase** is not essential to the meaning and can be separated by commas. Note the differences in the following examples:

Restrictive: I . . . saw a man's dead body *sprawling in the mud.*

Nonrestrictive: Some more women followed, *clicking their tongues and exclaiming . . .*

A. PRACTICE: *For each sentence, underline the participial phrase. On the line, indicate whether it is restrictive or nonrestrictive, and write the word it modifies.*

1. ". . . the insults hooted after me when I was at a safe distance got badly on my nerves."

   _____

2. "It was a very poor quarter, a labyrinth of squalid bamboo huts, . . . winding all over a steep hillside."

   _____

3. "An old woman with a switch in her hand came round the corner of a hut, violently shooing away a crowd of naked children."

   _____

4. "He was lying on his belly with arms crucified and head sharply twisted to one side."

   _____

5. "Here was I, the white man with his gun, standing in front of the unarmed native crowd . . ."

   _____

B. Writing Application: *In a few sentences, describe a situation in which you felt uncomfortable in front of an audience or crowd. Use at least one restrictive participial phrase and one nonrestrictive participial phrase in your description.*

   _____

   _____

   _____

   _____

   _____

   _____

   _____

© Pearson Education, Inc., publishing as Pearson Prentice Hall. All rights reserved.

"Shooting an Elephant" by George Orwell
Support for Writing

Make an outline of the experience you will describe in your essay written in Orwell's style. First, write a sentence identifying your experience. Then, list events that were part of the experience in the order they happened. Finally, go back and fill in details about each event.

Experience: _____
_____

Event: _____

    Details: **1.** _____

            2. _____

            3. _____

Event: _____

    Details: **1.** _____

            2. _____

            3. _____

Event: _____

    Details: **1.** _____

            2. _____

            3. _____

Event: _____

    Details: **1.** _____

            2. _____

            3. _____

On a separate page, as you begin to draft your essay in Orwell's style, first write about your response to the experience. Then, draw on information in your outline to illustrate and explain what happened. Present details in a clear order.

© Pearson Education, Inc., publishing as Pearson Prentice Hall. All rights reserved.

Name _____ Date _____

"**The Demon Lover**" by Elizabeth Bowen
Literary Analysis: The Ghost Story

During the nineteenth-century Romantic movement, the focus of literature turned to the personal lives of everyday people. Some of these stories were of people with dark or mysterious events in their lives. One of the offshoots of this movement was the development of gothic novels, so named for settings that often included castles or other buildings of gothic architecture. Inevitably such stories began to include tales of folklore and other metaphysical events. Others were written with an emphasis on the supernatural. The **ghost story**, long an oral tradition, became a popular literary form as well.

Part of the appeal of a good ghost story is that it is about normal people who do everyday things. Somehow, though, their normality is disrupted by something that cannot be easily explained or dismissed. Readers relate to the ordinariness of the characters, and are, therefore, intrigued when something unusual happens. Most writers of ghost stories build tension throughout the story by dropping hints or including small details that could be interpreted in more than one way.

DIRECTIONS: *Use the following chart to record the "normal" elements in "The Demon Lover" as well as the unusual aspects that creep in almost from the very beginning.*

Scene or Detail	What is normal?	What is unusual?
outside Mrs. Drover's house		
inside Mrs. Drover's house		
the letter		
the farewell, 25 years ago		
Mrs. Drover's marriage and family		
catching the taxi		

© Pearson Education, Inc., publishing as Pearson Prentice Hall. All rights reserved.

Name _____ Date _____

"The Demon Lover" by Elizabeth Bowen
Reading Strategy: Respond to the Story

When you are reading and interpreting fiction, try to find the relationship between the details the author presents and the meaning of the piece. One way to find that meaning is to think about your own **response.** Did the piece grab your attention? Were you frightened? Did it remind you of something in your own life? Identify your own reaction and judge whether your response was intended by the author, and how he or she evoked it.

DIRECTIONS: *Use the following questions to record your own response to "The Demon Lover."*

1. What was your response to the mood set at the beginning of the story?

   _____

   _____

   _____

2. What was your response to the letter sent to Mrs. Dover?

   _____

   _____

   _____

3. What was your response to the story's ending?

   _____

   _____

   _____

4. Were there parts of the story that reminded you of your own experiences? If so, what were they?

   _____

   _____

   _____

5. What parts of the story grabbed your attention or emotions? Why?

   _____

   _____

   _____

6. Do you think the author intended to get these responses from you? Why would the author want this kind of response?

   _____

   _____

   _____

© Pearson Education, Inc., publishing as Pearson Prentice Hall. All rights reserved.

Name _____ Date _____

Using the Root -loc-

A. DIRECTIONS: Each word in the following list contains the root -loc-, meaning "place." Choose the word from the list that correctly completes each sentence, and write it on the line.

allocation	localism	locality

1. Based on her accent, it was apparent that the _____ of her upbringing was the deep South.

2. The residents' customs gave the town its sense of _____.

3. Each employee received a memo about the _____ of bonuses at the end of the year.

Using the Word List

spectral	dislocation	arboreal
circumscribed	aperture	

B. DIRECTIONS: *Match each word in the left column with its definition in the right column. Write the letter of the definition on the line next to the word it defines.*

___ 1. spectral   A. a condition of being out of place

___ 2. arboreal   B. ghostly

___ 3. circumscribed   C. limited

___ 4. dislocation   D. opening

___ 5. aperture   E. of, near, or among trees

© Pearson Education, Inc., publishing as Pearson Prentice Hall. All rights reserved.

Name _____ Date _____

"The Demon Lover" by Elizabeth Bowen
Grammar and Style: Sentence Beginnings—Participial Phrases

A participle is a verb form that functions as an adjective. Most participles end in *-ing* or *-ed*. A **participial phrase** is made up of a participle and its modifiers and complements.

The Londoners, *dreading nightfall,* listened for the drone of the German planes.

In this sentence, the participial phrase "dreading nightfall" modifies *Londoners*.

To create variety in your writing, you can begin sentences with participial phrases. Make sure, though, that the word your participial phrase modifies follows soon after the phrase.

Confusing: Looking about her, the unfamiliarity of her own home perplexed her.

Clear: Looking about her, she was perplexed by the unfamiliarity of her own home.

A. PRACTICE: *Circle the number of each sentence that begins with a participial phrase. For each sentence that begins with a participial phrase, underline the phrase and circle the word it modifies.*

1. Everything smelled vaguely of ashes from the unused fireplace.

2. Proceeding upstairs, Mrs. Drover had not yet shaken her discomfort.

3. On the table lay a letter addressed to her.

4. Annoyed at the caretaker, she picked up the letter, which bore no stamp.

B. Writing Application: *Revise the following paragraph so that three of the sentences begin with participial phrases. You may either combine or rearrange the existing sentences, or add your own details to create the participial phrases. Rewrite the paragraph in the space provided.*

Elizabeth Bowen, described as a writer of "finely wrought prose," is praised highly for her stories. Her characters are mostly from the upper middle class in England and Ireland. Bowen "knew" her characters well, for she was born into that class. Her novel *The Hotel*, published in 1927, contains a typical Bowen heroine. The girl, trying to cope with a life for which she is not prepared, might remind some of a young Elizabeth Bowen.

_____

_____

_____

_____

_____

_____

_____

_____

_____

© Pearson Education, Inc., publishing as Pearson Prentice Hall. All rights reserved.

"The Demon Lover" by Elizabeth Bowen
Support for Writing

Plan your sequel using the graphic organizer that follows. First, write a question that "The Demon Lover" leaves unanswered. Then, answer the question with an action or event.

Question that needs to be answered:
Action or event that answers the question:

Question that needs to be answered:
Action or event that answers the question:

Question that needs to be answered:
Action or event that answers the question:

Question that needs to be answered:
Action or event that answers the question:

On a separate page, use information from your diagram to organize your ideas as you draft your sequel. Make sure that the events are in a logical order that helps you tell a story.

© Pearson Education, Inc., publishing as Pearson Prentice Hall. All rights reserved.

"The Soldier" by Rupert Brooke
"Wirers" by Siegfried Sassoon
"Anthem for Doomed Youth" by Wilfred Owen
"Birds on the Western Front" by Saki (H. H. Munro)

Literary Analysis: Tone

The **tone** of language conveys an attitude toward the audience or the subject. We recognize tone in spoken language quickly. The way in which words are spoken, as well as the speaker's volume and facial expressions help us sort out his or her attitude. Some of these advantages aren't available to the writer, who must create tone with language alone. In literature, tone is transmitted primarily through choice of words and details.

Details selected may imply an attitude about the subject. In "The Soldier," Rupert Brooke represents England with "her flowers to love" and "the suns of home." Apart from descriptive language, these choices tell us part of what Brooke feels for his country.

The particular words selected matter greatly. When Wilfred Owen writes of "shrill, demented choirs of wailing shells," we get a clear sense of his attitude toward war. A writer's manner of speaking, or voice, conveys tone, too. Is it formal or informal? Serious or light? Lofty or low? How does the language help you make these decisions?

DIRECTIONS: *Analyze the tone of each of the following passages. For each one, explain what impression details, word choices, and voice make. Then describe the overall tone of the passage.*

"Wirers"		
. . . I heard him carried away, / Moaning at every lurch; no doubt he'll die today. / But *we* can say the front-line wire's been safely mended.		
Details:	Word Choice:	Voice:
Tone:		

"Birds on the Western Front"		
. . . once, having occasion to throw myself down with some abruptness on my face, I found myself nearly on the top of a brood of young larks. Two of them had already been hit by something and were in rather a battered condition, but the survivors seemed as tranquil and comfortable as the average nestling.		
Details:	Word Choice:	Voice:
Tone:		

© Pearson Education, Inc., publishing as Pearson Prentice Hall. All rights reserved.

"The Soldier" by Rupert Brooke
"Wirers" by Siegfried Sassoon
"Anthem for Doomed Youth" by Wilfred Owen
"Birds on the Western Front" by Saki (H. H. Munro)
Reading Strategy: Make Inferences

An **inference** is a conclusion drawn by reasoning. We make inferences all the time in daily life. Someone stands in the hall with wet hair and a dripping umbrella, and we conclude that it has been raining outside. If the sprinkler system had gone off in the building ten minutes ago, however, we might make a different inference. In short, we infer based on all available evidence. In daily life, we do this quickly, almost automatically.

In literature, we may have to make inferences more consciously. Writers engage readers by portraying a world of details or evidence and understand that readers will draw conclusions from clues they read.

Much in literature is implied, especially in poetry, so picking up quickly on setting, images, language, tone, and theme is a valuable skill for a reader. What do you know about the setting and speaker? How do you know it? What's going on? How soon do you find out? What clues do you use? What is the tone and message of the work? What language lets you make the inference?

Use the following chart to practice making inferences.

DIRECTIONS: *Write down the inference you make about each element of "Birds on the Western Front." In the Clues column, identify specifically the evidence that you used to make the inference.*

Element	Inference	Clues
Setting (Where?)		
Speaker (Who?)		
Action/Topic (What?)		
Tone (Attitude)		
Theme (Message)		

© Pearson Education, Inc., publishing as Pearson Prentice Hall. All rights reserved.

"The Soldier" by Rupert Brooke
"Wirers" by Siegfried Sassoon
"Anthem for Doomed Youth" by Wilfred Owen
"Birds on the Western Front" by Saki (H. H. Munro)

Vocabulary Builder

Using the Root -laud-

The word *laudable*, which means "praiseworthy," originates from the Latin verb *laudere*, which means "to praise." Other related words are *laud*, *laudatory*, and *laudation*.

A. DIRECTIONS: *Complete the following sentences with one of the words in the preceding paragraph that use the -laud- root.*

1. Wilfred Owen's poem is powerful enough to _____ young soldiers and say that they "die like cattle" at the same time.

2. Is Brooke's _____ of England different in tone from one a homesick German might imagine for his country?

3. Saki's _____ remarks about birds gloss an ironic view of human beings.

Using the Word List

stealthy	desolate	mockeries	pallor
laudable	requisitioned	disconcerted	

B. DIRECTIONS: *Each item consists of a word from the Word List followed by four lettered words or phrases. Choose the word or phrase most nearly* similar *in meaning to the Word List word. Circle the letter of your choice.*

1. stealthy
   A. furtive
   B. luxurious
   C. pilfered
   D. invisible

2. desolate
   A. absent
   B. disconnected
   C. selected
   D. deserted

3. mockeries
   A. imitations
   B. farces
   C. symbols
   D. vanities

4. pallor
   A. salon
   B. friendship
   C. gloom
   D. paleness

5. laudable
   A. humorous
   B. flexible
   C. praiseworthy
   D. clamorous

6. requisitioned
   A. relocated
   B. investigated
   C. ordered
   D. recovered

7. disconcerted
   A. silenced
   B. confused
   C. detached
   D. failed

© Pearson Education, Inc., publishing as Pearson Prentice Hall. All rights reserved.

"The Soldier" by Rupert Brooke
"Wirers" by Siegfried Sassoon
"Anthem for Doomed Youth" by Wilfred Owen
"Birds on the Western Front" by Saki (H. H. Munro)

Grammar and Style: Using *Who* and *Whom* in Adjective Clauses

The pronouns *who* and *whom* sometimes cause confusion when they occur in clauses. A clause has both a subject and predicate and serves as a sentence element. In a sentence with an **adjective clause,** the entire clause modifies a noun or pronoun.

Determine which pronoun to use by what the pronoun is doing *within the clause.* If the pronoun serves as a subject, appositive, or complement in the clause, use *who,* the nominative form. If the pronoun serves as an object, indirect object, or object of a preposition in a clause, use *whom,* the objective form, regardless of how the entire clause functions. For example:

Sassoon, *whom* Owen met, published Owen's poetry after the war.

The pronoun *whom* serves as the object of *met,* the verb within the adjective clause. Because it is the object of a verb, *whom* is the correct pronoun, even though the clause is part of the subject.

A. PRACTICE: *Write either* who *or* whom *on the line to complete each of the following sentences.*

1. In World War I, the killing efficiency of modern machine guns shocked those _____ had romantic notions of the glory of war.

2. Brave soldiers, _____ unprepared generals thought would attack as they always had, were mown like grass.

3. Tanks and airplanes were dismissed as interesting novelties by strategists _____ four years of slaughter taught little.

B. Writing Application: *Write sentences with adjective clauses using* who *or* whom. *Follow the prompts provided.*

1. Write a sentence using *who* about Rupert Brooke and talented writers dying in World War I.

   _____

   _____

2. Write a sentence using *whom* about Siegfried Sassoon. The world discovered him in war and he wrote about peace in later life.

   _____

   _____

3. Write a sentence using *whom* about families that soldiers left behind—a subject on Wilfred Owen's mind as he writes his poem.

   _____

   _____

© Pearson Education, Inc., publishing as Pearson Prentice Hall. All rights reserved.

Name _____ Date _____

"The Soldier" by Rupert Brooke
"Wirers" by Siegfried Sassoon
"Anthem for Doomed Youth" by Wilfred Owen
"Birds on the Western Front" by Saki (H. H. Munro)

Support for Writing

Before writing your critical response, reread "The Soldier" and "Wirers." Record in the diagrams below which details about patriotism are sentimental and unsentimental. You may not fill every row.

Sentimental		Unsentimental
	"The Soldier"	

Sentimental		Unsentimental
	"Wirers"	

On a separate page, use the details you gather to analyze the two poems. Write a thesis statement that expresses your opinion about whether the poems are sentimental or unsentimental. Support your position as you write your critical response.

© Pearson Education, Inc., publishing as Pearson Prentice Hall. All rights reserved.

Name _____ Date _____

"Wartime Speech" by Winston Churchill

"Defending Nonviolent Resistance" by Mohandas K. Gandhi

Literary Analysis: Speech

Although different in rhetorical style, Churchill and Gandhi were excellent persuasive speakers. Both understood that the audience for a **speech** has needs different from the audience for a written work, and developed speaking styles to meet those needs.

The purpose of a speech may be to entertain, inform, or persuade, but to do any of these, it must capture and hold the attention of its audience. Features of an effective speech include:

An engaging introduction Depending on its purpose, a speech may begin with an announcement, brief statement of purpose, entertaining anecdote, or surprising declaration. The introduction serves as a "hook" to capture the interest of the audience. Churchill knows his audience is worried about war news, and begins there. Gandhi begins a "defense" by admitting guilt.

Clear organization The audience for a speech cannot stop and reread for information, so clarity and organization are especially important in a speech. Churchill uses simple statements followed by explanations and Gandhi addresses his points chronologically, but neither is hard to follow.

Concrete language and vivid images Although Churchill uses more formal rhetoric, his terms are familiar, and when he speaks of "gashed" Holland, or when Gandhi refers to "skeletons in many villages", the words have impact.

Examples Churchill gives specific examples of British heroism in the air and service at home, and Gandhi traces precisely the causes of his disaffection with British rule.

A strong conclusion In many speeches, the conclusion summarizes main points in an appealing way. In a persuasive speech, appeals to high ideals may be made. Gandhi and Churchill do both.

DIRECTIONS: *Cite specific examples or passages from each selection that correspond to features of an effective speech.*

1. Engaging Introduction: _____

_____

2. Clear Organization: _____

_____

3. Concrete Language/Vivid Images: _____

_____

4. Examples: _____

_____

5. Strong Conclusion: _____

_____

© Pearson Education, Inc., publishing as Pearson Prentice Hall. All rights reserved.

276

"Wartime Speech" by Winston Churchill
"Defending Nonviolent Resistance" by Mohandas K. Gandhi

Reading Strategy: Identify Main Points and Support

One of the most important reading skills is the ability to recognize **main points** and supporting details. Readers and listeners look for main ideas and supporting details almost intuitively. You can see the principle operating in even a single sentence:

Churchill was a great wartime leader who refused to quit and inspired his people.

The main idea is that Churchill was a great wartime leader. The rest of the sentence gives evidence for the idea. Here is a graphic representation of the idea and support:

Main Idea	Churchill was a great wartime leader
Support 1	He refused to quit.
Support 2	He inspired his people.

The same principles of analysis work in paragraphs. In most paragraphs, a topic sentence near the beginning identifies the main idea. Other sentences provide support.

You can extend this type of analysis even to whole documents. The main idea of the Declaration of Independence, for example, is that the bonds of government between the King and the colonies must be broken. Thomas Jefferson gives about twenty-five reasons.

DIRECTIONS: *Use the grid below to list the main idea and supporting features for the following paragraph. Label the supporting features S1, S2, and so on.*

We must not allow ourselves to be intimidated by the presence of these armored vehicles behind our lines. If they are behind our Front, the French are also at many points fighting actively behind theirs. Both sides are therefore in an extremely dangerous position. If the French Army, and our own Army are well handled, as I believe they will be; if the French retain that genius for recovery and counter-attack for which they have so long been famous; and if the British Army shows the dogged endurance and solid fighting power of which there have been so many examples in the past—then a sudden transformation of the scene might spring into being.

Main Idea	
S1	

© Pearson Education, Inc., publishing as Pearson Prentice Hall. All rights reserved.

"Wartime Speech" by Winston Churchill
"Defending Nonviolent Resistance" by Mohandas K. Gandhi
Vocabulary Builder

Using the Root -dur-

The Latin word *durus* is an adjective meaning "hard." It is an ancestor of the Word Bank word *endurance*, which means "stamina" or "resistance to wear." Most words with a *-dur-* root carry this connotation of toughness.

A. DIRECTIONS: *For each of the sentences, write the word from among the following that can replace the underlined words:*

duration endured obdurate

1. For the <u>time</u> the war wore on, Churchill never let show his fear. _____
2. Gandhi was <u>hard and unyielding</u> in not compromising his position. _____
3. Though they differed on the role of the British Empire, the resistance to corruption of their reputations has <u>lived</u> beyond both the men and the issues that divided them. _____

Using the Word List

intimidated	diabolical	retaliate	formidable	excrescence
invincible	endurance	extenuating	disaffection	

B. DIRECTIONS: *Complete each sentence with the best choice from the Word List.*

After the Germans tore through France early in World War II, there appeared no way to defeat them. The Nazi war machine looked (1) _____. Hitler, however, feared crossing water for military action, and the British Navy was still (2) _____. German planes began to bomb England in an effort to terrorize Britons. The British, however, were unafraid and not (3) _____. Churchill chose to bomb Berlin. Hitler was shocked that the English had the means to (4) _____. Bombing raids struck at civilians, an evil development in the (5) _____ history of war. This horrible tactic, an (6) _____ of previous military strategy, became common. With unbelievable stamina, civilians went about daily life with incredible (7) _____. In spite of their suffering, British citizens showed little (8) _____ with the war effort. The recognition that this was total war for both sides may be an (9) _____ factor in the decision to bomb civilians, but it doesn't make less terrible the death of innocent millions.

© Pearson Education, Inc., publishing as Pearson Prentice Hall. All rights reserved.

"Wartime Speech" by Winston Churchill
"Defending Nonviolent Resistance" by Mohandas K. Gandhi
Grammar and Style: Parallel Structure

Parallel structure is the use of matching grammatical forms or patterns to express related ideas. Parallel structure adds rhetorical power through rhythm, repetition, and balance. Writers may repeat single words, phrases, or clauses in parallel structure. In a parallel structure, each part of the coordinating structure must be of the same grammatical form.

A. PRACTICE: *Underline parallel structures in the following passages and identify the grammatical element of each.*

"Wartime Speech"

1. And if the French Army, and our own Army, are well handled, as I believe they will be; if the French retain that genius for recovery and counter-attack for which they have so long been famous; and if the British Army shows the dogged endurance . . . of which there have been so many examples in the past—then a sudden transformation might spring into being.

2. Only a very small part of that splendid army has yet been heavily engaged; and only a very small part of France has yet been invaded.

3. After this battle in France abates its force, there will come the battle for our island—for all that Britain is, and all that Britain means.

"Defending Nonviolent Resistance"

4. Nonviolence is the first article of my faith. It is also the last article of my creed.

5. No sophistry, no jugglery in figures can explain away the evidence that the skeletons in many villages present to the naked eye.

B. Writing Application: *Rewrite each of the following items to use parallel structure.*

1. Churchill wanted to explain the situation so he could encourage the Army and reassure the people. He also wanted to prepare both Army and people and inspire them for the long struggle he foresaw.

   _____

   _____

   _____

2. Gandhi did not dispute the British charges. He disputed the British right of administration. He objected to their application of the law and imposition of justice. He opposed British rule of India.

   _____

   _____

   _____

© Pearson Education, Inc., publishing as Pearson Prentice Hall. All rights reserved.

"Wartime Speech" by Winston Churchill
"Defending Nonviolent Resistance" by Mohandas K. Gandhi
Support for Writing

Use the graphic organizer that follows to gather and organize ideas for your persuasive speech.

Issue: _____

Audience: _____

What questions will my audience have?

_____

_____

_____

_____

Main Points	**Supporting Facts, Reasons, and Examples**
	←
	←
	←

On a separate page, use information from the organizer to draft your speech. Keep in mind your audience and the questions they will have. Strengthen your main points with examples.

© Pearson Education, Inc., publishing as Pearson Prentice Hall. All rights reserved.

"**Follower**" and "**Two Lorries**" by Seamus Heaney
"**Outside History**" by Eavan Boland

Literary Analysis: Diction and Style

Style refers to these poetic elements: **diction,** or word choice; imagery; rhythms; poetic form; and theme. How each poet *uses* these elements is that poet's style. The style of a poem adds meaning to the poem and affects how a reader responds to that poem. Though generalizations can be made, a poet's style varies from poem to poem.

Following is the first stanza of "Follower." Read it and then refer to the table for an explanation of Heaney's style.

My father worked with a horse plow,
His shoulders globed like a full sail strung
Between the shafts and the furrow.
The horses strained at his clicking tongue.

Elements of Style	Examples
Diction—Is the poet's word choice formal or informal, conversational or stilted, concrete or abstract?	Diction is informal and easy to read, just as if a boy were talking to the reader. Poet uses many concrete words.
Imagery—Is the imagery easily perceived by the senses? Or does it create unusual or abstract pictures? Do the images tell a story, or do they just stand next to each other?	The imagery appeals to the senses of sight and hearing. Poet creates a vivid image of the father's strong shoulders.
Rhythm—Does the poet use rhyme? Does the poet use rhythm? How much? Are they conventional or irregular?	Poet uses a traditional *abab* rhyme scheme.
Form—Are there stanzas? Are they regular or irregular? Does the poet write in free verse?	Poet uses regular, four-line stanzas.

DIRECTIONS: *Using the table on this page as a model, examine the first stanza of "Two Lorries" for style. Write your evaluation of each element of style in the space provided.*

Diction: _____

_____

Imagery: _____

_____

Rhythm: _____

_____

Form: _____

_____

© Pearson Education, Inc., publishing as Pearson Prentice Hall. All rights reserved.

"Follower" and **"Two Lorries"** by Seamus Heaney

"Outside History" by Eavan Boland

Reading Strategy: Summarize

A summary is a restatement of main ideas in a condensed, or shortened, form. Creating a summary is a useful study tool because it makes you think critically about material you've read, identifying main ideas and pushing aside unnecessary details or examples. When you **summarize** a poem you will do the same thing—identify and restate the main ideas aside from the poem's images.

For poetry, it may be helpful to note the main points of each stanza and then build a complete summary from there. Here is a portion of "Outside History" (lines 7–12), accompanied by notes about the main ideas of these two stanzas.

They keep their distance. Under them remains a place where you found you were human, and	discovery of humanness—being alive
a landscape in which you know you are mortal. And a time to choose between them. I have chosen:	discovery of mortality; must choose

DIRECTIONS: *Use the space on this page to note the main idea of each stanza of "Two Lorries" as you read. Then use your notes to summarize the essence of the whole poem.*

"Two Lorries"

Stanza 1: _____

Stanza 2: _____

Stanza 3: _____

Stanza 4: _____

Stanza 5: _____

Stanza 6: _____

Stanza 7: _____

Summary of "Two Lorries":

_____

_____

_____

_____

_____

© Pearson Education, Inc., publishing as Pearson Prentice Hall. All rights reserved.

"Follower" and **"Two Lorries"** by Seamus Heaney
"Outside History" by Eavan Boland
Vocabulary Builder

Using the Root -mort-

A. DIRECTIONS: *Each of the following words contains the root -mort-, meaning "dead" or "death." Match each word with its definition. Write the letter of the definition on the line next to the word it defines.*

___ 1. mortify

___ 2. mortally

___ 3. postmortem

A. in a deadly or fatal manner

B. to subject to severe embarrassment

C. after death

Using the Word List

furrow	nuisance	inklings
mortal	ordeal	

B. DIRECTIONS: *Choose the lettered word or phrase that is most similar in meaning to the numbered word. Circle the letter of your choice.*

1. furrow
   A. groove
   B. mold
   C. measurement
   D. ditch

2. inklings
   A. notes
   B. blotches
   C. suggestions
   D. ideas

3. mortal
   A. impermanent
   B. prone to error
   C. inexact
   D. everlasting

4. nuisance
   A. boredom
   B. excitement
   C. distress
   D. annoyance

5. ordeal
   A. comedy club
   B. severe test
   C. new freeway
   D. light supper

© Pearson Education, Inc., publishing as Pearson Prentice Hall. All rights reserved.

Name _____ Date _____

Grammar and Style: Concrete and Abstract Nouns

You already know that a noun names a person, place, thing, or idea. More specifically, a **concrete** noun names something that can be perceived by the senses. An **abstract** noun names an idea, a quality, or a characteristic. Following are some examples:

Concrete: salt, fire, field, clang, sunset

Abstract: ability, ego, wit, cleverness, certainty

The kinds of nouns you use in your writing affect the impact your writing has on your readers. Concrete nouns tend to create vivid pictures because readers can perceive with their senses the objects being named. The use of abstract nouns tends to create impressions rather than images, and readers have to grasp the meaning with something other than their senses.

A. PRACTICE: *Following are lines from the poems in this section. Above each italicized noun, write C if the noun is concrete or A if the noun is abstract.*

1. An *expert.* He would set the *wing*
   And fit the bright steel-pointed sock.
   The *sod* rolled over without breaking.
   At the *headrig,* with a single pluck

   Of *reins,* the sweating *team* turned round
   And back into the *land.*
       ("Follower," ll. 5–10)

2. And *films* no less! The *conceit* of a coalman . . .
   She goes back in and gets out the black lead
   And emery paper, this nineteen-forties *mother,*
   All *business* round her stove, half-wiping *ashes*
   With a backhand from her *cheek* as the bolted *lorry*
   Gets revved and turned and heads for *Magherafelt*
       ("Two Lorries," ll. 13–18)

B. Writing Application: *Write sentences using concrete and abstract nouns according to the instructions that follow.*

1. Describe the farmer in "Follower" using only concrete nouns.

   _____

2. Now describe the farmer using at least two abstract nouns.

   _____

3. Write a sentence about what the boy in "Follower" does, using only concrete nouns.

   _____

© Pearson Education, Inc., publishing as Pearson Prentice Hall. All rights reserved.

"Follower" and **"Two Lorries"** by Seamus Heaney
"Outside History" by Eavan Boland
Support for Writing

Use the cluster diagram to gather details for your poem. First, write your central image or topic in the center circle. Then, write thoughts, feelings, sensory images, and other details that remind you of the central image in the surrounding circles.

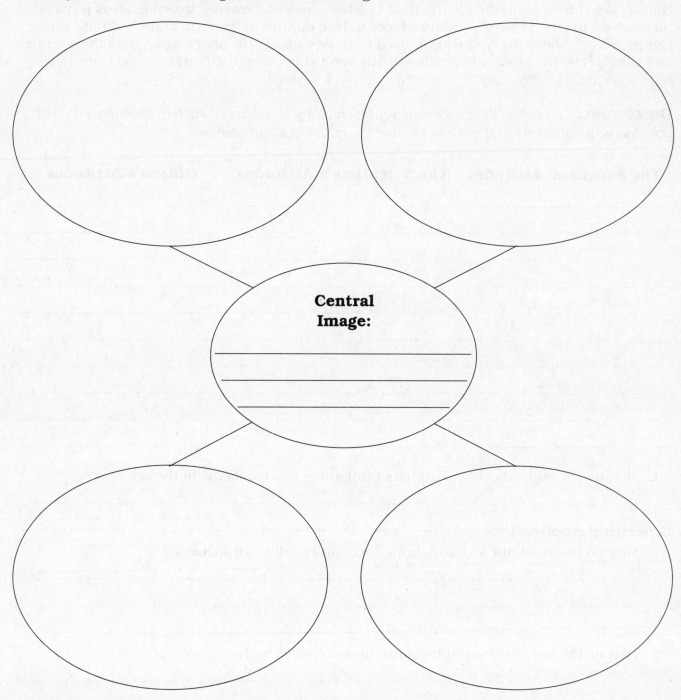

Use the information in your cluster diagram as you write your poem on a separate page. Remember your central image as you write.

© Pearson Education, Inc., publishing as Pearson Prentice Hall. All rights reserved.

Name _____ Date _____

Literary Analysis: Cultural Conflict

Doris Lessing's story is based on the premise that Gideon's culture and the Farquars' culture are in conflict. In spite of the fact that the characters seem accepting of their roles and live relatively compatibly, they possess different customs, ideas, and values.

Perhaps, in the workings of everyday life, the cultural differences between the Farquars and Gideon were invisible. In the aftermath of Teddy's accident, however, differing ideas revealed themselves. In fact, Lessing even introduces a third culture in the form of the scientist who comes to learn about the cure Gideon used for Teddy's eyes. His added ideas from the scientific and commercial world serve to emphasize the conflict between the Farquars and Gideon, who otherwise live harmoniously.

DIRECTIONS: *List below the viewpoints represented by members of each of the three cultures over the issue of the medicine. Then answer the questions that follow.*

The Farquars' Attitudes	The Scientists's Attitudes	Gideon's Attitudes

1. How do the attitudes of the Farquars bring them into conflict with the scientist?

   _____

   _____

2. How do the Farquars' attitudes bring them into conflict with Gideon?

   _____

   _____

3. How do the scientist's attitudes cause him to conflict with Gideon?

   _____

   _____

© Pearson Education, Inc., publishing as Pearson Prentice Hall. All rights reserved.

Name _____ Date _____

"No Witchcraft for Sale" by Doris Lessing
Reading Strategy: Analyze Cultural Differences

All short stories contain a conflict of some sort. Often the conflict is between two individuals or between an individual and nature. Sometimes, as is the case in "No Witchcraft for Sale," the conflict is between the characters' cultures. For the most part, the characters themselves are not in conflict. Differences in their cultures, however, lead to misunderstandings or actions that cause conflict.

Analyzing the cultural differences among characters can increase your understanding of the characters themselves as well as of the story as a whole. When comparing the similarities and differences of two things, it is helpful to do so in chart form.

A. DIRECTIONS: *In the Venn diagram, note details about the Farquars that are unique to them and their way of thinking in the circle labeled "Farquars." In the circle labeled "Gideon," note details that are unique to Gideon's culture and way of thinking. In the center, where the circles intersect, write ideas or attitudes that the Farquars and Gideon share.*

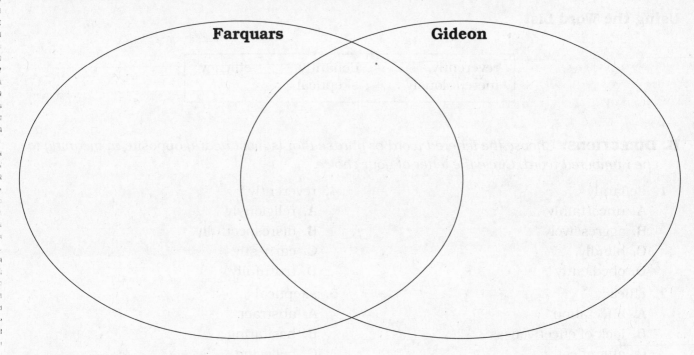

Farquars   **Gideon**

B. DIRECTIONS: *Now that you have analyzed the cultural differences in the story, answer this question.*

1. If the characters' cultural differences—that is, the cultural conflict—did not exist, what would be left of the plot? Describe what this story would be without the cultural differences. Would it still be an engaging story? Why or why not?

   _____

   _____

   _____

   _____

   _____

Unit 6 Resources: A Time of Rapid Change
© Pearson Education, Inc., publishing as Pearson Prentice Hall. All rights reserved.

"No Witchcraft for Sale" by Doris Lessing
Vocabulary Builder

Using Forms of *Skeptical*

A. DIRECTIONS: *The word* skeptical *means "doubting" or "not easily persuaded." Use one of the following words related to* skeptical *to complete each sentence correctly.*

skeptically   skeptic   skepticism

1. The pleasure of the circus may be somewhat deflated for an audience member who is a _____.

2. The child looked at the circus performer _____ after the clown had apparently pulled an egg out of the child's ear.

3. There was even more _____ on the part of the child's parents, whose eyes told them one thing, but whose minds told them another.

Using the Word List

reverently	defiantly	efficacy
incredulously	skeptical	

B. DIRECTIONS: *Choose the lettered word or phrase that is most nearly* opposite *in meaning to the numbered word. Circle the letter of your choice.*

1. defiantly
   A. uncertainly
   B. aggressively
   C. blindly
   D. obediently

2. efficacy
   A. affectation
   B. lack of effectiveness
   C. aftereffect
   D. self-sufficiency

3. incredulously
   A. trustingly
   B. curiously
   C. childishly
   D. massively

4. reverently
   A. religiously
   B. disrespectfully
   C. earnestly
   D. truthfully

5. skeptical
   A. abstract
   B. hesitating
   C. believing
   D. artificial

© Pearson Education, Inc., publishing as Pearson Prentice Hall. All rights reserved.

Name _____   Date _____

Grammar and Style: Correct Use of *Like* and *As*

The words *like* and *as* have become almost interchangeable in casual conversation. This informal usage can lead to errors in formal speaking or writing. Sometimes *like* is a verb meaning "to prefer." When used for comparisons, however, *like* is always a preposition. Remember that a prepositional phrase consists of a preposition followed by a noun or pronoun and any related words.

Gideon, *like the Farquars,* dotes on Teddy.

In casual speech, we often use *like* as a conjunction to introduce a subordinate clause. (Remember that a subordinate clause contains a subject and a verb, but does not express a complete thought and cannot stand alone.) In formal speaking or writing, use *as* in such situations.

As the scientist suspects, Gideon will not reveal the source of his medicine.

In general, use *like* to compare people or things. Use *as* to compare or demonstrate actions or states. If you are unsure about which word to use, look for a verb form. If the phrase in question contains a verb, use *as* to complete your subordinate clause.

A. PRACTICE: *Each of the following sentences uses* like *or* as. *Write* C *if a sentence is correct. Write* I *if a sentence is incorrect.*

_____ 1. As the other servants, Gideon calls Teddy "Little Yellow Head."

_____ 2. The Farquars, as many colonials, kept a number of servants to run their household.

_____ 3. Gideon, like many other Africans, had been educated in a mission school.

_____ 4. Later, Gideon was unable to be as comfortable with Teddy as he once had been.

_____ 5. As Teddy, Gideon's youngest son was fascinated with the scooter.

B. Writing Application: *Write comparative constructions using* like *and* as *according to the instructions that follow.*

1. Use *like* to compare Teddy with other young children.

   _____

2. Use *as* to compare Mrs. Farquar with other mothers.

   _____

3. Describe Teddy's treatment of Gideon's son, using a subordinate clause that begins with *as.*

   _____

4. Compare Mrs. Farquar's and Gideon's reactions to Teddy's accident, using the preposition *like.*

   _____

© Pearson Education, Inc., publishing as Pearson Prentice Hall. All rights reserved.

Name _____ Date _____

"No Witchcraft for Sale" by Doris Lessing
Support for Writing

Use the graphic organizer below to collect and organize ideas for your problem-and-solution essay. First describe the problem between the Farquars and Gideon. Then, brainstorm for solutions to the problem and list them in the first column of the chart. In the second column, state the conditions needed to implement them. In the third column, list the steps that must be taken.

Problem:

	Conditions that would have to exist for the solution to happen	*Steps* that people could take to make the solution happen
Solution 1:		
Solution 2:		
Solution 3:		

Use the details from you chart as you write your essay on a separate page. Add details such as *why, for how long, what kind,* and so on to elaborate on your ideas and to clarify the steps in your solution.

© Pearson Education, Inc., publishing as Pearson Prentice Hall. All rights reserved.

"The Lagoon" by Joseph Conrad
"Araby" by James Joyce
Literary Analysis: Plot Devices

In "The Lagoon," Conrad uses a **story within a story,** a plot device in which a character in a fictional narrative tells a story. Conrad's plot device focuses attention on Arsat's story by framing it with another narrative. In "Araby," Joyce uses an **epiphany,** a plot device in which a character has a sudden and profound revelation in an ordinary moment, to heighten the story's climax.

DIRECTIONS: *Write your answers to the following questions.*

1. As you read "The Lagoon," what clues signal the beginning and the end of the story within the story?

   _____

   _____

   _____

2. In "The Lagoon," is Arsat's story ever interrupted by the outside narrative? If so, what is the effect?

   _____

   _____

   _____

3. Would Arsat's story in "The Lagoon" have the same effect if it had been told on its own? Explain.

   _____

   _____

   _____

4. What is the epiphany in "Araby"?

   _____

   _____

   _____

5. In "Araby," what is the boy doing or looking at when he has an epiphany?

   _____

   _____

   _____

© Pearson Education, Inc., publishing as Pearson Prentice Hall. All rights reserved.

Name _____ Date _____

"The Lagoon" by Joseph Conrad

"Araby" by James Joyce

Reading Strategy: Picture the Action and Situation

Conrad and Joyce place great importance on the psychological states of their characters. As you read modernist fiction, pause to picture the action and situation. Pay particular attention to the characters' internal responses to what is happening. For example, in "The Lagoon," as the narrator details the crew's thoughts about Arsat, try to picture the physical scene and imagine what the white man might be thinking at the same moment.

DIRECTIONS: *Read the following passages from the stories. For each, write a few sentences describing what the characters do and see as well as what they might think or feel.*

1. The white man . . . murmured sadly without lifting his head—

   "We all love our brothers."

   Arsat burst out with an intense whispering violence—

   "What did I care who died? I wanted peace in my own heart."

   _____

   _____

   _____

   _____

2. At nine o'clock I heard my uncle's latchkey in the hall door. I heard him talking to himself and heard the hallstand rocking when it had received the weight of his overcoat. I could interpret these signs. When he was midway through his dinner I asked him to give me the money to go to the bazaar. He had forgotten.

   _____

   _____

   _____

   _____

3. Nearly all the stalls were closed and the greater part of the hall was in darkness. I recognized a silence like that which pervades a church after a service. I walked into the center of the bazaar timidly.

   _____

   _____

   _____

   _____

© Pearson Education, Inc., publishing as Pearson Prentice Hall. All rights reserved.

"The Lagoon" by Joseph Conrad
"Araby" by James Joyce
Vocabulary Builder

Using the Root *-vinc-*

A. DIRECTIONS: *In each sentence, cross out the italicized word or phrase and replace it with one of the following words:* convince, evince, invincibility.

1. I have doubts about this alarm system's *unconquerable quality.*
2. What can you do to *conquer the doubt in* me?
3. If you *show* clear, overwhelming evidence of the system's performance, perhaps I'll buy it.

Using the Word List

portals	invincible	propitiate	conflagration	august
imperturbable	litanies	garrulous	derided	

B. DIRECTIONS: *For each related pair of words in CAPITAL LETTERS, choose the lettered pair that best expresses a* similar *relationship. Circle the letter of your choice.*

1. PORTALS : ENTRANCES ::
   A. gates : iron
   B. locks : keys
   C. roads : pathways

2. INVINCIBLE : VICTORY ::
   A. strong : muscula
   B. confident : success
   C. fear : doubt

3. PROPITIATE : VICTORY ::
   A. welcome : greet
   B. confident : success
   C. hasten : hurry

4. CONFLAGRATION : SPARK ::
   A. flood : droplet
   B. burn : destroy
   C. thunder : lightning

5. AUGUST : REVERE ::
   A. November : spring
   B. authoritative : obey
   C. powerful : weak

6. IMPERTURBABLE : DISRUPT ::
   A. anger : hatred
   B. wealthy : inherit
   C. contented : dismay

7. LITANIES : PRAYER :
   A. clery : congregation
   B. songs : music
   C. snow : sleet

8. GARRULOUS : TALKATIVE ::
   A. sickly : healthy
   B. yawning : tired
   C. energetic : lively

9. DERIDED :TEASE ::
   A. ran : sprint
   B. stretched : squeeze
   C. grasped : release

© Pearson Education, Inc., publishing as Pearson Prentice Hall. All rights reserved.

Name _____ Date _____

"The Lagoon" by Joseph Conrad
"Araby" by James Joyce
Grammar and Style: Adverb Clauses

Adverb clauses are subordinate clauses that modify verbs, adjectives, and adverbs. As modifiers, adverb clauses add specificity and vivid detail to writing. In the following sentence from "The Lagoon," the adverb clause shown in italics modifies the adverb *paler*:

The stars shone paler *as if they had retreated into the frozen depths of immense space.*

A. PRACTICE: *Underline the adverb clauses in the following sentences. Circle the word each adverb clause modifies.*

1. ". . . his voice and demeanor were composed as he asked, without any words of greeting— 'Have you medicine, Tuan?'"

2. "She lay still, as if dead; but her big eyes, wide open, glittered in the gloom. . . ."

3. "But since the sun of today rose she hears nothing—she hears not me."

4. "He had known Arsat years ago, in a far country in times of trouble and danger, when no friendship is to be despised."

5. "When we returned to the street, light from the kitchen windows had filled the areas."

6. "She could not go, she said, because there would be a retreat that week in her convent."

7. "When he was midway through his dinner I asked him to give me the money to go to the bazaar."

B. Writing Application: *For each of the following, write a sentence containing an adverb clause that answers the question.*

1. Why does the white man stay with Arsat in "The Lagoon"?

_____

_____

2. In "The Lagoon" when do Arsat and his brother kidnap the young woman?

_____

_____

3. How does the boy in "Araby" feel about Mangan's sister?

_____

_____

4. In "Araby," what circumstance prevents the boy from going to the bazaar when he wants?

_____

_____

© Pearson Education, Inc., publishing as Pearson Prentice Hall. All rights reserved.

"The Lagoon" by Joseph Conrad
"Araby" by James Joyce
Support for Writing

Use the graphic organizer below to develop ideas for your literary essay on the concept of *nothing* in Arsat's tale and in "The Lagoon." Write details about images of silence and nothing in the left column. In the right column, jot down notes about the events surrounding each image.

Images of Silence and Nothing   **Events Connected to the Images**

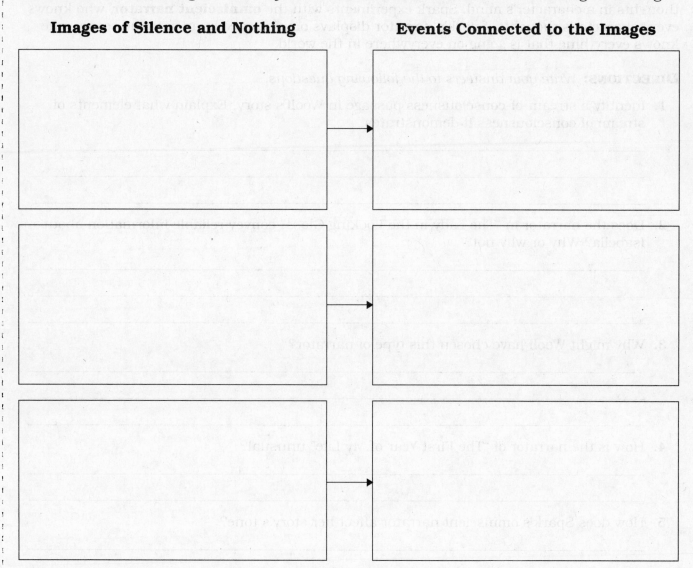

Draw on details and ideas from your graphic organizer as you draft your essay on a separate page. Present your ideas in a logical order, and make sure that the details you have selected support the points you wish to make.

Name _____   Date _____

"The Lady in the Looking Glass: A Reflection" by Virginia Woolf
"The First Year of My Life" by Muriel Spark
Literary Analysis: Point of View: Modern Experiments

Point of view is the perspective from which a writer tells a story. Many writers, including Woolf and Spark, have experimented with point of view to reflect the state of modern life. Woolf uses **stream-of-consciousness narration,** which attempts to convey the random flow of thoughts in a character's mind. Spark experiments with the **omniscient narrator,** who knows every character's thoughts. Spark's narrator displays omniscience in an extreme sense—she knows everything that is going on everywhere in the world.

DIRECTIONS: *Write your answers to the following questions.*

1. Identify a stream-of-consciousness passage in Woolf's story. Explain what elements of stream of consciousness it demonstrates.

   _____

   _____

   _____

2. Does the narrator in "The Lady in the Looking Glass" convey reliable information about Isabella? Why or why not?

   _____

   _____

   _____

3. Why might Woolf have chosen this type of narrator?

   _____

   _____

   _____

4. How is the narrator of "The First Year of My Life" unusual?

   _____

   _____

5. How does Spark's omniscient narrator affect her story's tone?

   _____

   _____

6. Why might Spark have chosen this type of narrator?

   _____

   _____

   _____

© Pearson Education, Inc., publishing as Pearson Prentice Hall. All rights reserved.

"The Lady in the Looking Glass: A Reflection" by Virginia Woolf
"The First Year of My Life" by Muriel Spark

Reading Strategy: Question

When reading experimental works, like those of Virginia Woolf and Muriel Spark, you must continually ask **questions** to find your way through each story and determine its meaning. Two areas of focus are *who* is narrating and *why* the narrator emphasizes an incident. For example, as you begin "The Lady in the Looking Glass," you must ask who the narrator is. Questioning and suggesting possible answers can help you determine the story's meaning.

DIRECTIONS: *Write a question and answer for each of the following passages.*

"The Lady in the Looking Glass: A Reflection"

1. As for facts, it was a fact that she was a spinster; that she was rich; that she had bought this house and collected with her own hands . . . the rugs, the chairs, the cabinets, which now lived their nocturnal life before one's eyes. Sometimes it seemed as if they knew more about her than we, who sat on them, wrote at them, and trod on them so carefully, were allowed to know.

   Question: _____

   Answer: _____

2. At last there she was, in the hall. She stopped dead. She stood by the table. She stood perfectly still. At once the looking glass began to pour over her a light that seemed to fix her; that seemed like some acid to bite off the unessential and superficial and to leave only the truth. It was an enthralling spectacle.

   Question: _____

   Answer: _____

"The First Year of My Life"

3. I wailed for my feed. . . . They rocked the cradle. I never heard a sillier song. Over in Berlin and Vienna the people were starving, freezing, striking, rioting and yelling in the streets. In London everyone was bustling to work and muttering that it was time the whole . . . business was over.

   Question: _____

   Answer: _____

4. . . . occasionally I beamed over to the House of Commons which made me drop off gently to sleep. Generally, I preferred the Western Front where one got the true state of affairs. It was essential to know the worst, blood and explosions and all, for one had to be prepared, as the boy scouts said.

   Question: _____

   Answer: _____

© Pearson Education, Inc., publishing as Pearson Prentice Hall. All rights reserved.

"The Lady in the Looking Glass: A Reflection" by Virginia Woolf
"The First Year of My Life" by Muriel Spark

Vocabulary Builder

Using the Prefix *trans-*

A. DIRECTIONS: *Knowing that* trans- *means "through" or "across," use the following words to complete the sentences.*

transatlantic   translucent   transom   transmutation

1. The glass panel is _____, allowing light to shine through it.

2. Opening the _____ above the door allowed the breeze to pass through.

3. The scientific experiment caused a _____ of the chemical substance.

4. During World War I, how many days did a _____ crossing require?

Using the Word List

suffused	transient	upbraidings	evanescence
reticent	omniscient	authenticity	discerned

B. DIRECTIONS: *Match each word in the left column with its definition in the right column. Write the letter of the definition on the line next to the word it defines.*

___ 1. suffused

___ 2. transient

___ 3. upbraidings

___ 4. evanescence

___ 5. reticent

___ 6. omniscient

___ 7. authenticity

___ 8. discerned

A. temporary; passing through quickly

B. gradual disappearance, especially from sight

C. silent; reserved

D. recognized as separate or different

E. filled

F. quality or state of being genuine

G. stern words of disapproval for an action

H. having infinite knowledge; knowing all things

© Pearson Education, Inc., publishing as Pearson Prentice Hall. All rights reserved.

Name _____ Date _____

Grammar and Style: Subject-Verb Agreement in Inverted Sentences

In inverted sentences, which often begin with *there* or *here,* the verb precedes the subject. However, the verb must still agree in number with its subject. Look at the following sentence from "The First Year of My Life":

There *were* those black-dressed people, females of the species to which I appeared to belong. . . .

The verb *were* agrees with the plural subject *people,* not with *There.*

A. PRACTICE: *Underline the subject or subjects of each sentence, and circle the verb that agrees with your choice.*

1. Here *(is, are)* a letter and an invitation delivered by the postman.

2. There *(was, were)* a suggestion of depth and intelligence in the occupant's room.

3. In the end, there *(is, are)* no interesting thoughts in Isabella's brain.

4. There *(was, were)* many soldiers scarred and killed by poisonous gas during the war.

5. In this anthology *(is, are)* poems by Wilfred Owen and Alan Seegar.

6. Here *(is, are)* an interesting theory on infant development.

B. Writing Application: *Write a paragraph describing the first birthday party you can recall, either your own or someone else's. Use at least two inverted sentences. Make sure to use the correct subject-verb agreement in your inverted sentences.*

_____

_____

_____

_____

_____

_____

_____

_____

_____

_____

© Pearson Education, Inc., publishing as Pearson Prentice Hall. All rights reserved.

"The Lady in the Looking Glass: A Reflection" by Virginia Woolf
"The First Year of My Life" by Muriel Spark
Support for Writing

Review "The Lady in the Looking Glass." List details about Isabella that tell about the "real" woman. Then, list details about the Isabella seen through the looking glass. Based on a comparison of the two sets of details, make a judgment about Woolf's ideas about knowing others, and write a response below.

Inference from "Mirror" View	Evidence

Inference about "Real" View	Evidence

Your response: _____

_____

_____

_____

On a separate page, use your response to help you write a topic sentence for your essay on a literary theme. Use information from the charts to explain and support your ideas.

© Pearson Education, Inc., publishing as Pearson Prentice Hall. All rights reserved.

"The Rocking-Horse Winner" by D. H. Lawrence
"A Shocking Accident" by Graham Greene
Literary Analysis: Theme and Symbol

In most short stories, a **theme** conveys a main idea or message about life to the reader. Writers often use **symbols** to enhance their themes. A symbol is a person or object that represents an idea or a connection point for several ideas. Lawrence uses the rocking horse as a symbol with multiple meanings. Greene, in "A Shocking Accident," strengthens his theme by using the pig as a symbol for what is out of place.

DIRECTIONS: *Write your answers to the following questions.*

1. What is the literal meaning of the rocking horse in "The Rocking-Horse Winner"?

_____

_____

_____

_____

2. What other meanings might the rocking horse have in Lawrence's story? In other words, what does the rocking horse symbolize?

_____

_____

_____

_____

3. How does the symbol of the rocking horse help you define the theme of "The Rocking-Horse Winner"?

_____

_____

_____

_____

4. How does the pig serve as a symbol in "A Shocking Accident"?

_____

_____

_____

_____

_____

© Pearson Education, Inc., publishing as Pearson Prentice Hall. All rights reserved.

"The Rocking-Horse Winner" by D. H. Lawrence
"A Shocking Accident" by Graham Greene
Reading Strategy: Identify With a Character

When you **identify with a character,** or put yourself in that character's place, you can better understand his or her thoughts, feelings, problems, or motivations. Identifying with a character can lead you to understand a writer's purpose and a literary work's overall theme. For example, identifying with Paul when he first discusses his winners with Uncle Oscar means putting yourself in the boy's situation. You imagine that Paul is proud of his luck, careful not to reveal too much, and concerned that an adult might disapprove of his actions. Empathizing with Paul makes it easier to understand his actions.

DIRECTIONS: *For each situation described, identify the character's thoughts, feelings, problems, or motivations. Then state how you would respond.*

"The Rocking-Horse Winner"

1. Paul proclaims to his mother that he is lucky, but she doesn't believe him.

   _____

   _____

   _____

2. After Paul's mother receives the five thousand pounds, Paul hears the house screaming for even more money.

   _____

   _____

   _____

"A Shocking Accident"

3. After his classmates learn the details of his father's death, Jerome is called Pig.

   _____

   _____

   _____

4. Jerome delays telling Sally the story of his father's death.

   _____

   _____

   _____

© Pearson Education, Inc., publishing as Pearson Prentice Hall. All rights reserved.

"The Rocking-Horse Winner" by D. H. Lawrence
"A Shocking Accident" by Graham Greene
Vocabulary Builder

Using the Prefix *ob-*

A. DIRECTIONS: *Replace the italicized word or words with the word* object, obscures, *or* obstacles.

1. During a solar eclipse, a celestial body *blocks* our view of the sun.
2. I *firmly am opposed* to your interpretation of the scientific findings.
3. We must remove any *items that block the way* before we can proceed.

Using the Word List

discreet	brazening	careered	obstinately	uncanny
remonstrated	apprehension	embarked	intrinsically	

B. DIRECTIONS: *For each numbered word, choose the word or phrase that is the most similar in meaning. Circle the letter of your choice.*

1. discreet
   A. showing good judgment
   B. behaving wildly
   C. showing favor
   D. acting mysteriously

2. brazening
   A. acting courageously
   B. thinking innovatively
   C. daring shamelessly
   D. accepting willingly

3. careered
   A. skidded
   B. dashed
   C. jumped
   D. glided

4. obstinately
   A. regretfully
   B. admittedly
   C. stubbornly
   D. happily

5. uncanny
   A. unique
   B. feverish
   C. unfamiliar
   D. eerie

6. remonstrated
   A. reverted
   B. exemplified
   C. protested
   D. approved

7. apprehension
   A. reluctance
   B. misgiving
   C. refusal
   D. avoidance

8. embarked
   A. made a start
   B. planned a party
   C. left the scene
   D. greeted a host

9. intrinsically
   A. thoroughly
   B. quickly
   C. superficially
   D. innately

© Pearson Education, Inc., publishing as Pearson Prentice Hall. All rights reserved.

Name _____ Date _____

"The Rocking-Horse Winner" by D. H. Lawrence
"A Shocking Accident" by Graham Greene
Grammar and Style: Subjunctive Mood

The **subjunctive mood** of a verb is used to state a wish or condition contrary to fact. It is usually expressed with the verb *were*. Notice the use of the subjunctive mood in the following sentence from "The Rocking-Horse Winner":

"I needn't worry, mother, if I *were* you."

The subjunctive is also used in *that* clauses of recommendation, command, or demand. Used with third-person singular subjects, the subjunctive form is the present form of the verb without *s*. For the verb *to be*, the present subjunctive form is *be* and the past is *were*.

Recommendation: It is suggested that Paul *go* to the seaside.

Demand: His mother insisted that the money *be* advanced all at once.

A. PRACTICE: *Circle the correct verb in parentheses for each of the following sentences.*

1. When he was on his rocking horse, Paul looked as if he (*was, were*) possessed.

2. Initially, Oscar recommended that Paul (*is, be*) cautious with his betting.

3. Paul wished that the house (*was, were*) satisfied.

4. The housemaster's shoulders shook as if he (*was, were*) laughing.

5. Jerome wishes that his father (*were, be*) remembered for his writing, not his bizarre death.

6. It is important to Jerome that Sally (*respond, responds*) appropriately to the story.

B. Writing Application: *Write a brief paragraph describing a dream, wish, or goal you have. Use the subjunctive mood at least twice in your description.*

_____

_____

_____

_____

_____

_____

_____

_____

_____

_____

© Pearson Education, Inc., publishing as Pearson Prentice Hall. All rights reserved.

Name _____ Date _____

Support for Writing

Collect ideas for your product description by sketching your idea for a new toy in the box below. Then, jot notes about its function, size, sounds, color, and moving parts in the surrounding circles.

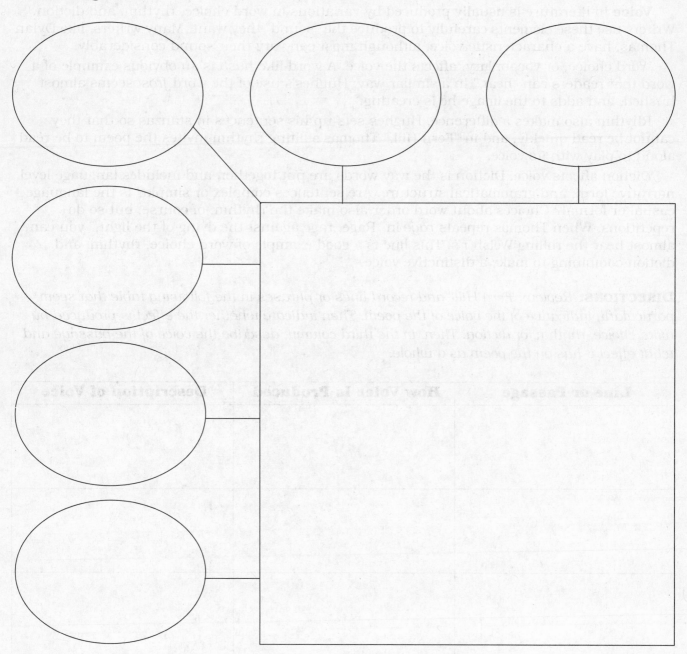

Use the information you have gathered in the graphic organizer as you write your product description on a separate page. Use vivid verbs and adverbs to describe the toy.

© Pearson Education, Inc., publishing as Pearson Prentice Hall. All rights reserved.

Name _____ Date _____

"Do Not Go Gentle into That Good Night" and **"Fern Hill"** by Dylan Thomas
"The Horses" and **"The Rain Horse"** by Ted Hughes

Literary Analysis: Voice

What did you "hear" when you read these poems by Dylan Thomas and Ted Hughes? Did you hear Thomas raging against death? Did you hear Hughes relishing his memory? What is it, exactly, that causes you to "hear" anything in a poem? What produces a poem's voice?

Voice in literature is usually produced by variations in word choice, rhythm, and diction. Writers use these elements carefully to produce the "sound" they want. Many writers, like Dylan Thomas, have a characteristic voice, although most can vary their sound considerably.

Word choice, or vocabulary, affects the voice. A word like *hush* is an obvious example of a word that readers can "hear." In a similar way, Hughes's use of the word *frost* seems almost hushed, and adds to the image he is creating.

Rhythm also makes a difference. Hughes sets up his sentences in stanzas so that they cannot be read quickly, and in "Fern Hill," Thomas's lilting rhythm invites the poem to be read aloud to play with its voice.

Diction affects voice. Diction is the way words are put together, and includes language level, narrative form, and grammatical structure. Are sentences rapid complex or simple? Is the language casual or formal? Choices about word order also make the rhythm, of course, but so do repetitions. When Thomas repeats *rage* in "Rage, rage against the dying of the light," you can almost hear the rolling Welsh *r*'s. This line is a good example of word choice, rhythm, and diction combining to make a distinctive voice.

DIRECTIONS: *Review "Fern Hill" and record lines or phrases in the following table that seem particularly indicative of the voice of the poem. Then indicate whether the effect is produced by word choice, rhythm, or diction. Then, in the third column, describe the voice of the passage and what effect it has on the poem as a whole.*

Line or Passage	How Voice Is Produced	Description of Voice

© Pearson Education, Inc., publishing as Pearson Prentice Hall. All rights reserved.

"Do Not Go Gentle into That Good Night" and **"Fern Hill"** by Dylan Thomas
"The Horses" and **"The Rain Horse"** by Ted Hughes
Reading Strategy: Judge the Writer's Message

Whenever you read a poem, a story, or an editorial, it is only natural to weigh the writer's ideas or events against your own experience. Does the writer's expression of an idea or an event match with your own experience, or have you had a different experience?

Readers should **judge the message** of what they read. Some ideas you come across simply won't make sense to you; other ideas will contradict what you may already believe or know to be true. Test a writer's message against your own experience and accept or reject ideas accordingly.

DIRECTIONS: *As you read each poem in this section, note its message in the appropriate area in the table. Then judge each message, deciding whether you agree or disagree, accept or reject the message.*

Poem	Message	Reader's Judgment and Explanation
"Do Not Go Gentle into That Good Night"		
"Fern Hill"		
"The Horses"		

"Do Not Go Gentle into That Good Night" and "Fern Hill" by Dylan Thomas
"The Horses" and "The Rain Horse" by Ted Hughes
Vocabulary Builder

Using the Root *-vol-*

A. DIRECTIONS: *The following words contain the root -vol-, meaning "to will" or "to wish." Complete each sentence by writing the appropriate word in the blank.*

volition   voluntary   voluntarism

1. The not-for-profit organization relied almost completely on _____ for its work among the community of homeless people.

2. Though her parents expressed their opinions, Sheila chose the field of social work of her own _____.

3. After seeing the news report, dozens of residents _____ turned out to show their support for preserving the historical building.

Using the Word List

grieved	transfiguring	exasperated
nondescript	malevolent	

B. DIRECTIONS: *Each numbered word is followed by four lettered words or phrases. Choose the word or phrase that is most similar in meaning to the numbered word, and circle the letter of your choice.*

1. exasperated
   A. out of breath
   B. without hope
   C. very irritated
   D. filled with longing

2. grieved
   A. sighed
   B. mourned
   C. hailed
   D. resented

3. nondescript
   A. lacking authority
   B. having no destination
   C. lacking form or shape
   D. without character

4. malevolent
   A. wishing harm
   B. hard or brittle
   C. against one's will
   D. clearly disinterested

5. transfiguring
   A. moving from place to place
   B. changing form
   C. performing experiments
   D. calculating values

© Pearson Education, Inc., publishing as Pearson Prentice Hall. All rights reserved.

Name _____ Date _____

Grammar and Style: Sentence Beginnings: Adverb Clauses

An adverb modifies a verb, an adjective, or another adverb. Similarly, an **adverb clause** is a subordinate clause that modifies a verb, an adjective, or an adverb, telling *how, when, where, why, to what extent,* or *under what condition.* In the sentence below, the italicized adverb clause modifies the verb *defend* and tells *under what condition.*

There were deep hollows in the river-bank, shoaled with pebbles, . . . perfect places to defend himself from *if the horse followed him out there.*

Adverb clauses are always introduced by subordinating conjunctions. Here are some common subordinating conjunctions.

after	as though	since	when
although	because	so that	whenever
as	before	than	where
as if	if	through	wherever
as long as	in order that	unless	while
as soon as	provided that	until	

To create variety—and, therefore, interest—in your writing, you can begin sentences with adverb clauses, as Ted Hughes does.

Since the horse seemed to have gone on down the wood, his way to the farm over the hill was clear.

A. PRACTICE: *Circle the number of each sentence that begins with an adverb clause. For each sentence that does begin with an adverb clause, underline the clause and circle the word it modifies.*

1. "At the woodside he paused, close against a tree."

2. "As he went, he broke a yard length of wrist-thick dead branch from one of the oaks."

3. "Through the bluish veil of bare twigs he saw the familiar shape out in the field below the wood."

4. "Whenever it seemed to be drawing off he listened anxiously until it closed in again."

B. Writing Application: *Write two sentences about "The Rain Horse." Begin each sentence with an adverb clause, and use three different subordinating conjunctions.*

1. _____

2. _____

© Pearson Education, Inc., publishing as Pearson Prentice Hall. All rights reserved.

"Do Not Go Gentle into That Good Night" and **"Fern Hill"** by Dylan Thomas
"The Horses" and **"The Rain Horse"** by Ted Hughes
Support for Writing

Use the following diagram to develop ideas for your parody of Thomas's or Hughes's voice. In the center circle, write your ridiculous subject. In each of the surrounding circles, write a detail about your subject that you can develop in your parody.

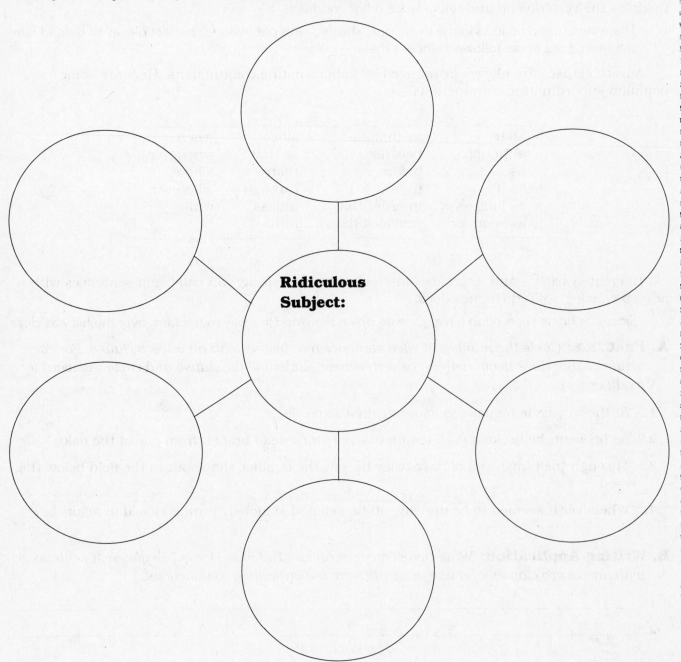

Ridiculous Subject:

On a separate page, use details that you have developed about your subject, as well as the poet's forms, rhythms, and words to help you write a parody. Use vivid language to exaggerate characteristics of the voice of the poet you have chosen.

© Pearson Education, Inc., publishing as Pearson Prentice Hall. All rights reserved.

"An Arundel Tomb" and **"The Explosion"** by Philip Larkin
"On the Patio" by Peter Redgrove
"Not Waving but Drowning" by Stevie Smith
Literary Analysis: Free Verse and Meter

Whether a poet uses free verse or a conventional form of poetry, the lines of poetry likely have some kind of rhythm, or alternation of strong and weak—or stressed and unstressed—syllables. That rhythm may or may not create a regular pattern, or meter. Whether it does or not, though, the poet probably uses the rhythm to add to the meaning of the poem.

The meter of a poem is measured in feet. One foot is made up of one stressed syllable and any number of unstressed syllables. Following is a summary of the kinds of meter Larkin uses in "An Arundel Tomb" and "The Explosion."

Meter	Pattern of Syllables	Example
iambic tetrameter	four sets of iambs per line (˘ ´)	The earl and countess lie in stone
trochaic tetrameter	four sets of trochees per line (´ ˘)	Shadows pointed towards the pithead:

When poets vary the rhythm of a conventional meter, they add emphasis to a line or give special significance to the meaning of the line. Free-verse poets vary their rhythms frequently to add to or create meaning in their poems.

DIRECTIONS: *Examine the rhythm and meter in the poems in this section, as directed by the following questions.*

1. Following is the first line of "An Arundel Tomb." Notice how the stressed and unstressed syllables fall.

   Side by side, their faces blurred,

   How is this line different from the other lines in the poem? Why do you think Larkin made this line different?

   _____

   _____

2. Scan line 15 of "The Explosion." How many feet does it have? What effect does its rhythm have?

   Scarfed as in a heat-haze, dimmed.

   _____

   _____

"An Arundel Tomb" and **"The Explosion"** by Philip Larkin
"On the Patio" by Peter Redgrove
"Not Waving but Drowning" by Stevie Smith
Reading Strategy: Read in Sentences

The key to reading and understanding poetry is to read the punctuation rather than the line endings. The rhythm or rhyme of a poem may seem to require a reader to pause at the end of each line, but one must think beyond the physical line endings to the sense of the words. If you **read in sentences,** ignoring the line endings, you will find that sense.

In Philip Larkin's "An Arundel Tomb," each of the first three stanzas is one sentence. Though some lines end with a comma, a dash, or a colon, the unit of thought does not end until the end of the stanza.

A. DIRECTIONS: *Write each sentence in stanzas 4–7 of "An Arundel Tomb." Do not pay attention to line endings; write the sentences in the space provided as if they are in narrative form.*

Sentence 1: _____

_____

Sentence 2: _____

_____

Sentence 3: _____

_____

Sentence 4: _____

_____

Sentence 5: _____

_____

Sentence 6: _____

_____

Sentence 7: _____

_____

Sentence 8: _____

_____

B. DIRECTIONS: *Now review the entire poem. Remember that each of the first three stanzas is one sentence. Practice reading them in sentences. Then continue to stanzas 4–7, which you have written on this page. Mark places to pause and breathe that fit with the meaning of the sentences. Practice several times, and then read the poem aloud to an audience.*

© Pearson Education, Inc., publishing as Pearson Prentice Hall. All rights reserved.

"An Arundel Tomb" and **"The Explosion"** by Philip Larkin
"On the Patio" by Peter Redgrove
"Not Waving but Drowning" by Stevie Smith
Vocabulary Builder

Using the Root *-fid-*

A. DIRECTIONS: *The root -fid-, meaning "faith," is included in each of the numbered words. Match each numbered word with its definition. Write the letter of the definition next to the word it defines.*

___ 1. confidant

___ 2. confidential

___ 3. perfidious

A. one to whom secrets are entrusted

B. faithless

C. private, secret

Using the Word List

effigy	supine	fidelity	larking

B. DIRECTIONS: *Complete each sentence by writing the appropriate Word List word in the blank.*

1. Without knowing anything about the earl and countess, it is hard to tell whether their _____ was the sculptor's imagination or not.

2. Many tombs of royalty traditionally include a(n) _____ of the noble person, in commemoration of his or her rank and importance.

3. The children were only _____; they hadn't meant to tramp through old Mrs. Wilson's flower garden.

4. When performing CPR, the victim should be lying _____ unless other injuries prevent him or her from being so positioned.

C. DIRECTIONS: *Choose a lettered pair that best expresses a relationship similar to that expressed in the numbered pair. Circle the letter of your choice.*

1. EFFIGY : LIKENESS ::
   A. canvas : easel
   B. water : wet
   C. portrait : painting
   D. horse : animal

2. FIDELITY : TRUST ::
   A. greed : money
   B. hope : future
   C. anger : calm
   D. betrayal : disloyalty

3. LARKING : PLAYFUL ::
   A. working : easy
   B. aiming : target
   C. troubling : avoidance
   D. studying : scholarly

4. SUPINE : ERECT ::
   A. recline : stand
   B. careful : mistake
   C. favorable : false
   D. run : jog

© Pearson Education, Inc., publishing as Pearson Prentice Hall. All rights reserved.

Name _____ Date _____

"An Arundel Tomb" and **"The Explosion"** by Philip Larkin
"On the Patio" by Peter Redgrove
"Not Waving but Drowning" by Stevie Smith

Grammar and Style: Sequence of Tenses

The tense of a verb indicates the time of the action or state of being expressed by the verb. Each verb has six tenses. The following summary focuses on just four tenses.

Tense	The tense expresses . . .	Examples
Present	an action that is occurring now	I *write* a story.
Past	an action that occurred in the past and did not continue into the present	I *wrote* a story.
Present Perfect	an action that occurred at some indefinite time in the past, or that began in the past and continues into the present	I have *written* a story. (Requires *has* or *have* + past participle.)
Past Perfect	an action that was completed in the past before some other past occurrence	I *had written* a story. (Requires *had* + past participle.)

When you write, it is important to make sure that your verbs express actions in the order in which they occurred. Writers must pay attention to this **sequence of tenses** to make sure their writing is clear and accurate. Using the sequence of tenses carefully can also add expressiveness to your writing, as it does to Philip Larkin's in "An Arundel Tomb."

A. PRACTICE: *Identify the tense of the italicized verb in each of the following sentences.*

1. Time *has transfigured* them into untruth. _____

2. The earl and countess *lie* in stone. _____

3. Rigidly they *persisted*, linked, through lengths of time. _____

B. Writing Application: *Write sentences according to the instructions.*

1. Use a past perfect verb in a sentence about a book you've read. Show that one action happened before another. _____

2. Use a present tense verb in a sentence about your morning routine. _____

_____

3. Use a past tense verb in a sentence about something you did yesterday. _____

_____

© Pearson Education, Inc., publishing as Pearson Prentice Hall. All rights reserved.

Name _____ Date _____

"An Arundel Tomb" and "The Explosion" by Philip Larkin
"On the Patio" by Peter Redgrove
"Not Waving but Drowning" by Stevie Smith
Support for Writing

Complete the organizer below to collect information for your reflective essay. Write the everyday sight or event that will be the subject of your essay in the center circle. In the surrounding circles, jot down the ideas, feelings, and comparisons that this event evokes in you.

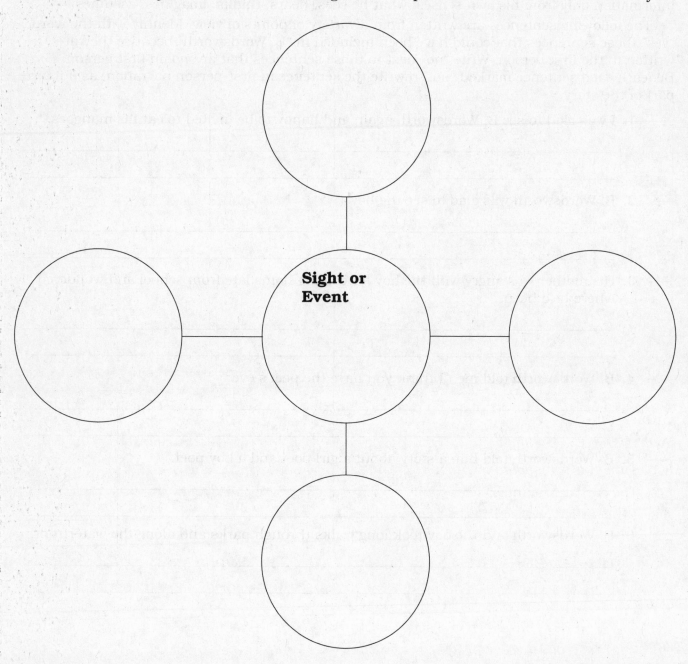

As you write your reflective essay on a separate page, draw on details you have recorded in the organizer. Use them to create deeper meaning about the event or sight you have experienced.

© Pearson Education, Inc., publishing as Pearson Prentice Hall. All rights reserved.

Name _____ Date _____

"B. Wordsworth" by V. S. Naipaul
Literary Analysis: First-Person Narrator

Point of view determines what the author can or cannot tell readers about a character's thoughts and actions. For instance, when we read a story written in **first-person narration,** we see, hear, and learn everything through the narrator. As a result, we can only guess why B. Wordsworth takes a liking to the narrator, what his motive might be, and whether or not he is what and who he says he is. We know only what the narrator tells us, and he can share information only from his own senses: what he sees, hears, thinks, imagines, assumes.

The following sentences are written from a variety of points of view. Identify with the word "yes" those sentences that could have been included in "B. Wordsworth" because they are written in the first person. Write "no" next to those sentences that are *not* in first person. Beneath each sentence marked "no," rewrite the sentence in first-person narration, as if it were part of the story.

_____ 1. I was glad to see B. Wordsworth again and happy to be invited to eat his mangoes.

_____

_____

_____ 2. B. Wordsworth was glad to see the boy.

_____

_____

_____ 3. His mother was angry with the boy for coming home late from school and wondered where he'd been.

_____

_____

_____ 4. B. Wordsworth told me, "I think you have the poet's eye."

_____

_____

_____ 5. B. Wordsworth told him a story about a girl poet and a boy poet.

_____

_____

_____ 6. B. Wordsworth and the boy took long walks through parks and along the waterfront.

_____

_____

© Pearson Education, Inc., publishing as Pearson Prentice Hall. All rights reserved.

Name _____ Date _____

"**B. Wordsworth**" by V. S. Naipaul
Reading Strategy: Respond to Characters

You can become a more active reader by envisioning the world a writer creates. One way to do this is to **respond to character** as you read. Each character reveals himself or herself through words, actions, personal qualities, and responses to other characters. For example, when B. Wordsworth asks the narrator if he may watch the bees, you are alerted to the character's unusual behavior. Then, when B. Wordsworth says, "I can watch a small flower like the morning glory and cry," you experience a glimpse of the man's sensitivity to the world around him.

DIRECTIONS: *As you read "B. Wordsworth," record in the following chart your responses to the behavior, words, and qualities expressed by B. Wordsworth and the narrator as they encounter specific events.*

Character: B. Wordsworth

Behavior/Words/Qualities	My Responses
Event:	
Event:	
Event:	

Character: the narrator

Behavior/Words/Qualities	My Responses
Event:	
Event:	
Event:	

Unit 6 Resources: A Time of Rapid Change
© Pearson Education, Inc., publishing as Pearson Prentice Hall. All rights reserved.
317

"B. Wordsworth" by V. S. Naipaul
Vocabulary Builder

Using Related Forms of *patron*

The Word Bank word *patronize* is a form of the word *patron*, which means "customer, supporter, or benefactor."

A. DIRECTIONS: *Write the form of the word* patron *that best completes each of the following sentences. Use context clues and your knowledge of the word* patron *to choose the correct word.*

patronize   patronizing   patronage   patroness

1. The wealthy _____ entered the gallery dressed in jewels and a lavish gown.
2. Unfortunately, the shopkeeper's _____ manner turned away many customers.
3. The wisest shopkeepers appreciate the _____ of each and every customer.
4. We decided to _____ the new Italian restaurant in our neighborhood.

Using the Word List

rogue   patronize   distill   keenly

B. DIRECTIONS: *Match each word in the left column with its definition in the right column. Write the letter of the definition on the line next to the word it defines.*

___ 1. keenly   A. to be a customer of a store
___ 2. rogue   B. to obtain the essential part
___ 3. patronize   C. sharply or intensely
___ 4. distill   D. scoundrel

C. DIRECTIONS: *Complete each of the sentences with the most appropriate word from the Word List.*

1. The poet sought to _____ life in a single line of poetry.
2. "What a _____ am I!" exclaimed Don Juan.
3. Writers seek to express thoughts and feelings _____.
4. Great minds _____ the resources of great literature.

© Pearson Education, Inc., publishing as Pearson Prentice Hall. All rights reserved.

Name _____ Date _____

Grammar and Style: Pronoun Case in Compound Constructions

Pronoun case refers to the different forms a pronoun takes to indicate its function in a sentence. The subjective case is used when the pronoun performs the action—acts as the subject of the sentence—or when it renames the subject. The objective case is used when the pronoun receives the action of the verb—as a direct or an indirect object—or is the object of a preposition.

Subjective case pronouns: *I, we, you, he, she, it, they*

Objective case pronouns: *me, us, you, him, he, it, them*

The following sentences show the use of subjective and objective pronoun cases:

Subjective case: The narrator eats a fresh mango.

  He is delighted with the flavor.

Objective case: B. Wordsworth tells the narrator a secret.

  The poet asks *him* to keep a secret.

When **personal pronouns** are used in **compound structures**, that is, when they are linked by conjunctions such as *and* or *or,* they use the case that would be correct if the pronoun were used alone.

Subjective case: *He and B. Wordsworth* become friends.

  B. Wordsworth and I talked about poetry.

Objective case: Orion shined brightly in the sky for the *poet and him.*

  The yard on Miguel Street is a secret between *B. Wordsworth and me.*

A. PRACTICE: *Circle the correct pronouns for each sentence.*

1. The poet and (*I, me*) live on Miguel Street.

2. The narrator's mother and (*he, him*) do not have a close relationship.

3. They became friends, B. Wordsworth and (*he, him*).

B. Writing Application: *Each of the following sentences contains a compound pronoun construction. Rewrite each of these sentences, replacing the italicized word or words with a pronoun in the correct case.*

1. Mr. Wordsworth and *the narrator* take long walks together.

  _____

2. *Mr. Wordsworth and the narrator* live on the same street.

  _____

3. The relationship between the narrator and *his mother* is not loving.

  _____

© Pearson Education, Inc., publishing as Pearson Prentice Hall. All rights reserved.

"B. Wordsworth" by V. S. Naipaul

Support for Writing

Use the diagram to collect details for your account of a remarkable person. Write the person's name in the center circle. In the surrounding boxes, write words and phrases to describe the person's remarkable qualities. Also, imagine the person in the scene you will describe. Jot notes about the person's reactions, words, and actions.

Remarkable Qualities   **Reactions, Words, Actions**

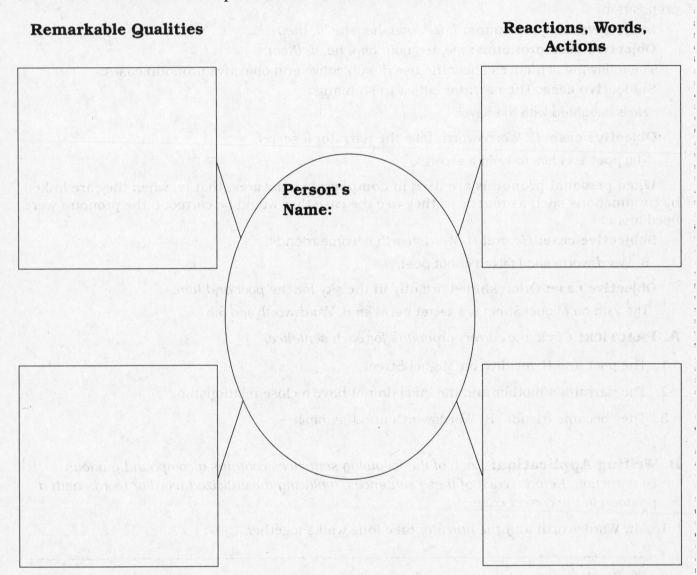

Person's Name:

As you write your first-person account of a remarkable person on a separate page, draw on ideas from your diagram. Use the details to help your readers see and understand the character and the situation.

© Pearson Education, Inc., publishing as Pearson Prentice Hall. All rights reserved.

320

Name _____ Date _____

"The Train from Rhodesia" by Nadine Gordimer
Literary Analysis: Conflict and Theme

A **conflict** in a literary work is a struggle between two characters, or between a character and some outside force, such as society or nature. A **theme** is a literary work's central idea. To bring alive a theme for readers, writers often dramatize it by showing a character struggling with a conflict. The writer's theme is developed through the way in which a character resolves, or fails to resolve, the conflict. In simple stories with simple themes, the resolution may be straightforward. In more complex stories, the conflict may remain unresolved.

In Gordimer's story, there are many conflicts. The main character, a young woman, is not able to resolve the major conflict, but she finally does, through her own inner struggle and that with her husband, reach an understanding of what the true conflict is.

DIRECTIONS: *For each of the following passages from "The Train from Rhodesia," explain how conflict helps dramatize the theme.*

1. . . . she thought of the lion and smiled. That bit of fur round the neck. But the wooden buck, the hippos, the elephants, the baskets that already bulked out of their brown paper under the seat and on the luggage rack! How will they look at home? Where will you put them? What will they mean away from the places you found them? Away from the unreality of the last few weeks? The man outside. But he is not part of the unreality; he is for good now. Odd . . . somewhere there was an idea that he, that living with him, was part of the holiday, the strange places.

   _____

   _____

   _____

2. She was holding it [the lion] away from her, the head with the open jaws, the pointed teeth, the black tongue, the wonderful ruff of fur facing her. She was looking at it with an expression of not seeing, of seeing something different.

   _____

   _____

   _____

3. If you wanted the thing, she said, her voice rising and breaking with the shrill impotence of anger, why didn't you buy it in the first place? If you wanted it, why didn't you pay for it? Why didn't you take it decently, when he offered it? Why did you have to wait for him to run after the train with it, and give him one-and-six? One-and-six!

   _____

   _____

   _____

© Pearson Education, Inc., publishing as Pearson Prentice Hall. All rights reserved.

Name _____ Date _____

"The Train from Rhodesia" by Nadine Gordimer
Reading Strategy: Read Between the Lines

Writers do not always explain the meaning or significance of an event in a story. Just as a character needs to reflect and consider the significance of events that occur, the reader needs to **read between the lines** of the story to discover clues to meaning. Consider the following passage from the story:

> All up and down the length of the train in the dust the artists sprang, walking bent, like performing animals, the better to exhibit the fantasy held toward the faces on the train. Buck, startled and stiff, staring with round black and white eyes. More lions, standing erect, grappling with strange, thin, elongated warriors who clutched spears and showed no fear in their slits of eyes.

What is significant in the passage's contrasting description of the artists "walking bent" and the fearless "elongated warriors"?

DIRECTIONS: *As you read "The Train from Rhodesia," record in the first column events that you or a character do not fully understand. After you read between the lines, explain in the second column the full meaning or significance of the event.*

Event	Meaning of Event

© Pearson Education, Inc., publishing as Pearson Prentice Hall. All rights reserved.

"The Train from Rhodesia" by Nadine Gordimer
Vocabulary Builder

Using the Prefix *a-*

One of the meanings of the prefix *a-* is "without or not." When using this meaning of the prefix *a-*, the meaning of the base word is negated. For example, the Word Bank word *atrophy* means "without nourishment."

A. DIRECTIONS: *Complete each of the following sentences. Form the missing word by using the italicized context clue and your knowledge of the prefix a-.*

1. The _____ character in the story displayed a *lack of moral judgment.*

2. *Without a tonal center or key,* the _____ composition sounded like a chorus of squabbling birds.

3. Our _____ meal of popcorn was *not typical* of our dinner eating habits.

Using the Word List

impressionistic	elongated	segmented
splaying	atrophy	

B. DIRECTIONS: *Match each word in the left column with its definition in the right column. Write the letter of the definition on the line next to the word it defines.*

___ 1. atrophy   A. conveying a quick, overall picture

___ 2. impressionistic   B. separated into parts

___ 3. elongated   C. waste away

___ 4. segmented   D. spreading

___ 5. splaying   E. lengthened; stretched

C. DIRECTIONS: *Rewrite each sentence using an appropriate word from the Word List.*

1. Her memories of the incident were sketchy.

_____

2. After long hours on the train, he felt his muscles begin to lose strength.

_____

3. The suitcase fell, spreading its contents across the corridor.

_____

4. The journey was more restful because it was broken into manageable parts.

_____

5. Her face sagged, stretched by fatigue.

_____

© Pearson Education, Inc., publishing as Pearson Prentice Hall. All rights reserved.

"The Train from Rhodesia" by Nadine Gordimer
Grammar and Style: Nominative Absolutes

A **nominative absolute** is a group of words containing a noun or pronoun modified by a participle or participial phrase. In the following sentence from "The Train from Rhodesia," the nominative absolute is italicized.

The stationmaster was leaning against the end of the train, *green flag rolled in readiness.*

As you can see in the preceding example, a nominative absolute modifies the rest of the sentence in which it appears, instead of modifying a particular word. A nominative absolute is always set off by a comma. The details included in the phrase can heighten suspense and bring a scene to life.

A. PRACTICE: *Underline the nominative absolute in each of the following sentences from Gordimer's story.*

1. "A man passed beneath the arch of reaching arms meeting gray-black and white in the exchange of money for the staring wooden eyes, the stiff wooden legs sticking up in the air."

2. "Joints not yet coordinated, the segmented body of the train heaved and bumped back against itself."

3. "She was holding it away from her, . . . the wonderful ruff of fur facing her."

4. "He stood astonished, his hands hanging at his sides."

5. "She sat down again in the corner and, her face slumped in her hand, stared out of the window."

B. Writing Application: *Revise each of the following sentences by adding a nominative absolute.*

1. The train pulled into the station.

_____

_____

2. The young woman stood on the platform.

_____

_____

3. The stationmaster rang the bell.

_____

_____

© Pearson Education, Inc., publishing as Pearson Prentice Hall. All rights reserved.

Name _____ Date _____

"The Train from Rhodesia" by Nadine Gordimer
Support for Writing

Use the chart below to develop ideas for your analysis of storytelling technique in "The Train from Rhodesia." First, review the story, and find examples of imagery and dialogue. Record them in the chart, and jot notes on how they relate to the theme.

	Examples	**How It Relates to Theme**
Imagery		
Dialogue		

On a separate page, draft your analysis of storytelling technique, using details from the chart. Organize your ideas logically. Discuss how Gordimer's technique works.

Name _____ Date _____

from **Midsummer, XXIII** and *from* **Omeros** *from* **Chapter XXVIII** by Derek Walcott

Literary Analysis: Theme and Context

The **theme** is the main idea or basic meaning that a writer communicates in a literary work. Theme expresses a clear point of view about some aspect of life and human experience. The theme is understood through exploring the **context**—the local conditions from which it comes. Very often poets and other writers choose to reveal their themes indirectly—thorough characters' behavior, figurative language, details of setting or atmosphere, dialogue, and other elements—rather than to state their message directly.

DIRECTIONS: *Answer each of the following questions.*

1. One of Walcott's themes in both *Midsummer* and *Omeros* concerns the brutality and injustice that result from racial prejudice. Put the theme in context by listing the images and phrases from these poems in which Walcott touches on this idea.

   from *Midsummer,* XXIII: _____

   _____

   _____

   _____

   _____

   _____

   from *Omeros,* from Chapter XXVIII: _____

   _____

   _____

   _____

   _____

   _____

   _____

© Pearson Education, Inc., publishing as Pearson Prentice Hall. All rights reserved.

from **Midsummer, XXIII** and *from* **Omeros** *from* **Chapter XXVIII** by Derek Walcott
Reading Strategy: Apply Background Information

Sometimes it is helpful to **apply background information** to extend your understanding of a literary work. The fact that Derek Walcott was in England, for example, probably explains Brixton rather than Miami or Los Angeles, as a setting for a poem. First, focus closely on the words the writer has chosen to use in the work. After considering what exists on the page, you might seek more information from the larger context of the artist's life.

It is not always safe to assume that a writer's work gives the exact story of his or her life, or that events in a writer's life adequately explain his or her work. Having knowledge of a writer's life may help explain references and attitudes, though, such as Walcott's disappointment in English theater. Applying background information can enlarge your understanding and expand your comprehension of the artist's world and yours.

DIRECTIONS: *Use the background information from the biographical material and footnotes in your text to consider the following passages. For each, write what background information may apply, and how you think it affects the particular passage or how it may have influenced the ideas represented.*

Passage	Background Information	Effect or Influence on the Passage
1. "I was there to add some color to the British theater." *Midsummer*		
2. "Now he heard the griot muttering his prophetic song/ of sorrow that would be the past." *Omeros*		

© Pearson Education, Inc., publishing as Pearson Prentice Hall. All rights reserved.

from **Midsummer, XXIII** and *from* **Omeros** *from* **Chapter XXVIII** by Derek Walcott
Vocabulary Builder

Using the Root *-duc-*

The Word Bank word *inducted* contains the Latin root *-duc-*, which means "to lead." Many other words, such as *education* or *ductwork*, that connote "leading" or "bringing something toward" also share this origin.

A. DIRECTIONS: *Match each word with the -duc- word root in the left column with its meaning in the right column. Write the letter of the definition on the line next to the word it defines.*

___ 1. ductile   A. to lead or take away

___ 2. ducat   B. to trace a course of thought

___ 3. deduce   C. a cutting back in number or amount

___ 4. abduct   D. easily drawn or shaped, as metal

___ 5. reduction   E. a coin bearing the image of a duke

Using the Word List

antic	rancor	eclipse	inducted

B. DIRECTIONS: *Each item consists of a related pair of words in CAPITAL LETTERS, followed by four lettered pairs of words. Choose the pair that best expresses a relationship similar to that expressed in the pair in capital letters. Circle the letter of your choice.*

1. ANTIC : DIGNIFIED ::
   A. comic : funny
   B. rushed : sedate
   C. crazy : oddity
   D. frantic : nervous

2. RANCOR : ANIMOSITY ::
   A. malice : generosity
   B. spite : jealousy
   C. kindness : courtesy
   D. revenge : charity

3. INDUCTED : MEMBER ::
   A. honored : hero
   B. called : answer
   C. gave : donor
   D. rejected : quality

4. ECLIPSE : LIGHT ::
   A. darken : darkness
   B. dim : bright
   C. orbit : planet
   D. shade : sun

© Pearson Education, Inc., publishing as Pearson Prentice Hall. All rights reserved.

Name _____ Date _____

from Midsummer, XXIII and **from Omeros from Chapter XXVIII** by Derek Walcott
Grammar and Style: Commonly Confused Words: *Affect* and *Effect*

Two words commonly confused are **affect** and **effect**. The words sound similar, and although *affect* is a verb, *effect* may be a noun or a verb, adding to the confusion.

Affect is nearly always a verb. The usual meaning of *affect* is "to influence." For example, "Caribbean backgrounds strongly *affect* the poetry of Walcott." You could substitute *influence* without changing the meaning.

Effect is usually a noun meaning "result." For example, "The *effect* of Walcott's poem is a new perspective of England." You can substitute *result* without changing the meaning.

When *effect* is a verb, it means "to bring about," or "achieve." The sense of *effect* when used as a verb is one of completion, as in "Walcott hopes to effect political change in England."

A. PRACTICE: *Indicate whether each sentence uses* affect *or* effect *correctly. Write* C *in the blank if the sentence is correct or* I *in the blank if the sentence is incorrect.*

_____ 1. One *effect* of England's economic problems of the 1980's was increased competition for scarce jobs.

_____ 2. This competition could not fail to *effect* an already tense racial climate.

_____ 3. In order to *affect* reform, the country needed to improve its entire economy.

_____ 4. The tension had its *effect* on every aspect of a long-overlooked issue.

B. Writing Application: *Write sentences using* affect *or* effect *according to the instructions given for each item.*

1. Write a sentence about the result of reading the selection from *Omeros* and your imagination of the slave trade.

   _____

   _____

   _____

2. Write a sentence about what change Walcott had hoped to bring about in British theater.

   _____

   _____

   _____

© Pearson Education, Inc., publishing as Pearson Prentice Hall. All rights reserved.

from **Midsummer, XXIII** and *from* **Omeros** *from* **Chapter XXVIII** by Derek Walcott
Support for Writing

Use the graphic organizer below to collect and organize ideas for your multimedia presentation of either Walcott poem. First, write the poem you have chosen. List the theme and main images in the boxes on the left. Then, list ideas for photographs, artwork, music, video clips, and sound effects that may illustrate the poem.

Poem: _____ **Audiovisual Aids**

Theme:

Image:

Image:

Image:

Draw on details from your graphic organizer as you draft your script on a separate page. Show the line-by-line relationship between the text and the aids you will use.

© Pearson Education, Inc., publishing as Pearson Prentice Hall. All rights reserved.

From the Author's Desk

Anita Desai Introduces "A Devoted Son"

DIRECTIONS: *Use the space provided to answer the questions.*

1. According to Anita Desai, why does writing a short story resemble writing a poem?

   _____

   _____

2. What examples does Desai give of "moments" that serve as inspiration or "seeds" for short stories?

   _____

   _____

   _____

   _____

3. Briefly explain Desai's process of writing a short story. How is this process like "planting seeds"?

   _____

   _____

   _____

   _____

4. According to Desai, what was the "seed" for her story "A Devoted Son"?

   _____

   _____

   _____

5. Desai claims that art can render complex and mysterious things "utterly pure, clear, and transparent." Do you agree with her claim? Briefly explain your answer, using at least one example from literature, painting, or music to support your opinion.

   _____

   _____

   _____

   _____

   _____

   _____

   _____

   _____

© Pearson Education, Inc., publishing as Pearson Prentice Hall. All rights reserved.

Anita Desai
Listening and Viewing

Segment 1: Meet Anita Desai
- What other languages does Anita Desai speak, and how does she incorporate them into her writing?
- Why do you think knowledge of other languages is important in character development?

_____

_____

_____

Segment 2: The Short Story
- What experience inspired Desai to write "A Devoted Son"?
- What truth about life does the story reveal?
- What experience would you write about that would express a truth about life?

_____

_____

_____

Segment 3: The Writing Process
- According to Anita Desai, why are writing and playing music similar activities?
- Why do you think it is important to practice writing consistently?

_____

_____

_____

Segment 4: The Rewards of Writing
- Why does Anita Desai consider reading her "lifeline"?
- How can entering books add "another dimension" to your life?

_____

_____

_____

© Pearson Education, Inc., publishing as Pearson Prentice Hall. All rights reserved.

"A Devoted Son" by Anita Desai
Literary Analysis: Static and Dynamic Characters

Anita Desai's "A Devoted Son" presents an unusual example of **static** and **dynamic** characters. A static character is one who does not change during the course of a work, and a dynamic character is one who undergoes change as a result of what happens in the work. Readers might expect that the young man would be the one to change, but Desai reverses our expectations.

To understand static and dynamic characters, we need to consider what we mean by change. Varma never leaves the village. Yet he is not the same person at the end of the story as he was when Rakesh first showed him his test results. His feelings about the world and his son have altered dramatically. By contrast, Rakesh has many experiences, for he begins the story as a student, studies in America, returns, marries, raises a family, and founds a successful clinic. Yet Desai presents him as the same dutiful son at the end of the story as at the beginning, apparently unaffected internally by the things he has done.

How does Desai show the changes in Varma and the lack of change in Rakesh? Because the change occurs emotionally, we can look at descriptions of characters' feelings or responses to situations to follow each character's progress.

DIRECTIONS: *Answer the following questions by analyzing indications of change in Rakesh and Varma in "A Devoted Son."*

1. Describe Varma's emotional state at the beginning, middle, and at the end of the story.

   _____

   _____

   _____

2. Identify three paragraphs from the beginning, the middle, and the end of the story that indicate this change. Write phrases or sentences from the paragraphs that evidence change.

   _____

   _____

   _____

3. Describe Rakesh at the beginning and at the end of the story.

   _____

   _____

   _____

4. Identify three paragraphs from the beginning, the middle, and the end of the story that support your description of Rakesh. Write phrases or sentences from the paragraphs that support your interpretation.

   _____

   _____

   _____

© Pearson Education, Inc., publishing as Pearson Prentice Hall. All rights reserved.

Name _____ Date _____

"**A Devoted Son**" by Anita Desai
Reading Strategy: Evaluate Characters' Decisions

In good writing, characters and the situations they face often seem real. One test of a good story is whether you wonder about the characters outside the context of the story. Is Rakesh's father still alive? What is Rakesh like now? Has he learned what his father really needs?

As you read, you compare the things that characters do to what you think they ought to do, and develop attitudes about them. In much fiction, just as in life, actions have consequences, some of them not foreseen by the characters (or the reader). When Rakesh first did well on his exams, could his father have anticipated how success might affect his relationship with his son? Could you? As you read, try to **evaluate characters' decisions** in terms of the world of the story. What is being decided? What are the choices and consequences? How is each decision made? What are the values on which the decision is based?

DIRECTIONS: *Use the following chart to help you consider decisions the characters make in the story. The first column lists a decision that has been made. In the second column, write what you think the reason for that decision is, and how the decision is made. In the third column, write the consequences of the decision. What does it lead to in terms of events, and what effect does it have on this or other characters? In the fourth column, note your assessment or thoughts about the decision and the character.*

Decision	Motivation	Consequences	Evaluation
1. Rakesh pursues a career in medicine			
2. Rakesh seeks advanced education in America.			
3. Rakesh returns to India and sets up a clinic.			
4. Varma becomes increasingly irritable.			
5. Varma decides he wants to die.			

© Pearson Education, Inc., publishing as Pearson Prentice Hall. All rights reserved.

"A Devoted Son" by Anita Desai
Vocabulary Builder

Using the Root -fil-

The Latin word *filius* means "son," and *filia* means "daughter." The Word Bank word *filial* comes from these roots, literally meaning "of or befitting a son or daughter." Words formed from the root -fil- imply obligation and association.

A. DIRECTIONS: *Match each word derived from the -fil- word root in the left column with its definition in the right column. Write the letter of the definition on the line by the word it defines.*

___ 1. affiliate (verb)   A. relationship between parent and child

___ 2. filiation   B. voluntary connection

___ 3. affiliate (noun)   C. to join or associate

___ 4. affiliation   D. a member or colleague

Using the Word List

exemplary	filial	encomiums	complaisant	fathom

B. DIRECTIONS: *Each item consists of a word from the Word List followed by four lettered words or phrases. Choose the word or phrase most nearly similar in meaning to the Word List word. Circle the letter of your choice.*

1. exemplary
   A. model
   B. necessary
   C. released
   D. principal

2. filial
   A. equine
   B. teeming
   C. belated
   D. respectful

3. encomiums
   A. campgrounds
   B. tributes
   C. environments
   D. savings

4. complaisant
   A. protesting
   B. supplement
   C. agreeable
   D. courtesy

5. fathom
   A. assist
   B. comprehend
   C. deny
   D. create

© Pearson Education, Inc., publishing as Pearson Prentice Hall. All rights reserved.
335

"A Devoted Son" by Anita Desai

Grammar and Style: Sentence Variety

Just as effective speakers change voice inflection to hold audiences, effective writers vary sentences to keep language moving.

Sentences vary by length. Some paragraphs begin with a short crisp sentence to make a point, followed by longer ones to provide details. Others may begin with long sentences to set the scene, and drive home a point with a single, blunt insight.

Sentences vary by type. Beginning a paragraph with a question or exclamation grabs readers' attention. Sentences are declarative, interrogative, imperative, or exclamatory.

Sentences vary by structure. Simple sentences, compound sentences (two or more independent clauses, but no subordinate clauses), or complex sentences (at least one independent and one subordinate clause) mix to vary the cadence of a paragraph.

Sentences vary in placement of elements. Within these types of variation exist options for more variety. Clauses, phrases, subjects, and predicates may shift for sentence diversity.

A. PRACTICE: *Identify the length, type, and structure of each sentence in the following passage. Then describe how all of the sentences work together to dramatize events in the paragraph.*

The old man who had been lying stretched out on his bed, weak and feeble after a day's illness, gave a start at the very sound, the tone of these words. He opened his eyes—rather, they fell open with shock—and he stared at his son with a disbelief that darkened quickly to reproach. A son who actually refused his father the food he craved? No, it was unheard of, it was incredible. But Rakesh had turned his back to him and was cleaning up the litter of bottles and packets on the medicine shelf and did not notice while Veena slipped silently out of the room with a little smirk that only the old man saw, and hated.

1. Sentence 1: _____

2. Sentence 2: _____

3. Sentence 3: _____

4. Sentence 4: _____

5. Sentence 5: _____

6. Paragraph Description: _____

_____

B. Writing Application: *Experiment with sentence variety by rewriting the third-to-last paragraph of "A Devoted Son." Reorder or recast sentences in the paragraph that begins "Varma's mouth. . . ."*

_____

_____

_____

_____

_____

© Pearson Education, Inc., publishing as Pearson Prentice Hall. All rights reserved.

Name _____ Date _____

"A Devoted Son" by Anita Desai
Support for Writing

As you brainstorm, record ideas for your proposal for a program for the elderly in the organizer below.

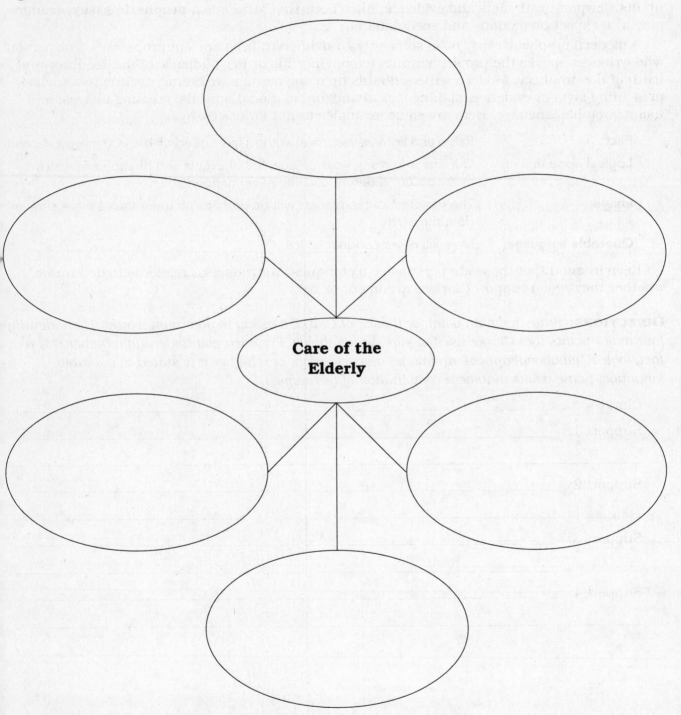

Use details from the diagram to draft your proposal for a program for the elderly on a separate page. State your objectives clearly, and use positive verbs.

© Pearson Education, Inc., publishing as Pearson Prentice Hall. All rights reserved.

Name _____ Date _____

from "We'll Never Conquer Space" by Arthur C. Clarke
Literary Analysis: Prophetic Essay

It is not hard for readers to guess what Clarke's viewpoint is as they begin to read *We'll Never Conquer Space*. Clarke's title makes it no secret. As in any essay, though, Clarke needs to back up his viewpoint with facts and evidence. Also, because Clarke's is a **prophetic essay,** readers may also expect predictions and speculations.

A modern prophetic essay is, in some ways, no different from ancient prophecies. The person who writes or speaks the prophecy wants to convince his or her audience of the accuracy and truth of the prophecy. Modern writers do this by using persuasive literary techniques such as presenting facts or evidence, making logical and/or emotional appeals, creating images, and using quotable language. Here are some examples from Clarke's essay.

Fact:	Radio and light waves travel at the same speed of 186,000 miles a second.
Logical appeal:	Our age is in many ways unique, full of events and phenomena which never occurred before and can never happen again.
Image:	The remotest of the planets will be perhaps no more than a week's travel from the earth.
Quotable language:	Man will never conquer space.

Keep in mind that these are persuasive techniques. Your job as a reader is to determine whether they *really* support Clarke's argument or not.

DIRECTIONS: *State the main point, or thesis, of Clarke's essay in your own words. Then identify four major points that Clarke uses to support his thesis. For each point, identify whether it is a fact, logical/emotional appeal, an image, a speculation, or whether it is stated in quotable language. Some points may be a combination of techniques.*

Clarke's thesis: _____

Support 1: _____

_____

Support 2: _____

_____

Support 3: _____

_____

Support 4: _____

_____

© Pearson Education, Inc., publishing as Pearson Prentice Hall. All rights reserved.

from **"We'll Never Conquer Space"** by Arthur C. Clarke
Reading Strategy: Challenge the Text

Do you believe, and accept, everything you read? Books, magazine articles, newspapers, office memoranda, and corporate newsletters all convey information. Is the newspaper's reporting unbiased? Does the memo address the heart of the issue, or just someone's side of it? Is the company revealing what employees have a right to know?

When you read an essay, even one by a famous, well-respected writer, you should **challenge the text,** just as you should challenge materials you read at school and home. Clarke's essay, in particular, addresses a controversial subject and should raise questions as you read. Some of Clarke's statements are straight facts. Others are opinions, assumptions, or speculations about what might—or might not—come to be. Test his ideas by raising those questions.

DIRECTIONS: *Following are some statements from Clarke's essay that are worthy of being challenged. For each statement, write a question with which to challenge the statement. (You need not know the answer to the question.) An example has been done for you.*

Because we have annihilated distance on this planet, we imagine that we can do it once again.

Have we really "annihilated distance" on earth? Do people assume we can do it again, as Clarke claims?

1. ". . . when the satellite communication network is established, we will be able to see friends on the far side of the earth as easily as we talk to them on the other side of the town."

   _____

   _____

   _____

2. "We have abolished space here on the little earth; we can never abolish the space that yawns between the stars."

   _____

   _____

   _____

3. "This achievement [using nuclear energy for spaceflight], which will be witnessed within a century, might appear to make even the solar system a comfortable, homely place . . ."

   _____

   _____

   _____

Unit 6 Resources: A Time of Rapid Change
© Pearson Education, Inc., publishing as Pearson Prentice Hall. All rights reserved.
339

Name _____ Date _____

from "We'll Never Conquer Space" by Arthur C. Clarke
Vocabulary Builder

Using the Suffixes -*ible* and -*able*

A. DIRECTIONS: *Many words in the English language contain the suffixes -ible or -able, meaning "able to," "having qualities of," or "worthy of." Match the following words with their definitions. Write the letter of the definition next to the word it defines.*

____ 1. applicable   A. capable of being traversed or dealt with

____ 2. commendable   B. able to be disregarded

____ 3. negligible   C. capable of being brought into action

____ 4. negotiable   D. worthy of praise

Using the Word List

ludicrous	irrevocable	instantaneous
enigma	inevitable	zenith

B. DIRECTIONS: *Each item consists of a Word List word followed by four lettered words or phrases. Choose the lettered word or phrase that is most nearly opposite in meaning to the Word List word, and circle the letter of your choice.*

1. enigma
   A. query
   B. widely known
   C. negative image
   D. solution

2. inevitable
   A. sure
   B. unavoidable
   C. satisfied
   D. unsafe

3. instantaneous
   A. delayed
   B. lacking attention
   C. rough-skinned
   D. precise

4. irrevocable
   A. without words
   B. changeable
   C. finely tuned
   D. permanent

5. ludicrous
   A. boring
   B. serious
   C. miserable
   D. not playful

6. zenith
   A. lowest point
   B. farthest point
   C. nearest point
   D. distant point

© Pearson Education, Inc., publishing as Pearson Prentice Hall. All rights reserved.

Name _____ Date _____

from "We'll Never Conquer Space" by Arthur C. Clarke
Grammar and Style: Linking Verbs and Subject Complements

A **linking verb** connects its subject with a word that identifies or describes that subject.

Arthur C. Clarke *is* a writer. (The word *writer* identifies the subject, *Clarke*.)

Following are the most commonly used linking verbs.

all of the forms of *be* (*am, is, are, was, were, will be, has been, could have been,* and so on)	*appear*	*seem*
	become	*smell*
	feel	*sound*
	grow	*stay*
	look	*taste*
	remain	*turn*

The word or words that identify or describe the subject, such as *writer* in the previous example, are called the **subject complement.** There are two kinds of subject complements, the predicate nominative and the predicate adjective. A predicate nominative refers to the person or thing that is the subject of the verb. The previous example has a predicate nominative. Here is another example.

Arthur C. Clarke *was* once a radar *instructor*.

A predicate adjective is an adjective that follows a linking verb and modifies, or describes, the subject of the verb.

Clarke's essay *is interesting.* (The adjective *interesting* modifies the subject, *essay*.)

A. PRACTICE: *In each sentence, circle the linking verb and underline the subject complement. Indicate whether the subject complement is a predicate nominative or a predicate adjective by writing* PN *or* PA *above the complement.*

1. "The facts are far otherwise."

2. "In all earlier ages than ours, the world was wide indeed."

3. "Once again we are face to face with immensity."

4. "The velocity of light is the ultimate speed limit."

5. "Again they are wrong."

B. Writing Application: *Use two different forms of the verb* be *and two other linking verbs to write sentences about Arthur Clarke or his essay. Underline the subject complement in each sentence.*

1. _____

2. _____

3. _____

© Pearson Education, Inc., publishing as Pearson Prentice Hall. All rights reserved.

from **"We'll Never Conquer Space"** by Arthur C. Clarke
Support for Writing

Use the chart below to gather details for your analysis of an argument. Review the essay, and identify Clarke's assumptions. Write them in the left column. Then, analyze each assumption. In the right column, list evidence and reasons that support or contradict each assumption.

Clarke's Assumptions	Support or Evidence For or Against

Use information from the chart as you draft your analysis on a separate page. As you write, include an evaluation of whether Clarke's assumptions make sense.

© Pearson Education, Inc., publishing as Pearson Prentice Hall. All rights reserved.